MW01484895

The Loan Guide

How to Get the Best Possible Mortgage

By Casey Fleming

Copyright 2014 by Casey Fleming

All rights Reserved. No part of this book may be reproduced or transmitted in any form or by any means, electronic or mechanical, including photocopying, recording, or by any information storage and retrieval system, without permission in writing by the publisher.

Published by Casey Fleming, San Jose CA

Interior text design: Casey Fleming

First Edition

ISBN-13: 978-0615980706

This book is dedicated to all of my clients, who have been my best teachers over the years. By asking sharp questions and holding my feet to the fire, you have made me a better mortgage advisor.

Table of Contents

Forward

Before you take on the largest debt you'll ever have, you should have more information than you've ever had before. This book was written to help you make that happen.

Because I work in Silicon Valley my clients tend to be smart people with lots of smart questions; they want to make informed decisions. By asking very sharp questions my clients have helps me learn how to help people make confident, informed decisions through my practice. The purpose of this book is to share what I've learned with you - to empower you to make informed, intelligent decisions about your mortgage financing, and to help you negotiate the best possible loan product, rate, price and terms for your family.

While getting a mortgage has always been a somewhat complicated affair, in the last few years it has become much more so. I began this book in 2007, at the beginning of the Great Mortgage Meltdown. It has become a little like trying to write a guide book to European travel in the middle of World War II. The rules, the boundaries, and the best practices kept changing. Consequently, I have learned much from writing this book, and I hope you learn something too.

I have been originating loans since 1995, and have been in the mortgage business since 1979, so I've had time to make observations about how the mortgage industry works (or doesn't work) in the best interest of its clients. While the rules, the products, the disclosures and the interest rates change dramatically over time, the basic principles of intelligent, thoughtful personal real estate finance have not.

As you begin to read the book it may seem like there is a lot of information in the book that isn't relevant to you. In fact, there is a lot of information in this book that you in particular won't need and wouldn't use anyway. But everything in the book has been included for a purpose; different sections will apply to different needs.

Therefore, this book is organized so that you don't need to read the whole book. I have tried to make each section stand alone as much as possible, referencing other sections where necessary. Use this as a reference book and reference the sections that are relevant to what you want to achieve.

Because I work with a lot of Silicon Valley engineers the analyses I use can get pretty complex. These are smart folks who have taught me a lot, and I have done my best to keep up with them by refining my analyses to a deeper and deeper level. In the process though, sometimes I give clients more information than they want.

So, in certain sections I'll present two different ways of looking at the problem: the more general view for those who want a basic understanding of the particular issue, and the detailed view for those who want to dig into the nuances. Both approaches are valid, and in my experience the highly detailed analysis does not usually lead to a different conclusion than a more general one. However, some clients really want the resolution that the more detailed analysis allows.

I will also present commonly-used analyses that are very weak and can be misleading, and explain how they can be used improperly by poorly trained or unethical loan officers. I will give you the tools to recognize when someone is using a marketing gimmick or a sales closing presentation that isn't leading you to the solution that is in your best interest so that you can walk away and find an ethical loan officer that has your best interests in mind.

If you want to jump right in and don't want a history of mortgage lending, start by reading the sections of Chapters four through seven that are relevant to your situation. These chapters cover whether you should acquire financing or not, whatever your purpose. In my experience the worst mistake most folks make is not getting the wrong mortgage at the wrong price, but rather getting financing when they shouldn't do it at all.

Chapters one, two, and three will help you understand how the industry has evolved since Grandma's day, and how to navigate today's much more complicated landscape. If you already know where you intend to go for your next mortgage you can skip these chapters – but you may not want to.

Chapters Nine through twenty is where the meat of the book lies. It is everything you ever wanted to know about mortgages but were too afraid (or too bored) to ask.

If it sounds at times like I am criticizing my colleagues in the mortgage business, I want you to know there are many professional, ethical and competent mortgage professionals out there who are primarily motivated by serving their clients well and doing the right thing. I personally know many professionals in the industry that care as much about your welfare as they do about their commissions. Some, however, do not feel that way.

As someone who has originated loans, mentored new loan officers, coached experienced loan officers, been responsible for the production of up to 300 loan officers at a time and taken a leadership role in the California Association of Mortgage Professionals, I do have information that can be useful to you. But the single most valuable thing I can give you is enough information to know when a loan officer is on your side, and when he or she is not and it's time to walk away.

My hope is that the dramatic changes our industry is undergoing right now will bring back a sense of connection between the mortgage professional and you; that, as mortgage originators, we remember that we are not just making a loan; we are making a huge difference in the quality of lives of real people, real families. When we remember to connect, on a human level, with your needs and concerns, when we build a relationship with you rather than seeing you as another transaction, you will be able to trust us.

I will refer throughout this book to the Boom Times, the Mortgage Boom, the Great Meltdown, and the Great Recession. These are general terms that I use to describe certain periods in the mortgage industry and in our economy in general. I do not intend for them to refer to any particular period of time as described by others. Besides, I still haven't figured out what was so great about the great recession.

In general, I consider the Boom Times to have been during the early to mid 2000s when we went through one refinancing boom after another, each one dragging us successively lower in rates. But also during this time lenders introduced more and more creative (read "risky") mortgage products with looser and looser underwriting guidelines, a trend which undoubtedly led to the disastrous Great Meltdown.

The Great Meltdown is the period during which the vast majority of mortgage bankers collapsed, roughly early 2007 through mid-2009. During this time the industry was in chaos and frankly, it became terribly difficult to actually complete a loan because lenders were never sure exactly what underwriting guidelines they could use and still sell a loan to an investor.

The exact time period that the Great Recession covers I will leave to history to decide, but there is no doubt in my mind that the collapse of the mortgage industry during the Great Meltdown led directly to the Great Recession, so while I believe the meltdown started first, I also believe they are inexorably intertwined.

Nothing in this book is terribly exciting or sexy. Reading about mortgages won't keep you up at night tearing through pages excitedly, wondering how it will all turn out. If I had my druthers I'd rather be reading a tabloid.

Yet, a mortgage is almost certainly the largest debt you will ever have. There are some sobering implications to this:

- You will probably spend more money on your mortgages over your lifetime than you will on anything else. I repeat: *You will spend more money on your mortgages over your lifetime than you will on **anything** else.*
- More of your working hours will be spent earning money to pay your mortgage than any other debt.
- Families that manage their mortgage portfolio properly can have tens of thousands, if not hundreds of thousands, more in assets when they retire than those who don't.

The implication is terrible, and exciting: making intelligent choices about your mortgage may have more impact on your financial health when you retire than anything else you do in your lifetime.

So yes, this may be a boring subject, but not unimportant. Drink some coffee, stay with me, and I promise that you will have more confidence, make smarter choices, and be far happier with the outcome of obtaining a mortgage after you have finished this book.

Casey Fleming

Acknowledgements

This book has been an enormous challenge to write, and it would not have happened without a little help from my friends.

First, I must say thank you to my editors. Steve Lawlor is an accomplished textbook author and provided invaluable technical editing input that dramatically improved the clarity of the information and ideas that I am trying to convey, particularly in the more technical areas.

Roberta Greenlaw is an experienced, competent mortgage originator who also has experience in editing and publishing. She recommended major realignment of some of the sections that at first glance I thought were terrible ideas – until I tried them and saw that they worked really well. Roberta's comments regarding the value of the information in the book were a prime driving factor in giving me the motivation to finish it.

Elizabeth Milligan is an experienced writer, editor and publisher in a completely different field and provided fantastic feedback principally because she is not familiar with mortgage origination terms and principles. She's very bright, so if something wasn't clear to her I knew I needed to re-work it.

Finally, my clients have taught me a great deal over the years by asking me really smart questions and forcing me to learn how to analyze options from a client's point of view and explain them to smart people who don't get mortgage very often, and so only need this information when they need it. I have learned from you, and the results made this book possible.

Thank you.

Quick Guide to Your Concerns

This is a big book and you don't need all of it. Think of it as a reference book.

When all the noise is filtered out, there are five things you need to do well to get the best possible mortgage.

Here is where to find the information in this book to make the best decision for you to get the best possible product:

Choosing whom to do business with: Chapter 3

Decide whether you ought to get a loan or not: Chapters 4 through 8

Choose the right loan product: Chapters 8 through 20

Choose the right tradeoff between fees and interest rate: Chapter 3, 19

Lock your rate at the right time: Chapter 3

Do these five simple things correctly and you will end up with a loan that serves you and your family well, and tens of thousands of dollars more money in your pocket.

Finally, you may see some words or phrases italicized in the text. These are things with which you might not be familiar, so they are defined in the Glossary.

Chapter One

Your Grandparents' Mortgage

In my opinion, the chief difference between mortgage lending after the Great Depression and mortgage lending since the 1980s is that the loan officers who made Grandma's loan cared about the results; the end results of profit to the bank and a successful outcome to the customer were really the only two things that mattered to them. Let me explain.

The concept of a mortgage broker would be foreign to my grandmother. In her world, you went to the bank, got a loan, paid it for 20 (or maybe 30) years and then burned your mortgage. Interest rates were set by the bank.

The concept that one would shop for a mortgage, use a broker, occasionally refinance, and maybe even use an adjustable rate were totally foreign to her.

Is our system better today? I think that is debatable, but it's what we have to work with.

Mortgages Were Made By Local Banks

There were some significant advantages to Grandma's mortgage system:

Simplicity: Not having choices meant that you didn't have to research, shop, analyze or even think. Grandma never needed this book.

Loan officers knew their borrowers: Grandma knew her banker, and he knew her. He may not have known, without checking, exactly how much she made, but he certainly knew where she worked, how long she had been there, and how stable her job was. He probably even knew if she paid her bills on time – she lived in a small town. The important thing was, his decision to make the loan was based less on numbers than it is today, and more on a human factor – was she going to pay back the loan, or not?

Bank officers were responsible for their lending decisions. The money that banks lent really belonged to their community – the customers who deposited money into the bank. (Admit it, you cried at the end of "It's a Wonderful Life", didn't you?) A bad loan impacted the profitability of the bank, and probably the bonuses, and maybe even the job stability of the bank officers and the loan officer. It wasn't exactly their own money they were lending, but they were responsible for it, and accountable for their decisions.

The system was bound to be manipulated, however, and favoritism, bigotry, and personal bias affected the decisions loan officers made. Plus poor communities tended to stay poor, since there was little money available to develop a local economy. They lacked the national sourcing of funds that we have today to provide liquidity for the housing market, and thus the American Dream.

There were certainly drawbacks to the old system. But we just might do well today if we gave less attention to the numbers and more attention to the question: "Are these folks likely to pay this loan back?"

This was a significant advantage of Grandma's system over ours. Today, as we will explore shortly, decision-makers are not required – or even allowed – to use their judgment in most cases, are not really responsible to investors for the quality of their lending decisions, and are rarely held accountable except in cases of extreme fraud. These fundamental changes in the nature of mortgage lending decisions were, in my opinion, the prime contributing factors to the Great Mortgage Meltdown.

Your Lender, Banker and Financial Advisor Were One and the Same

Along the same lines, you counted on the financial wisdom of your personal banker. Grandma might have assumed that her banker was not just someone good at taking loan applications; she might have assumed he understood finances better than most, and certainly better than her.

The loan officer at the bank might have given you advice not only on your mortgage and your investment options, but also on whether you ought to be committing to a mortgage at all. The answer was often "no." After all, they were accountable for how the loan performed.

Interest Rates Stayed the Same for Years

In Grandma's day mortgage interest rates rarely changed – in fact they were sometimes posted on a **permanent** sign out in front of the bank. Over the years there were changes, to be sure, but they were incremental and glacial in nature.

Today, interest rates change daily. Actually, it isn't unusual for us to receive notifications from lenders several times a day that rates have changed due to market conditions. While this particular piece of the puzzle – rate movement and locking strategy – isn't discussed by very many professionals, it is the area where a competent mortgage planner or loan consultant can make the biggest difference in the lifetime cost of a loan for his or her clients. It's also the most difficult area to master, and is rarely taught to loan originators.

One Loan, Pay it Off

I remember when Grandma and Grandpa had a party to burn their mortgage, because they had paid it off. Grandma never refinanced as far as I knew. But there were reasons that this was so.

First, with only one loan product in general, they never had a chance to refinance to improve the terms of their loan. With interest rates painted on a permanent sign out in front of the bank there was never a reason for them refinance to get a lower rate. And, our grandparents for the most part rarely moved if they owned their own home.

It was really pretty simple. Save up enough cash to put 20% down, buy a home, make payments for 20 or 30 years, and then host a mortgage-burning party. There wasn't much strategy to it, but there wasn't a lot of effort either.

Summary

The good news is that today, although we have fewer options than we did during the Mortgage Boom in the early 2000's, we have many more options than did Grandma and Grandpa. The bad news is that because we have more options we need to have a much deeper understanding of how mortgages (and the mortgage industry) work in order to make the best choice for our family, and to avoid being sold a bill of goods.

Chapter Two

What Went Wrong?

Where did things go wrong? When I was growing up homeownership was the American Dream – a reward for which you worked hard and saved. Over time it seemed to evolve into something you were entitled to. We went from earning the right to own your own home to believing that anybody should be able to get a mortgage – whether they could afford to pay it back or not. And then we witnessed the collapse of the American Dream, and a lending industry in such serious disarray that it can only be described as severely dysfunctional.

People want answers, of course, especially in light of the dramatic damage done to the world's economy by the Mortgage Meltdown. When a building collapses or a plane crashes due to mechanical failure, a team of highly trained engineers converges on the site, forms a commission, conducts a very thorough failure analysis, and issues a report so that we don't repeat the mistakes in the future.

Imagine how the conclusion might be different, however, if the engineers on the commission all had a hand in designing the thing that failed. How credible would the report be? This is the case with almost everything written about the Mortgage Crisis so far. Almost all the literature that claims to identify who was responsible (in my opinion) has been written to deflect blame or to advance a political agenda.

As a result, I've heard folks argue that the banks were responsible, or the mortgage brokers, or the investment bankers. Who is right?

Plenty of Blame to Go Around

In my opinion, we can lay blame on bad choices made by individuals in every layer in the system.

There were borrowers who wanted to buy more house than they could afford.

There were originators who packaged fraudulent loans or sold toxic loan products that should never have been offered to most borrowers.

There were underwriters who colluded with the originators to assemble fraudulent loan packages, or who approved loans that could never be paid back when they knew (or should have known) that the loans were bound to fail.

There were executives in mortgage lending companies who created loan products designed to sell more loans regardless of whether the products made sense for borrowers or the ultimate investors.

There were investment bankers who directly asked mortgage lenders for pools of mortgages comprised of toxic loan products, and who knowingly sold securities backed by these toxic loans to institutional investors.

And these things happened within the wholesale (broker) channel, the retail mortgage banking channel, and at banks. (See Chapter 3 – "Choose Your Lender, Nail the Deal.")

It was all about volume and profit, and never about what made sense for the borrowers, the communities, or the economy. There were bad players on every layer and at all types of lenders. Some saw opportunity and grabbed it, and others chose to not participate in toxic practice. But the important point is that the blame cannot be assigned to only one layer of players. No one could have pulled off such a massive scam without help from the entire system.

So, the "real story" is probably that many players at every level in the industry conspired to create, knowingly participated in, or willingly sold products that they knew (or should have known) were toxic to consumers, and toxic to investors.

Moving From Responsibility to Profitability and Back

The blood-letting is pretty much over at this point, so let's examine how the mortgage industry today is different than it was forty years ago, different than it was in 2008, how and why it changed and how it works today.

If you're looking for more practical advice for your particular situation, skip ahead to the next chapter. On the other hand, this is a short chapter and will give you a good understanding of what is going on now in our industry and why.

As we discussed in Chapter 1 there was a time when your bank had to be sure that the loans it made were secure, because they had to answer to the stockholders, and eventually to regulators as well. The loan officer back then was a relatively low paid employee whose primary responsibility was to help the bank decide if the loan was a prudent investment or not. But the loan officer had another job, too, although more subtle. *It was his job to help you manage your debt by not taking on too much.* What was bad for **your** financial situation was, in theory, bad for the bank, too. This system had built in to it important features that were missing during the Mortgage Boom: the bank's interests and yours were in alignment, and the decision-maker at the bank was judged not on production, but on the quality of the loans he wrote.

So what happened? Over time we moved away from a focus on making safe, profitable investments for the bank while serving the client. The industry began to focus intensely instead on making sales and driving revenue.

Because it makes sense for modern-day companies to motivate their sales force, professional sales is now one of the highest-paid career paths available. Those of us in commissioned sales work are thrilled that we are now paid much more than clerks. And, let's be honest – we love the compensation. But there is a dark side to this profound shift in the role of your loan officer: the trusted advisor sitting across the desk from you may no longer be primarily concerned with your financial health, but may be more concerned about the potential profit he can make on the deal.

While it could be argued that the loan originator was never exactly on **your** side, he had a vested interest in making sure you didn't get a loan that you couldn't pay back. After all, his paycheck was signed by the bank that would lose money if the loan went bad.

Lenders had to answer for the quality of their work even as late as the 1990s. Ultimately, if a loan went bad someone had to pay for it, so everyone in the transaction at least had to consider the quality of their decisions.

Sometime in the late 1990s an interesting shift began to happen in terms of where money came from. To understand this change, you need to know where ultimately your loan goes, and where the money comes from.

Middlemen Move the Money

Keep this in mind. There are ultimately two primary parties in a mortgage transaction: the borrower, who needs the use of money for a period of time, and the lender, who is willing to meet that need in exchange for a profit, or interest. The borrower is, well, you, and the lenders are institutional investors moving billions of dollars at once. They might be pension funds, insurance companies, and the like. Everyone else – the broker, the mortgage banker, the bank, the savings and loan, Fannie Mae, Freddie Mac, and Wall Street investment bankers are middlemen – nothing more.

All of the middlemen have two things in common: **it's not their money they are lending, and they aren't the ones paying it back.** They simply move paper one direction and cash in another, and take a toll as both go by.

While the new channels opened up a plethora of options for borrowers and created competition that steadily drove down mortgage rates, they also disassociated all the middlemen from responsibility for the borrower and the ultimate investor. Ultimately, it wasn't **their** money. They didn't have to pay it back, and they didn't have to be paid back. They collected their fees and moved on. If the loan became a problem for you or for the investor, well, it wasn't *their* problem.

It is this disassociation that was one of the prime causes of the Great Mortgage Meltdown in my opinion. We will never go back to your only option being to go to your local bank, and we shouldn't. Today's system of moving money has many benefits to consumers. The trick is going to be to getting the retail loan officer - whether he or she works for a broker, a broker / banker, or a bank - to once again own a relationship with you. (See Chapter 3 – "Choose Your Lender, Nail the Deal" for a discussion of types of lenders.)

Regulation – The CFPB

The Dodd-Frank Act, signed into law in 2010, created the Consumer Financial Protection Bureau (THE CFPB). The express purpose of the CFPB is to enforce regulations created to protect consumers from all types of financial fraud or abuse, including mortgage lending.

The ambitious methods used to protect consumers includes the education and licensing of mortgage loan originators, strict regulations regarding compensation of originators, disclosures to borrowers, and a prohibition on "toxic" loan terms.

In short, the abandonment of concern about your welfare that occurred during the structural changes in the industry over 50 years and the resulting cultural shift toward profits over people is now being replaced by regulation and enforcement. ("If we can't make them think right, we'll make them act right!")

You might notice I have my doubts about the efficacy of regulation – not because I am opposed to regulation, but because I know my colleagues in the industry pretty well. They have a way of working around the rules.

However, I have met some of the top players in the CFPB and have to say, I'm impressed. I think these are folks who care about the consumer, care about their work, and intend to make a difference.

Having said that, I still believe regulation is, at best, second best. In an ideal world, you would only deal with ethical, competent mortgage originators. In the real world, you're really going to have to rely on protecting yourself through education and vigilance. Protecting consumers can only be accomplished through educating and empowering them.

So, it is you, the consumer, who has the power to clean up our industry. Educate yourself so that you can make informed decisions, and then hold our feet to the fire. If your loan officer is not on your side – and if you are well-informed you will know – fire him, and find one who is.

Chapter Three

Choose Your Lender, Nail the Deal

As a consumer you have a choice – many choices, in fact – as to where to go for your mortgage. Your grandmother probably went to her local bank. But in later years she might have gone to her *savings and loan* or her *credit union*. You might still go to a bank or a credit union, but you are just as likely to look to a mortgage banker or mortgage broker for your mortgage.

The history of the development of the industry is beyond the scope of this book, but an understanding of the nature of the different lending channels will be very useful to you.

Before we begin, however, the most important thing I can tell you is that **no lender has a special "magic" source of funds.** Some lenders make this claim, but the truth is, we all get our money from the same sources; either *Fannie Mae* or *Freddie Mac*, or from Wall Street investment bankers who assemble pools of funds from private institutional funds, like pension funds.

Remember there are two parties to the mortgage transaction; you, the borrower, and the institutional investor, wanting to invest billions of dollars at a time in investments that yield a good return but are as safe as possible. Your mortgage is an excellent investment (statistically speaking) but a Norwegian pension fund is not in the business of **making** loans; they only want to **invest** in them.

Thus we have middle men. Lots of them. Let's take a look.

How the Money Flows Through the System

You apply for your loan either to a mortgage banker, a mortgage broker, or a bank.

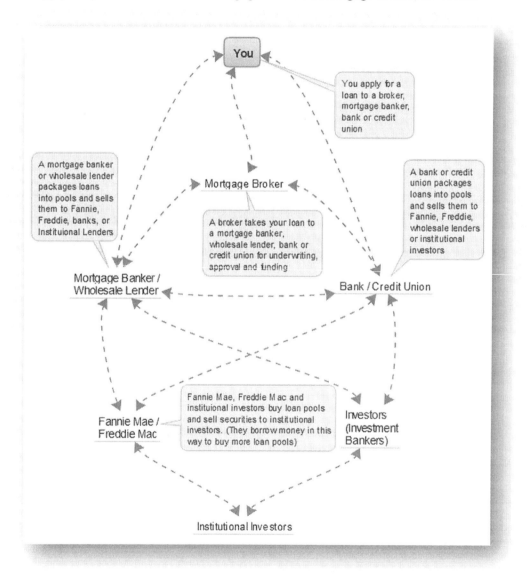

Brokers get their money from a wholesale lender, which could also be a mortgage banker or a bank.

Mortgage bankers and banks get their money from Fannie Mae or Freddie Mac, or from Wall Street investment bankers.

Fannie, Freddie and investment bankers all get their money by pooling thousands of mortgages and selling securities backed by the pools.

In essence, they borrow against the pools to raise money to make more loans.

Applications flow down the arrows in this diagram; money flows up.

Institutional investors (think state retirement funds, pension funds, insurance company funds, etc.) effectively set your interest rate by deciding what they need to earn on their investment.

There is quite a bit of cross-over among the players in the above diagram, but let's take a closer look at each of them.

Mortgage Brokers

A mortgage broker is a company that has no money of its own to lend. This company develops business relationships with *wholesale lenders* – who could be mortgage bankers or banking institutions as well - that provide funds to the brokerage community to make loans. When you apply to a mortgage broker for a loan, the broker will check with the various wholesale lenders to see which company has good pricing on a program for which you qualify that suits your needs. For instance, if you have "bruised" credit, some lenders will still entertain funding your loan, but many will not. The broker sorts this out and then finds the best price, rate and terms combination for your needs.

In theory the two greatest advantages that a broker has over a mortgage banker or a banking institution are more options and, in most cases, better pricing. Why is this?

Because a broker can take your loan to many different sources, he can shop your loan aggressively and, if you are turned down for any reason, can usually take your loan somewhere else. Any given lender may have a few loan programs, but a broker with access to dozens of lenders may have access hundreds of different programs with different terms and features that might be helpful to you. Furthermore, brokers are usually entrepreneurs with lean staffing who can keep their expenses low and expand or contract nimbly with the market in order to contain costs. Large banks or institutions simply cannot compete with the broker's cost structure and cost flexibility.

But there can be a disadvantage, too. Because brokers want to make every loan possible and wholesale lenders want to make every **good** loan possible, wholesale lenders have to *underwrite* loan packages from some brokers with a high degree of due diligence. In some cases your loan -- which **might** be approved quickly and easily if submitted directly to a bank or a mortgage banker -- could be subjected to far greater scrutiny if submitted to the same lender by a broker (particularly a broker with a bad reputation among the mortgage bankers) and your loan may not even be approved.

Therefore, submitting your loan through a mortgage broker may, in some cases, mean longer processing times and being turned down when you might not otherwise be. But only in some cases; in others, your loan may have a much better chance of being approved if submitted to the lender through a competent, ethical broker.

Banking Institutions

Ask your grandmother where to go for a loan, and she will likely point you to the bank, savings and loan, or credit union she's done business with for years. Banks are perceived by some people as being "safer" to do business with. Because the loan officers are the bank's employees, the bank in theory has more control over the behavior of the loan officers. Of course, that could work for you, or against you.

Banks also have (in theory) more control over the quality of the loan package (meaning whether or not fraud is present.) Therefore, banks can be less rigorous about underwriting internally-originated loans, and perhaps more flexible in which loans they approve.

Banks are also subject to less rigorous disclosure requirements than brokers. In other words, they do not have to disclose as many rights to you as brokers do. This has advantages and disadvantages. You are extended fewer rights in the transaction, but you sign a lot less paperwork, too. If you are a well-qualified borrower the overall process of getting a loan from the bank **might** be easier than going through a broker.

On the flip side, banking institutions are highly regulated and must make prudent, conservative lending decisions so as not to have too many bad loans in the event of a recession. So, banks are typically less creative and less flexible than brokers and wholesale lenders working together. If they don't approve your loan, that's it – you are declined and told to move on. You cannot recover the time or money you've invested in the process.

So banking institutions might be more flexible in underwriting – up to a point – and then much less flexible once that point is passed.

Another consideration is that bank loan officers are generally not free to negotiate terms or price (whether paid as fees or in the interest rate) on your behalf. They are either given the price, including the profit margin the bank wants, or at best a small range within which they can work. They work for the bank, remember, not you.

However, if you are a qualified investor with enough savings that the bank would want your banking relationship, you have a good chance of being able to get the bank to be more flexible in pricing, terms and process on your mortgage. Dangle the banking relationship in front of them, and ask for what you want. (This is usually handled by the "private client" division of the bank.)

One final note on banking institutions: you think of a bank as being just a bank. You might think they make loans from the money they have in their vaults from checking, savings, CDs, etc. In fact, most banks today operate in essence as mortgage bankers. Acting as wholesale lenders they offer their products through brokers or mortgage bankers in addition to their own loan officers, and sell their loans to investors as mortgage bankers do, as described below.

In short, the bank today really isn't your grandmother's bank. Banks are generally perceived as the "safe" route, and they do offer an easier process in some cases, but as a generalization the loan officer's job at the bank is to sell you a product and move on to the next client. That might be fine in your circumstance.

Wholesale Lender

Pure wholesale lenders are not likely to have a retail presence, meaning they don't offer loans directly to you. I include them in this discussion because of the important role they play in moving money to make brokers more competitive. These institutions create loan programs and underwriting guidelines, and raise money to make loans. They then offer their programs to you through the brokerage community. They offer the brokers a "wholesale" rate, leaving enough room in the price for the brokers to make a profit and still compete with direct lenders, such as banks. Brokers originate loans and the wholesale lender underwrites the loans to ensure compliance with the program guidelines. Then they approve and fund the loans.

Once the wholesale lender has made enough loans, they are packaged together as a loan pool. Think of each loan from the lender's perspective as being the right to collect a monthly payment from you, the borrower, for the next 30 years. The right to collect that money has value. A pool (or portfolio) of many loans is then offered to investors; the money generated by the wholesale lender by the sale is then used to fund more loans.

During the Mortgage Boom wholesale lenders were plentiful. Through mortgage brokers they offered a wide array of creative loan products and created significant competition, greatly benefitting consumers. In retrospect, many will argue that it was not good for consumers that wholesale lenders became as significant a source of funding as they did because it played a large role in precipitating the subprime mortgage crisis through toxic loan products. While this is true, many wholesale lenders offered only safe products, and they played a valuable role in making us all more competitive, too. A well-managed wholesale lender working through brokers can often offer you terrific options and terms today.

Mortgage Banker

The mortgage banker has a "warehouse" of someone else's money to lend, and works directly with the consumer. You could walk into a mortgage banker's office and not know whether or not you are dealing with a broker or a banker. The banker has a number of lenders with whom they work, much like a broker. But when you go to a mortgage banker your loan isn't underwritten or funded by the ultimate lender.

The mortgage banker has their own underwriting staff and underwrites the loan "in-house" according to the rules of the investor to whom they intend to sell the loan. They then fund your loan from a *warehouse line of credit* issued to them from a lending source (often the wholesale lender to whom they will sell the loans in question.) The mortgage banker then sells the completed package to the wholesale lender, pays off the line of credit and keeps a little as a profit.

If you have ever gotten a mortgage from ABC Mortgage, and all the paperwork when you closed escrow was in the name of ABC Mortgage, but the loan was sold to XYZ Mortgage within two or three months, you were working with a Mortgage Banker, or basically a slightly different kind of broker.

Three really important points:

- Mortgage bankers often claim they lend their own money and the decisions are made in-house. Actually, they lend you someone else's money and they do make the decisions in-house, but do so in accordance with someone else's rules.

- Because they have more control over the process it **can** be (but isn't always) faster than working with a broker.

- Nowadays, many brokers have become broker / bankers, meaning that they can lend in either capacity. They will fund your loan "in-house" if they have the loan program because their margins are higher if they do. If they don't have the right loan program through their banking channels they will broker your loan to a wholesale lender that does have the right program, rather than lose your loan.

From your perspective, there should be little difference between working with a broker, a mortgage banker, or a broker / banker.

However, do remember that disclosure rules for brokers are more stringent. If you want to know exactly what your lender is actually earning on the loan, for instance, you must use a broker. Banks and mortgage bankers do not disclose what they earn on your loan.

The Best Choice

Ultimately, the important thing will be the honesty, integrity and competence of the mortgage advisor with whom you work, and secondarily the programs and lenders they have access to. Since we all draw our money from the same pool, so you should be able to get close to the best pricing possible by becoming well-informed and asking the kind of questions that make it clear how well informed you are. But work with a competent, ethical professional.

Relationship of Brokers to Bankers

Are brokers cheaper?

What about pricing? Are brokers cheaper? It depends. As a broker I have almost always been able to get better pricing for my clients through particular banks than my clients could get through the same bank going directly to them. It helps to remember that bank loan officers are employed by the bank, and in most cases are told what to charge. They work for the bank; they can be terminated at any time, for any reason.

Brokers, on the other hand, work for you. If you aren't satisfied enough to sign off at the end of the deal they earn nothing at all. While a bank may fire their loan officer at any time for any reason, you may fire your broker at any time, for any reason, even **after** you have signed off your final loan documents in some cases.

So for years banks have been reasonably competitive because they've had to be. Brokers simply represented too large a share of the market, and banks had to compete with them.

As of this writing, that has changed somewhat. Many mortgage brokers have had to leave the business. At the same time many of our funding sources – the wholesale lenders from whom we get our funds – have shut down, cutting off a significant source of the funds available to the brokerage community. Many traditional banks eliminated their wholesale operations, so they no longer offered their loans through brokers, and instead hired hundreds or thousands of loan officers.

Brokers can still be cheaper, but most no longer hold the primary advantage they held for so long over banks and mortgage bankers – access to hundreds of lenders to shop.

How do brokers make money?

Many folks assume that brokers simply shop for the best deal for you and add on their commission. This is not true (and actually never was.) Today brokers are paid in most cases by the wholesale lender, and not by you. (And remember, often our wholesale lender is the bank that you might walk into.) Why would a bank work with brokers?

A bank or mortgage banker may have their own offices and employees and make loans directly to consumers, but what if they want to expand rapidly and grow their market share? They have two options:

1. They could spend a lot of money and take huge risks opening up branches and hiring loan officers, processors, managers, HR people, etc.

2. They could take their product to the brokers and sell through them, too.

All they need to do is pay the broker what they would otherwise pay for their own staff, and in doing so multiply their reach to the public many times over instantly, with virtually no risk. The bank gets instant exposure to many times the number of customers and still earns the same margin on the loans, and the broker absorbs all the costs and risk of expansion. (And the bank still keeps their retail origination staff too, so they don't cannibalize their own production, they just enhance it.)

So, while brokers do earn money on the deal as a middleman, they are paid by the banks from the money the bank saves by **not** having to hire more staff. If you find an aggressive enough broker you should be able to get a price as good, or better, than any retail bank or mortgage banker.

Why "good" brokers get better pricing

There is more to it than that, however. Not all brokers get the same price from even the same lenders. From a wholesale lender's perspective, business from some brokers is more profitable and less risky than business from other brokers. To see this you must understand that a wholesale lender is paid only when (and if) your loan closes. Yet, every loan submitted costs money to process and underwrite, whether it closes or not. A broker who submits only loans that are likely to close is much more profitable than one who submits any old loan to the lender to "see what sticks to the wall." Likewise, a broker that submits clean, non-fraudulent deals represents far less risk and higher profit than one who is willing to work in the "gray" area.

Wholesale lenders are smart people moving tens of millions, if not hundreds of millions of dollars per month. If one broker is less costly and less risky to do business with than another, the "good" broker will get special pricing and usually higher-priority service.

The implication is obvious. If you find a "good" broker to work with, they get better wholesale prices and can pass all or some of those savings on to you. It is not unusual for a good broker to get pricing as much as 0.50% of the loan amount better than what we call "street" pricing. ½ of 1% doesn't seem like much, but on a $500,000 loan that amounts to $2,500 in up-front costs, which can be used to offset other costs or buy down your interest rate. It adds up.

However, a broker lands in a wholesale lender's good favor by submitting good, honest loan packages, so don't count on one to lie, cheat and steal for you to get the deal done. It is their integrity that has afforded them the better pricing.

So then whom do I choose?

The answer to this question depends on your profile and circumstances. Do you fit neatly into one of the descriptions below?

- If you are a highly qualified borrower and **minimal hassle** is the most important thing to you and price is secondary, you might be happiest going to your bank or credit union for your mortgage.
- If you have very large liquid deposits that you can tempt the bank with, and in particular if you also happen to need a very large mortgage, go to the bank and dangle the deposits in front of them. Ask for their **private client** division.
- If your situation is a little complicated, go to a broker or a broker / banker so that your loan officer can sift through a number of lenders to find one comfortable with your scenario.
- If you want the very best price and ease of the transaction is not that important to you, go to a small mortgage broker.
- If you want great advice so that you feel comfortable with the decisions you make about your loan program, whether you should buy down your rate, or whether you should even get the loan at all, go to a broker or broker / banker that comes highly recommended by folks whose judgment you trust.

Getting the Best Possible Deal

What most folks say want then they come to me is the lowest **interest rate** possible. The second-most common response is the lowest **cost** possible. Few people, however, tell me they want the lowest possible costs over their anticipated life of the loan. My job, as a mortgage advisor, is to make sure you do consider this, whether you know you ought to or not.

The lowest possible lifetime cost for you will be most likely if you complete the following steps:

1. Choose a mortgage advisor, rather than a mortgage seller.
2. Match the loan product with your needs and situation.
3. Choose the right trade-off of price against interest rate for your needs.
4. Lock intelligently with the help of your mortgage consultant.
5. Manage your loan intelligently to pay it off as quickly as possible.

Choosing a Loan Consultant

After reading all about the different types of lenders above you've decided what type of lender you want to work with. But even at any given lender all loan officers are not the same. The choice you exercise by choosing the right mortgage advisor will have a greater impact on your lifetime costs than any other choice you make in the loan process, in my opinion.

All things being equal, I would choose my loan consultant based on the following criteria (in order of priority):

1. Referral – did someone I know and trust refer me to this professional?
2. Quality of Advice – does this professional know his or her stuff, and is he or she on my side? Does he or she understand the big picture and are they able to communicate that to me?
3. Price.
4. Who they work for – reputation of organization.

Negotiate what you can, and certainly shop for price to a degree, but good advice and great locking strategy will save you multiples over the lifetime of your loan compared to what going to a cheaper provider will.

Yet, in many cases consumers make their decision about whom to work with based on the lowest cost quote. For many reasons, you could not use a less reliable standard to choose your mortgage advisor.

Many of the reasons should become clear to you as you read the rest of this book. But here we will discuss this specific issue in a very direct way.

First, let's ask the question, "What makes a **great** mortgage advisor?"

I believe it is the quality of the advice they give you. Your advisor should understand what concerns you ought to have, whether you know of them or not.

A great mortgage advisor will ask him or herself "What is it that this borrower really needs?" Note that I didn't say want, but **need**. Most borrowers would answer this question with "the lowest cost or rate possible." However, when asked what "the lowest cost" means, many will give me an answer that tells me they don't understand what the true cost of financing over time really is.

Let's examine what I mean by that. We'll assume we need a $200,000 mortgage and examine a very simple illustrations of this concept.

Bill and Lois are doing their last refinance on the home they plan to retire in. They shop the loan and they tell both prospective lenders they want the best interest rate on a zero-point loan.

Loan officer Bob recommends a zero-point 15-year fixed loan at 5.500% and other costs of $3,500. Their payment would be $1,634.17.

Comparison of Lifetime Cost of Two Loan Options

	Option: 5.500% @ -0- points	5.000% @ 1.25 points
Loan Amount:	$ 200,000	$ 200,000
Non-Lender Fees:	$ 3,500	$ 3,500
Points:	$ -	$ 2,500
Total Up-Front Loan Costs:	$ 3,500	$ 6,000
Term:	15	15 (Years)
Monthly Payment:	$ 1,634.17	$1,581.59
Lifetime Cost:	$ 297,650	$ 290,686
Initial Investment:	$	2,500 (Difference between up-front cost of two options)
Monthly Savings:	$	52.58 (Difference in monthly payment)
ROI:		24.58% (Yield on the "investment" of paying points.)

Loan officer June understands that this couple will never refinance again. She offers Bill and Lois the same deal Bob offers them, but also suggests and recommends a 15-year fixed loan at 5.000% at 1.25 points, and $3,500 in other costs. The payment on this loan would be $1,581.59.

If Bill and Lois take Bob's offer their lifetime cost of the loan would be:

$3,500 + (15 x 12 x $1,634.17) = $297,650.

If they take June's recommendation, their lifetime cost of the loan would be:

$3,500 + ($200,000 x 1.25 / 100) + (15 x 12 x $1,581.59) = $290,686.

June's recommendation would save Bill and Lois nearly $7,000 over the next 15 years.

Another way of looking at it is to say that June wants Bill and Lois to "invest" $2,500 (the 1.25 points) to buy the interest rate down, saving Bill and Lois $52.58 per month for 15 years. This equates to an ROI of 24.58%. Not a bad return on investment.

When a client tells me they want the lowest possible cost, they usually think that they mean the lowest cost **up front**. Since I'm helping them make what is likely to be the largest financial decision of their life, I have an obligation to think of the bigger picture.

I'm biased, of course, but I think thoughtfulness is the most important quality a loan consultant can have. In practice, there are a number of pieces to this puzzle. Your loan officer should be an expert in all of the following areas. If he or she is not, find another one.

Ability to understand your financial picture

Loan consultants are **not** financial planners or CPAs, as a rule. However, we deal every day with very large financial transactions, and our advice can save or cost you tens of thousands of dollars in your lifetime.

While we are not qualified to give you advice on taxes, insurance, investments, etc., we absolutely should be able to look at your overall financial picture and understand your strengths and weaknesses and how they might relate to your ability to qualify for a loan and which loan products and pricing would be advisable in your case.

Your initial conversation with your loan consultant should give you confidence that he or she is capable of and interested in understanding your needs and concerns.

Ability to communicate complex financial principles to you

An ability to understand your financial picture must translate into an equally strong ability to communicate those principals to you, especially to the extent that they drive his or her recommendations.

Not only should your loan consultant understand why a certain course of action is best for you – he should be able to help you understand why your choice is right for you, and what the costs and risks are. Being able to have an intelligent conversation with your financial advisor is a bonus.

Knowledge of underwriting guidelines and programs

This might seem obvious, but you'd be surprised how many loan officers are weak in this area. ("Let's throw this against the wall and see if it sticks…") No loan officer has an encyclopedic knowledge of underwriting guidelines, but if they can't determine quickly if your loan is feasible then they ought to be able to find out very quickly and without putting you through a wringer. If your loan officer submits your loan to a lender for underwriting and it is turned down once, be wary. If it is turned down by a second lender, find a different loan officer.

Understanding of how interest-rate markets work

A loan officer can save or cost you more money by how and when they lock your loan than with anything else within their control, including pricing. The interest rate market is quite a bit like the stock market, however. On most days we see new pricing in the morning. But on many days the pricing changes once, twice or even three times again during the course of the day.

Over the course of the time your loan is in process pricing will have changed dozens of times. It will have gone up, and down, and up, and down.

There are factors that drive rates up and down, just like certain news or trends drive stock prices up and down. You would not place your investments with a stock broker that didn't understand what drove stock prices; you would be wise to trust your mortgage to someone who has a clear understanding of what drives interest rates, so that he or she will know when to lock your loan.

On the other hand, just as a stock broker cannot possibly hit the lowest possible price of a stock every time you want to buy and the highest when you sell, no loan officer will hit "the bottom of the dip" every time. But even small changes can make a huge difference in your lifetime cost.

When you are interviewing your loan officer, ask him or her "Are interest rates going to go up or down in the short term, and why?" If you don't feel confident in the answer, keep shopping.

Willingness to watch the market daily

No amount of competence in understanding interest rate markets will matter if your loan officer isn't willing or able to watch interest rates every day until you lock. If your loan officer recommends that you lock your loan on the day of the application, ask why. While once it a while it is a good idea, that is rare.

A good advisor will re-price all unlocked, approved loans every morning, and send an analysis to clients via email upon doing so. They should include a short analysis on where they think rates are going in the next day or two, and why. Clients should always be in control of when they lock, and at what price and cost. There are many competent, ethical loan officers out there who follow this practice. Ask your loan officer if he or she is willing to do this and, if not, find another one.

Matching the Product to Your Needs

Once you've chosen the best mortgage advisor for your needs, you now have to choose the right product. Almost everyone has a clear idea of the type of loan they want and the price they want to pay. I always offer my clients the best deal I can find on exactly what they ask for. I also provide them, however, guidance about other products or alternative price points that I think they should consider and my thoughts on why.

Throughout this book you'll find real-life examples of clients who initially wanted one type of loan but chose another when they understood the benefits, costs and risks of all their options.

The most important decision you'll make about your loan is which loan to get. You'll have to choose between:

- One loan or two

- Adjustable-rate (and its various flavors) or fixed (and it's various flavors)
- 10, 15, 20 or 30 year term
- Accepting or avoiding mortgage insurance

In Chapter 11, "Fixed-Rate Mortgages", for example, I examine how choosing a 20-year term instead of a 30-year term will save you nearly $100,000 on a $200,000 mortgage over the lifetime of the loan. Would that surprise you? I know many of my clients are shocked to learn there is a way to have $100,000 (or in many cases much more) cash when they retire.

In my case my compensation has always been the same no matter what product (or price level – see below) you chose. In this way I could give you options and let you select what is best for you without any question about my motivation.

Today, all mortgage brokers have to work this way. The amount that mortgage bankers and banks can earn can still vary, but a mortgage broker will earn the same amount (expressed as a percentage of the loan amount) on every loan.

So do pay attention if your broker suggests an alternative product for you. The choice is still yours. (Insist on it.) But the suggestion just might save you money.

Paying the Right Price

You always have the option to trade off your up-front costs against your interest rate. You can buy a lower interest rate (and therefore lower payments) by paying a little more up front, or you can reduce (or possibly even eliminate) up-front costs by accepting a higher interest rate and higher monthly payments. Which is the right choice for you?

Many clients come to me having done their research on the internet. They have learned rules of thumb that make them very confident about whether they want to pay points or costs or not.

The thing is, calculating your lifetime costs involves math. Using rules of thumb just seems silly when you can build an Excel spreadsheet and calculate **exactly** how much one option will cost versus another. As I mentioned, I work with a lot of engineers.

The great thing is that you don't even have to be able to do the math, but your loan officer should be able to do it. The difference between paying or not paying points can amount to thousands of dollars over your lifetime. This is money that ends up in your pocket when you retire, rather than your lender's.

If you want to pay zero points, by all means pay zero points. If you want a no-point, no-fee loan then you shall have one. But if you are working with me I would like to give you options to consider so that I know you are making an informed decision. Then choose whatever you want.

Locking Strategy

Locking refers to the process whereby you commit to the lender that you will take a particular interest rate at a specified price, and the lender commits that it will deliver that rate and price to you provided you are approved and close by a certain day. The longer the period for which you ask the lender to commit, the higher the price will be for a given interest rate at any given point in time.

I want to make an outrageous claim here. A competent loan officer can save you – or cost you – more money by being great or terrible at locking strategy than any other part of the transaction. The fees charged by your lender, the interest rate they ultimately give you, even the choice you make around the trade-off between up-front costs and the interest rate, all pale in comparison to locking strategy when it comes to the sheer amount of money good practice can save you.

I like to play the market when locking my clients' interest rates. I usually do not lock in the interest rate immediately upon taking the application. (I always explain the concept and give the client the choice.) Most of the time it works out great, and my clients get a lower rate and / or lower cost than they would have had I locked them immediately.

The interest rate market is an odd beast, though, and interest rates tend to jump up fast, but settle down slowly. An unexpected move in the market can make rates jump through the roof in a matter of minutes. So, while most of my clients end up with a better deal for playing the market, a small percentage of them lose the opportunity to lock in a low rate.

I have had clients who are philosophical, to be sure. One couple buying a fourplex wasn't sure how long it would take to close escrow, and so decided (it is always the client's call) to wait to lock their interest rate. Some unexpected event came along in the market and sure enough, rates jumped up. By the time we had to lock in order to close their purchase on time rates had settled down a bit, but they were higher than they would have been had we locked them right away. They saw the event as having taken a chance, and although it made it slightly more difficult to make the investment cash flow, it was tax-deductible after all. They were philosophical – the event didn't ruin their experience with the investment or ruin their life.

I've noticed that others, however, are less philosophical. They need to know that in every single case they have received the lowest possible rate and cost combination that was ever available during their escrow – maybe even before or after. Anything less than a bull's eye is a miss, so to speak.

I recall one gentleman where everything went perfectly. We tracked the rates every day, followed them up and down, and locked at the last possible moment – and exactly hit the lowest cost available during our escrow period. Rates rose after we locked and were higher when he signed his loan papers. After signing, however, and before closing, interest rates started to slide and looked like they would probably go lower – so he demanded a lower interest rate. (0.125% or 1/8 better, by the way, which would have saved him less than $30 per month.) The thing was, we would have had to start his loan from scratch and taken him to a new lender, and, if rates went up during that time, he would have been worse for the experience, not better.

We told him no, so he cancelled his loan which was his right. We declined to start his loan up again and he went elsewhere – I hope he got what he was looking for, but I doubt it as rates started rising again.

Playing Partners in a Game of 3-D Chess

You can probably see that getting the best possible mortgage is a little like playing 3-D Chess. When you only play once in a while it's a daunting game, and you aren't likely to play well. A great mortgage advisor, however, has played this game hundreds of times. Between choosing the product, picking the right price and timing your lock, you can save tens of thousands, if not hundreds of thousands of dollars over your lifetime. But you need to choose wisely, and you need a great advisor to do that.

The more you share with us what you want and why and what is important to you about the transaction the better we can deliver the product, price and process you want.

If you are like most people, you will not remember how much you paid for your loan six months after you close. If I ask you your interest rate you'll have to look it up. If you are happy with the transaction and feel good when it comes time to close, however, you'll be happy with the result, and if you feel like you've been strung along you will be unhappy.

My happiest clients are those who worked with me like a partner. Those who distrusted me all along because of bad experiences they had with other lenders in the past were never happy no matter how good a price or rate they got.

Clients who work **with** me, however, are usually very happy down the road because they knew they were the ones making the decisions, they understood their options, and they chose wisely and confidently. In retrospect they knew they had saved a ton of money. **That** you'll remember.

My advice, therefore, is to be as honest with your mortgage advisor as you would be with your doctor. (Unless you lie to you doctor about your smoking.) Tell us everything that might be important to us, and tell us everything that is important to you.

If we are not on your side, you will almost certainly know it intuitively. If you have a bad feeling, fire your mortgage advisor and get one you trust, because we're about to commit you to more debt than you've probably ever had before; we should be working together.

Managing Your Mortgage

Finally, getting your mortgage is only half the story. When it comes to spending as little as possible on your mortgage over your lifetime, managing your mortgage is at least as important at getting the best mortgage to begin with.

There are a number of different strategies you can employ to reduce your lifetime costs:

- Bi-weekly payments
- Additional principal every month
- Extra payments when possible

Bi-Weekly Payments

The bi-weekly plan saves you money by paying down your principal balance faster in two ways.

First, your payments are sent to the lender sooner than they are due, so when they are made less interest has accrued and more of the payment goes to principal. Since the interest accruing is calculated based on your current principal balance, less interest accrues each month and more of the payment goes to principal, creating a positive feedback loop.

Second, you'll make 26 payments each year, since there are 52 weeks in a year. That amounts to 13 monthly payments, so you are making one additional payment each year. Think of it as sending in an extra check each year equal to your monthly payment, but it all goes to principal.

There are a number of third-party companies that will set up and make bi-weekly payments for you for a small monthly fee. I'll start this discussion by saying there's no reason you need to hire someone to do it for you. The only value they add to the equation is discipline, which you can do yourself through your bank's bill pay system. Here's how hiring someone else compares to doing it yourself:

Bi-weekly payments on your own: The bi-weekly plan works best for those who are paid bi-weekly. To put this plan in place:

1. Pay your mortgage on the 1st of the month as soon as it is due, so that you are current.
2. Have your paycheck automatically deposited into your checking account.
3. Using your bank's bill-pay system, set up an automatic payment from your checking account to the lender equal to one-half of your mortgage payment, to be paid the day after your paycheck is deposited into your account. Be sure to include "Apply overage to principal curtailment" on the memo line. (I say pay this from your bank's auto-pay system because that forces the discipline on you that you would pay for with a bi-weekly service, but it costs you nothing.)

By the following month you will have made two half-payments, so your next monthly payment will have already been made. You have to get ahead of the payment first, though, or else a portion of your payment will be late each month.

Hiring a company to do this for you works like this:

- The company sets up an escrow account for you, and you make payments which are placed in the escrow account.

- You send the company one-half of a mortgage payment every two weeks, plus a small processing fee. (The fee is charged every time they accept a check from you.)
- They send in the payments to the lender, hopefully in a timely manner.

You can see there is no real benefit to you in hiring a company to do this for you. You must pay a fee every time, and your payment is credited to your mortgage later than it would if you sent it directly to the lender yourself.

How much can paying bi-weekly save? It depends on your interest rate and term of the loan, but let's use our example from earlier in this chapter and calculate the savings.

Our $200,000 30-year mortgage at 6% will have monthly payments of $1,199.10. Over 30 years the scheduled total of your payments (if you pay exactly according to the original plan) will be $1,199.10 x 360 = $431,676.38.

> Note, however, that a bank doesn't have to credit partial payments or even full payments if they are made before the due date. Instead, some banks escrow the payments and then apply then when they are due. If this is the case your lifetime savings will be less.
>
> Check with your lender before making bi-weekly payments.

If we pay it bi-weekly, we will pay $599.55 every two weeks. We will have the loan paid off in 24.51 years (in this example) and we will have paid a total of $382,052.24.

Paying bi-weekly we will shave 5 ½ years off of our loan, and save about $50,000 over our lifetime.

Additional Principal

If we are disciplined we can also pay extra principal every month as an alternative to bi-weekly payments. This is very simple – simply add a certain amount to your payment every month, and add "Apply overage to principal curtailment" on the memo line.

Many of my clients simply "round up" their payments. If their mortgage payment is $1,199.10, for instance, they might send in $1,300. I choose this number because, in our bi-weekly example above, you would be sending in the equivalent of $1,299.02 per month. ($599.55 x 26 weeks /12 months = $1,299.02) So a payment of $1,300 is almost exactly the same.

Let's see how this stacks up. We already know that:

Our $200,000 30-year mortgage at 6% will have monthly payments of $1,199.10. Over 30 years the total of your payments will be $1,199.10 x 360 = $431,676.38.

If we pay $1,300 each month on our regular due date, we will pay off our loan in 24.50 years, and pay a total of $382,199.96. The results are almost **exactly** the same as the bi-weekly payment plan, which makes sense since we're sending in about the same number of dollars every year.

Extra Payments When Possible

Finally, many of my clients have windfall income from stock options or bonuses. They will take the windfall income and apply it to the principal balance of their loan when they receive it. The lifetime savings depends on the amount and timing of the extra payments, but can be calculated. One of the tools described in Chapter 22 – "Tools" is called "Effect of Extra Payments" and is available on www.loanguide.com. This tool will help you determine how any one individual additional payment will affect your lifetime costs.

Summary

My job is to help you keep as much money in your pocket as possible over the anticipated life of your loan by getting you the best possible mortgage. You can take it from where I leave off. You can manage your debt in such a way as to get out of debt as quickly as possible and spend as little as possible in your lifetime paying money to the banks.

However, I will say this: many of my clients are so intent on paying off their mortgage, they will pay down their mortgage while keeping other debt. Your mortgage is probably the least expensive and usually the most stable debt you have. For most folks it is also the only tax-deductible debt that they have. (Consult your tax advisor for your specific situation.)

If you have any other debt, it is likely that you should retire that debt first, and then begin working on your mortgage debt. Your financial planner can help you with this, but keep one singular focus in mind: the best way to save money over the course of your lifetime is to get rid of all of your debt as fast as you possibly can.

Keep this in mind, and you will get the best possible mortgage.

Chapter Four

Should You Get a Mortgage?

Any discussion about mortgages needs to start with the question: "Should I?" Most of the meetings I had with prospective clients during the Great Meltdown have ended with the conclusion that no, they should not (or could not) do anything. It is not uncommon for a client to question me when my recommendation is to do nothing. But remember, I am on commission. If I do a loan for you, I earn money. If I don't do a loan for you, I get paid nothing for my time. I am incented to recommend "Yes," not "No."

So why would I say no? There are two reasons. First, I say "no" when it is the right thing to do. That is reason enough for me, and for many of the mortgage professionals that I know.

Second, for most top-notch mortgage professionals, virtually all of our business comes from referrals and past clients. While we may give up income today when we recommend you not refinance or buy, we are building our professional practice. It is simply good business practice to guide you to making the right decision, so that you will think of us when you need financing in the future, or when a friend, family member or co-worker mentions they are in the market. (Can you imagine how long a dentist would stay in business if they recommended pulling healthy teeth in order to make more money?)

So before we examine how to get the best mortgage for your needs, let's look at whether you even *should* get a mortgage in the first place. There are four very different scenarios to consider:

1. Buying a home
2. Refinancing
3. Buying an investment property
4. Getting a Reverse Mortgage

Let's take a look at each situation separately.

Chapter Five

Should You Buy A Home?

Very few folks can afford to pay cash for a home, and so if you want to buy a home you'll need a mortgage.

Common wisdom is that your home is the best investment you'll ever make, and the sooner you can get into the market the better. Up to a point, I agree. The value of real estate invariably has risen *given enough time*, and it has historically been an excellent hedge against inflation.

But owning a home isn't necessarily for everyone, and it often happens that folks that should buy a home are sold into homes that they cannot really afford.

So what do you consider?

Reasons to Buy

Following is a list of the reasons traditionally used to argue that you **should** buy a home. All of them are often true, but have to be considered in context; are they true for **you**? The reasons not to buy a home may outweigh the reasons to buy a home. We can break down the various reasons to buy a home into two categories: Financial and emotional.

Financial

Tax Advantages

When you finance a new home, the interest you pay on your mortgage is usually tax deductible, and it can be significant. For an example, let's assume you are buying a $250,000 house with 20% down. You decide to put $50,000 down and get a $200,000 mortgage to finance the balance of the purchase price. Assume you are able to get a 30 year fixed loan at 6.000%. Your interest cost for the first year would be about $11,933. If your marginal tax rate were 28%, you would save $3,341 ($11,933 x 28%) on your income taxes. Quite literally, the IRS is paying for 28% of your interest cost.

Furthermore, your property taxes are deductible as well. In California your taxes equal roughly 1.25% of the purchase price, depending on where the property is located. In this case, your property taxes would run $3,125 per year. Your deduction would save you an additional $875 per year, courtesy of the IRS. Isn't it nice for the IRS to be giving *you* money for a change?

If you are making such a good income that your tax bills are killing you and you have no other deductions, the U.S. tax code is written in such a way as to encourage you to buy a home.

What is not usually said, however, is that if you do not have a tax problem, the tax benefits are less meaningful to you. Also, if you don't itemize deductions now when you file your income tax return, you currently take the standard deduction. When you itemize in order to take advantages of the tax deductibility of your home mortgage interest deduction, you lose the standard deduction, so the tax benefits estimated with this example would be overstated.

If you want good information here you'll need to examine your specific situation and do a more in-depth analysis. In order to be sure what your homeownership tax benefits will be, you absolutely must consult your tax advisor, as your situation is unique.

Appreciation

Prior to originating mortgages, I was an appraiser for 17 years. When I hear folks tell me that real estate *always* goes up in value, I have to chuckle. Of course, I hear that less these days than I used to. From an historical perspective, values in our area (The San Francisco Bay Area) **declined** from about 1982 through 1985, and declined again from 1989 through 1994 or so. During the Great Meltdown and the Great Recession our values slid quite dramatically, but began recovering in 2012.

Even so, over time real estate has certainly risen in value, and has done so pretty reliably. If you buy a home, the chances are very good that given enough time the value of your home will rise, and you will make money on the property. There are stories, of course, of folks making hundreds of thousands of dollars on their homes in a very short period of time. Don't count on it. Buy a home because you want to own your own home. If you hold it long enough, the appreciation is a bonus.

Leverage

If your property's value does rise, you will benefit from the principle of *leverage*. What this means is that while the entire property is appreciating at a certain rate, only a small portion of the purchase price was your cash to begin with. The bulk of the price is usually fronted by a lender in the form of a mortgage. If the property is appreciating at, say, 3% per year on average, you are earning 3% on the money you invested. But since the entire property is appreciating, you are also earning 3% on the money the bank invested.

A simple illustration follows that might make this clear.

A $50,000 investment without leverage earning 3% per year grows to $61,494 after seven years.

With leverage, the same investment grows to $107,468!

In this example, you have the option to invest your down payment of $50,000 at 3% somewhere safe – a

Simple Leverage Example			
	Without Leverage	With Leverage	
Purchase Price:	N/A	$ 250,000	
Down Payment:	N/A	$ 50,000	(@ 20%
Loan and Purchase Costs:	N/A	$ 2,500	Down)
Initial investment:	$ 50,000	$ 52,500	
Yield / Appreciation:	3%	3%	
Holding Period:	7	7	(Years)
Balance / Value after 7 years:	$ 61,494	$ 307,468	
Pay Off Financing:	$ -	$ 200,000	
Net Proceed:	$ 61,494	$ 107,468	
Less Initial Investment:	$ 50,000	$ 52,500	
Net Profit:	$ 11,494	$ 54,968	
ROI:	3.00%	10.78%	

respectable rate of return. After 7 years you now have $61,494, for a 3.000% yield, or rate of return.

If, on the other hand, you invest it in the example we've been using as a 20% down payment on a $250,000 home, you are earning 3% on your money **plus** 3% on the lender's money. At the end of seven years you will have $107,468, compared to $61,494 if you simply put the money in the bank.

Because *compounding* makes it even better, the net result is an annual return of almost 11% on your original investment of $52,500, an impressive annual yield.

This example is simplified to make the concept easy to see. We are ignoring the payments you'll be making on the mortgage, the payoff of your mortgage principal, the rent you will **not** be paying as a result of owning your own home, and the costs of the sale of the home. But you can see that leverage is a very powerful tool, and one of the reasons that folks want to buy real estate.

However, the flip side of leverage is **risk**. The lender is guaranteed their rate of return; you are not. As millions of families have learned during the Great Recession, if your property declines in value instead of appreciating, your equity – the initial $50,000 investment -- can be wiped out in a very short time, and you may even owe the bank more than your home is worth.

Lifetime Housing Costs

You're going to live somewhere, and you'll have to pay for it. The conundrum for most first-time homebuyers is that renting almost always costs less to get in and less each month. But if we look closer, how accurate is that perception?

Is buying a home less or more expensive than renting? With both rents and home prices going up faster than they have in years, this is becoming a very interesting question.

For years real estate agents have used a common analysis that accounts for the tax advantages of home ownership to show that indeed, owning a home is as cheap, or nearly as cheap, as renting the same home. I've built a similar analysis and used it a number of times myself.

Because I work with a lot of Silicon Valley engineers, however, I always like to look deeper. (Because my clients do, and I need to keep up with them.) Consequently, I have two different ways of answering the question posed by this chapter.

First, the simple method

The classic way of looking at this question is to acknowledge that there are tax benefits to home ownership, and to account for them to compare the *net, after-tax, initial* monthly cost of home ownership versus the monthly cost of rental.

Let's use our ongoing example:

We'll assume we are currently renting a home in a middle-class neighborhood. The identical home next door is for sale and we're wondering how much more it would cost us each month to own it than we currently pay in rent.

We currently pay a monthly rent of $1,050. Nowadays most renters have renter's insurance to cover their personal belongings and liability, so we'll assume that we have a renter's insurance policy with an annual premium of $360, or $30 per month.

The identical home next door is listed with an asking price of $250,000. We have enough cash on hand to put 20% down, and we can qualify for a 30 year fixed mortgage at 5.000%. The monthly payment on this loan will be $1,073.64, slightly more than the rent we currently pay to rent. However, we'll also need to pay for homeowner's insurance and property taxes, which boost our monthly pre-tax housing cost well above the cost of renting.

When we apply our tax benefits, however, we find that the net after-tax cost of ownership is about the same as renting. The easiest way to see this is visually; here's what the analysis looks like:

You'll note that the monthly payment (*Principal and Interest*, or P &I) has two parts: *Principal*, and *Interest*. The interest portion of your payment is generally deductible, the principal portion is not. Property taxes are also deductible, but homeowner's insurance is not. (All of these rules are subject to change and may or may not apply to your circumstances. Consult your tax advisor.) Take a look at the example on the next page.

Your total pre-tax housing payment is $1,394.06 per month, over $300 more than renting. But assuming a 28% marginal tax rate (consult your tax advisor) you'll see that Uncle Sam pays for $233 of your interest and $73 of your property tax. Your net after-tax housing payment is only $8 more in this example than renting.

Tax Advantages of Owning Real Estate

Assumptions

Purchase Price:	$ 250,000	Interest Rate:	5.000%
Down Payment (%:)	20.0%	Loan Term (Years:)	30
Down Payment ($:)	$ 50,000	Property Tax Rate:	1.25%
Loan Amount:	$ 200,000	Income Tax Rate:	28%

Monthly Payment (Principal & Interest:)   **$1,073.64**

Ongoing Tax Deductibility (Rent Vs. Own)

	Own	Deductible?	Rent	Deductible?
Principal:	$ 240.31	No	$ 1,050	No
Interest::	$ 833.33	Yes		
Mortgage Insurance:	$ -	Yes		
Homeowner's Insurance:	$ 60.00	No	$ 30	No
HOA Dues:	$ -	No		
Property Taxes:	$ 260.42	Yes		
Total Pre-Tax Payment:	$ 1,394.06		$ 1,080.00	

Tax Benefit

Item	Amount	Benefit
Interest:	$ 833.33	$ 233.33
Mortgage Insurance:	$ -	$ -
Property Taxes:	$ 260.42	$ 72.92
Tax Savings:		$ 306.25
Net Monthly Payment:		$ 1,087.81	$ 1,080

Your current total housing payment:	$	1,080
Your proposed net after-tax housing payment:	$	1,088

There are other considerations, but in this example the monthly cost of ownership works out to about the same as renting. This type of analysis has been used for decades to illustrate the cost of ownership relative to renting.

Now, the more complex method

Any good Silicon Valley engineer considering buying a home would tell you, however, that there are several deficiencies in this analysis. (I know this, because they've told *me*.)

First, the amount of interest you pay declines over time: slowly at first, but eventually your tax benefits are reduced considerably. So, in time the benefits of owning are overstated.

Second, we're not taking into account inflation. Even with the relatively benign inflation we've had over the last decade, a reasonable estimate for inflation over time might be 2% to 3% per year. Which costs will rise? Property taxes for sure and insurance almost certainly. But here's the kicker: your **rent will certainly rise, and your mortgage payment will not**. In fact, eventually your mortgage payment will drop to zero when you pay off your loan. In the long view, the above analysis **significantly understates** the financial benefits of home ownership.

It's complicated, but let's see if we can clarify it. First, here's the analysis taking into account inflation. If you continue to rent, your housing costs will rise throughout your lifetime. Even with a relatively benign inflation rate of 3%, you will be spending almost *three times* as much on your annual housing expense after 30 years than you do today.

Rent vs Own, Long Term View		
Assumptions		
Rent		**Own**
Monthly Rent: $ 1,050		Purchase Price: $ 250,000
Renter's Insurance: $ 30		Down payment: (%) 20%
		Down Payment: ($) $ 50,000
Other Assumptions		Loan Amount: $ 200,000
		Interest Rate: 5.000%
Inflation Rate: 3.00%		Loan Term: 30 years
Property Appreciation: 3.00%		P & I Payment: $1,073.64
Marginal Tax Rate: 28%		Prop Taxes: (%) 1.25%
		Prop Taxes: ($) $ 260.42 Increase: 2% annually
Savings Rate: 6.00%		Insurance: $ 60.00 montlhy
		Total Monthly Housing Pmnt: $1,394.06
Results		
Total housing cost after 30 years		
	Annual	Cumulative
Cost of Renting:	$ 30,053	$ 610,250
Cost of Owning:	$ 20,034	$ 495,318
Annual and Cumulative Cost After 5 and 9 years	Renting	Owning
First Year Owning Is Less Than Renting (Annual Cost): 5	$ 14,541	$ 14,478 (Annual)
Years to Break-Even (Cumulative Cost): 9	$ 131,245	$ 130,438 (Cumulative)
Asset Value After 30 years: Renting: $ 254,993	Owning:	$606,816

If you buy a home your housing costs still rise because taxes and insurance costs rise, but since your mortgage payment stays the same the total monthly housing costs rise much more slowly. And look what happens by year 30! In fact, in year 31 the principal and interest payment drops to zero – you only have to pay taxes and insurance.

Going back to the analysis above, you'll see that over 30 years the cumulative cost of renting is estimated to be $610,250, while the cumulative cost of owning a home is estimated at $495,318. And then the annual savings skyrocket.

The most significant benefit can best be seen graphically. What happens to your annual housing costs after your mortgage is finally paid off?

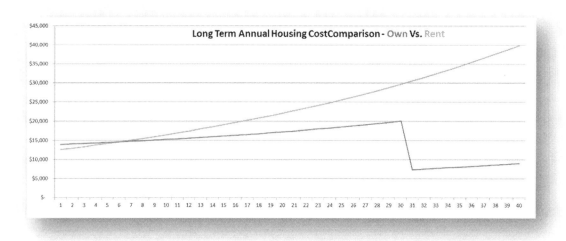

After 30 years your annual housing cost as a homeowner drops to about $7,500, while the renter is paying just over $30,000. When you need it most – in retirement, when your income is probably fixed – your housing costs drop to almost nothing.

> Many of the tools I use throughout this book are available to readers for free on the book's web site, www.loanguide.com. The tools are written in Microsoft Excel 2010, so you will need to be able to read Excel files to use them.

Simple or In-Depth?

So let's compare the two analyses – the simple and the more in-depth – to see what they tell us and how they differ.

The simple analysis shows that the after-tax net cost of buying a home will be about $8 per month more than renting.

The in-depth analysis shows that buying a home will save you $114,932 over the next 30 years.

They are both "right" in that the math is correct. Which is more meaningful to you?

But Wait! There's More! What About Net Worth?

Finally, one more benefit of investing in Real Estate is a by-product of the principles of leverage and annual cost of ownership over time. Real estate will appreciate and, when it does, you will gain equity in the property. Using our example above, what if you compared buying versus renting a home and looked at how much you would have in assets after a period of years?

If you rent, you won't have to put $50,000 down, so let's assume you put $50,000 in cash into a savings account. If you rent you'll be spending less than if you buy, at least for the first few years, so let's assume you invest the money you save renting into the same account. Let's also assume that you earn 6% interest on your account as well. (I want that account today! As of this writing, a 6% APY on a safe savings account would be spectacular, but I'm trying to make a point.) Eventually renting becomes more expensive than if you bought the home, so we'll assume that when that time comes you'll take the difference **out** of your savings each month because your rent is now higher than your mortgage payment would have been.

In essence, by investing the difference when renting is cheaper and then using savings to supplement the rent after renting becomes more expensive, we're making your cash flow for the next 30 years for housing expense the same for renting as it would be if you were to own your home.

We'll assume that the property is appreciating at the inflation rate, which we've set at 3%. Let's look at this graphically:

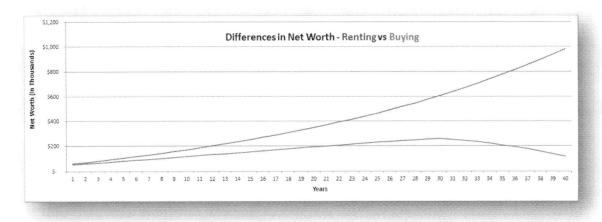

At first your net worth is the same – you have either invested $50,000 in purchasing your new home, or you've invested $50,000 into your savings account.

By the end of year three, however, you'll see there is already a noticeable difference in your net worth. If your home is appreciating at 3% per year, and your bank account is earning 6% *and* you're contributing money to it, how can that be? *Leveraging!* (See section on leverage earlier in this chapter.) If you rent you have $50,000 growing at 6%, plus your small monthly contribution. If you buy you have $250,000 growing at 3%, plus some of your monthly payment is buying even more equity by paying down the principal balance on your mortgage.

Remember from our analysis above by year six you'll spend more renting than if you own, although it won't be much. But from then on, not only are you spending more money on housing to rent (and therefore having to pull money from your savings account to make up the difference) but the difference grows every year.

After 15 years you'll have about $100,000 more equity as a homeowner than the renter would in their savings account. After 30 years you'll have almost $450,000 more, and that's when your housing payment drops dramatically.

All this happens from an initial investment of $50,000 to buy a $250,000 home.

Summary

What is clear to me – and I admit I'm biased – is that in the long run, owning your own home is a very good financial investment. If you are ready to buy your first home, however, I ask that you read the section on why **not** to buy a home. I personally believe most families will benefit from buying a home, but I am serious when I say it's not for everyone, and not everyone should.

But first, we haven't covered all the reasons you **should** buy a home.

Emotional

Changing direction, as we said above there are two components to the decision as to whether to buy or rent your own home: financial and emotional. The financial considerations are important, and I would never work with a client that has not fully considered them. This might surprise you, though: I would also never work with a client that has not fully considered the emotional reasons for owning your own home. It is just as likely that not being emotionally ready for home ownership will destroy a deal as it is not being financially ready. If you are emotionally ready to buy you can overcome many challenges that arise that financial strength alone cannot solve. Let's explore this.

Stability

A perfectly valid reason many of my clients mention for wanting to buy a home is stability. If you are a renter, chances are you don't live in one place very long. Even if you have, you know that you could be asked to move anytime, for any reason.

Whether you are just ready for some stability in your life, want a home to raise a family, or are just sick and tired of moving, having the stability of knowing that you own your own home and nobody can ask you to leave affords peace of mind that many families find very comforting.

Pride of Ownership

Along the same lines, there is something nice about being able to make your home your own, which is difficult to do if you are a renter -- although I can think of one notable example.

I own a small four-unit apartment building as an investment. I had one tenant who decided that she wanted to "personalize" her apartment. She repainted walls, tore out flooring, replaced lighting fixtures, etc. I could certainly understand her need to nest and be comfortable in her own home, but when I discovered that the changes had been made and went to see them I was not pleased. She did not ask permission to make the changes. Her taste was – unique – at best, and would almost certainly not appeal to any other prospective tenant. When I reminded her that her lease agreement said she could not make modifications without written permission she ignored me and continued to do whatever she wanted.

When she informed me she was going to tear out the kitchen because a contractor friend of hers was remodeling someone's kitchen and these great used cabinets were going to be available, I could not ask her to leave fast enough. Renovating the apartment to get it ready for the next tenant cost me thousands of dollars. The point is this woman needed her own place.

When you have your own place you can make it your own. When counseling first-time homebuyers, I often advise them to make sure all their credit cards are paid off before buying their first home – because for sure they'll be run up again soon enough.

But this is a good thing. When you buy your own home you can personalize it to your heart's content and make it your own sanctuary for when you come home from a hard day's work. If you want purple walls, by all means paint your walls purple. Put polka dots on it. Buy some shag carpeting.

But if you're renting from me, please ask permission first.

Reasons Not to Buy

My job is to sell loans. So why would I give you reasons to not buy a home? Because buying a home is not in everyone's best interest. If the time is not right for your family to buy a home now, I would much rather counsel you properly and trust that I've earned your business in the future.

Having said that, there have been cases where I counseled my clients not to buy but they chose to buy anyway. In some cases I chose to provide the financing because even though I thought it was not a good decision I decided they could handle it if they were committed. In other cases I have declined to provide the financing where I believed that they would not be able to handle the payments.

It all comes down to commitment and risk. Most folks think they can handle the commitment of owning a house, but do they understand the risk?

A young couple – I'll call them Bob and Sally – came to me wanting to buy a condominium together. Bob had inherited some money (enough for a small down payment) and both were employed in fairly steady jobs; they were anxious to start a life together. The bad news was that Bob's income was largely commission and was not sufficient to qualify for the loan, plus he had very little credit established. Sally had excellent credit and higher income, and could basically qualify on her own, but she didn't have any money of her own for the down payment and closing costs. They had been to see another loan officer, who had recommended a sub-prime loan of the type we've since learned was very dangerous. The recommended loan was an *adjustable-rate loan* with a *prepayment penalty*. (More on these terms later in Chapter 12, "Adjustable-Rate Mortgages.")

A good example of a suicide loan

The interest rate was locked for **two** years, and would then begin rising (a lot) and the prepayment penalty would last for **five** years. In other words, their payments would begin rising at the beginning of year three, but it would cost them a great deal of money (in the form of a pre-payment penalty) to get rid of the loan prior to year six.

The loan officer counseled them that they could obtain 100% financing and refinance out of it when they were making more money and get better financing then because their home would be worth a lot more through appreciation.

I recommended that they not proceed. First, there was reason to suspect by the time we were meeting that the appreciation we had been experiencing was fading. I reasoned that they may not **have** any more value when the time came to refinance, and they would not be able to get rid of their adjustable loan; they would be stuck with whatever rate (and payment) their contract gave them at that time.

Also, without trying to get into their personal business, I pointed out that responsibilities can be stressful on relationships, and that if the relationship didn't work out they would be stuck with each other because of their financial commitment.

I'm known for my romantic nature.

They decided they wanted to move forward with or without me. I agreed to work with them because I could structure a loan that would at least be far more favorable than the one offered by my competitor. Because of their circumstances I couldn't get rid of the pre-payment penalty altogether and they couldn't qualify for a fixed-rate mortgage. However, I knew that it would be smart for them to have a pre-payment penalty period **shorter** than the period for which their interest rate was fixed. (You want to be able to refinance without penalty before the rate begins to adjust.)

I arranged a loan where instead of the rate being fixed for two years and the prepayment penalty lasting for five, (the very dangerous proposal from the first loan officer) the rate was fixed for **three** years and the prepayment penalty was in force for **two**. Once the prepayment penalty expired they would still have 12 months to refinance before their interest rate adjusted. The two-year pre-pay gave them a lower *margin*, which meant when the rate did adjust it would do so less violently. (For more on margins read Chapter Eleven – "Adjustable-Rate Mortgages.") In other words, I gave them the best chance at success possible under the circumstances.

You know what happened. The economy turned, their incomes went down and the value of their condo declined. They were underwater (their home was worth less than what they owed on their mortgage) and in trouble. I got a call from Sally, who said she and Bob were breaking up and asked me how she could "get off the loan." I had to tell her that she couldn't. It doesn't work that way.

Do I regret making this loan? No, because they would have had no chance at all if they had used the other lender. I do wish I had done a better job of talking them out of buying the condo in the first place, but the next Bob and Sally I meet will definitely get the story of the first Bob and Sally.

Sometimes the decision not to buy a home – yet – is the right one.

Long-Term Debt

In almost all cases, the mortgage I arrange for you is the largest debt you've ever had. You most likely can't pay it off in any reasonable amount of time, and it will take a huge chunk of your paycheck for as long as you can imagine.

Some financial authors write about "good debt" and "bad debt." They will argue that good debt is debt that you use to invest, such as your mortgage when you buy a home. I think that needs refining a bit. It is only good debt if you can afford to make the payments, plus invest for the future, plus live your life with some level of comfort. For many years most conventional underwriting assumed that your monthly payments on all your debt should not exceed 45% of your monthly gross income. (As of 2014, the *Federal Housing Finance Agency, or FHFA,* has implemented a rule which effectively sets a benchmark of 43% of your gross income as the max that lenders should consider "safe.") Situations vary, but for many folks I think even that is way too high.

People ask me what payment they can afford all the time. They shouldn't ask me; they need to ask themselves. Here's a simple exercise if you aren't sure what you can afford:

If the home you want to buy will take a payment (principal, interest, taxes and insurance) of $2,000 per month, and your rent is currently $1,000 per month, stay where you are, pay your rent and put $1,000 per month in the bank for a year. If at the end of the year you have been able to do this comfortably then you'll know how you have to live to afford $2,000 per month. As an added bonus to the exercise, you'll have an extra $12,000 for your down payment.

This is a simple example, and your tax situation, the amount of interest you can earn on your savings and your income patterns all may have an impact on what your specific example would look like, but you get the idea. There is a saying that first-time homebuyers are "house poor," meaning they can't afford to live because they've stretched so far to buy their first home. Unless it means a great deal to you to own a home, don't be house poor.

Long-Term Commitment (Liquidity)

It costs a lot of money and takes time to get out of a piece of real estate. If you make a mistake and buy the wrong shoes you can return them, or maybe you're out $50. If you make a mistake and buy the wrong car you may lose a thousand or two unwinding the deal, or drive a car you don't like for a couple of years.

But if you buy the wrong house, or buy a home and then discover you really weren't ready, you will probably be out tens of thousands of dollars and you might destroy your credit. This is not a decision to be taken lightly, and if you feel you are being pushed to make a decision that feels too rushed, take a step back, breathe, and ask yourself if you are truly ready.

Ongoing Maintenance

Remember when you first moved out of your parent's house and discovered that toilet paper cost money? And it didn't replace itself? And the fridge wasn't magic after all - you had to fill it?

Owning your first home is like that. Grass needs mowing, trees need trimming, walls need painting and then a few days, weeks or years later *they need it again.* Appliances break down, too, and when your first plumbing leak happens you just might call your real estate agent to ask how much you can get for the house if you sold now.

If you buy a condo at least your homeowner dues pay someone else to handle the outside for you, but those HOA dues can be steep, and they tend to go up over time.

The point is, when the typical renter buys their first home it can be a shocking experience. Don't get me wrong, it can be fun, too. I love to try to fix things with my hands. Notice I said "try." I often fail. But I still love doing it.

However, please be ready for this. If you rent today and spend all your time and money traveling to exotic locales to scuba dive, your life will change dramatically when you own a home.

Conclusion

Buy a home if you are ready for the commitment, can realize a substantial tax benefit, and it would make you happy to personalize your home. If you hate maintenance problems, are not highly stable in your job and relationships, or have to stretch so far that you would have to live meagerly to make your house payments, think it over carefully.

Chapter Six

Should You Refinance?

Folks refinance for one of two reasons:

    1.   To reduce their payments or change their terms (known in the industry as a *rate and term refinance*) or

    2.   To pull cash out for some reason (known as *cash-out.*) The decision points for rate and term and for cash out are very different, so we will handle them separately.

> For a separate discussion about *reverse mortgages* see Chapter 8 "Reverse Mortgages." I will treat them separately because the mechanics of the analysis are completely different than they are for a cash-out refinance.

Rate and Term

There could be two reasons to consider a rate and term refinance: Reducing your interest rate, and changing the terms of your loan.

Rate

Considering rate, of course, means that you are considering refinancing to reduce your interest rate and (usually) therefore your payments. I have heard many "rules of thumb" about when to refinance for a lower rate:

- You must lower your rate by 0.500% (1/2%) or more;
- You must lower your payment by $100 or more;
- You should not pay points; etc.

Nonsense. It's all nonsense. These rules are much too simple, and none of them considers how much longer you have to go on your current loan, how long you intend to keep the house (or the loan,) whether you have plans in the near future that might create a need to pull cash out, or even what the cost of the new loan would be.

Here is my rule of thumb: consider all of these things, and only refinance if it will save you money **when looking at the life of the loan**. What is the life of the loan? The length of time you think you will have this loan in place. It may or may not coincide with how long you intend to stay in the property. Let's consider those factors that should impact your decision.

Before we begin, however, keep in mind that I work with a lot of Silicon Valley engineers, and I also get referrals from financial advisors and planners who work with engineers. These men and women are great to work with, because they demand a rigorous analysis of the facts and situation, and really hold my feet to the fire when it comes to giving them extraordinarily well-considered advice and rich detail. They're very smart, and I've learned a great deal from them.

My clients who are not engineers, however, often don't appreciate and usually don't even want the depth of analysis that engineers want. It's not that they aren't smart, but rather that they are often not interested in knowing the mechanics of how the finance works; they just want to know what the best deal is.

I understand this. When I take my car in to a mechanic, I know that in most cases if I really tried I could understand the mechanics of why the engine is making that scraping sound, but really I just want it fixed.

When it comes to the question of whether or not you should refinance to a lower rate to save money, there are a number of ways you can analyze the options. The more in-depth you go the more informed your decision will be, but at some point more information only points out the solution that is mathematically more refined; it does not necessarily lead to the best decision for your family. (You'll see why as you keep reading.)

Consequently, I have come up with two different methods to look at the question, "Should I refinance to lower my rate or not?"

The (Overly) Simple Method

Let's start with the method you **shouldn't** use. The most common method used by loan originators – the payback analysis - to help you decide whether you should refinance or not is very simple to use and understand, and is usually very misleading. The concept is simple: How much will the loan cost, and how much will you save every month? If you divide the monthly savings into the cost of the loan you find out how long it will take to "pay back" the cost of the loan. It's all savings after that. Right? Well, no. Let's take a look.

We assume you have a 30 year fixed mortgage that you've been paying for five years. You have 25 years left to run on it. You are currently at 6% and your payments are $1,288.60 per month. You can get a new 30 year mortgage at 5.500%. Should you do it?

In this analysis your mortgage advisor shows you that the loan will cost a total of

Simple Refi Benefit Analysis		
	Current Loan	Proposed Loan
Principal Balance:	$ 200,000	$ 200,000
Interest Rate:	6.000%	5.500%
Term (Years):	25.00	30
Payment:	$ 1,288.60	$ 1,135.58
Monthly Savings:		$ 153.02
Cost of New Loan:		$ 3,000
Paybay (Months):		19.6

$3,000 and your monthly payment will go down by $153.02. You'll earn your costs back in less than 20 months. As long as you plan to stay in the house at least this long, this looks like a good deal. So what's wrong with it?

The primary problem is that you've just added five years to the life of the loan. The lesser (but still important) problem is that you are paying your loan down more slowly (usually) after you refinance than you would if you just kept your current loan.

As you pay your mortgage off over time a larger portion of your monthly payment goes to principal, and you begin to pay your loan off faster. If you refinance, however, you "reset" the loan, and you will pay very little principal on your loan each month. You have extra money each month, but you might be paying down your loan more slowly and, if you make only the new, the smaller payments, will certainly pay more over a lifetime because you'll have to make payments for five more years. You are not just refinancing your mortgage; you are mortgaging your future.

So how do we fix this?

I will first outline a very simple modification of the payback analysis that can help you decide if you should refinance, and then I'll outline a much more in-depth approach. If you are in the market you may want to use one or the other, or both. But after the numbers are crunched, remember that there may not be one "right" answer. It may be that several options available to you are suitable and there are less tangible issues (non-mathematical) that make one more desirable than the others.

The Simple Method

So back on task: what issues do you need to consider if the reason you are considering refinancing is to save money?

How long do you have left on your current loan?

If you have 25 years left on your 30-year loan and you get a new 30-year loan, you add five years of payments to the end of your loan. Does this mean it's a bad idea? Not necessarily, but the question must be asked. Let's review a simple way to answer that question by asking two other simple questions:

1. For the new 30-year loan that is proposed, what payment would you need to make in order to pay it off in 25 years rather than 30? In other words, let's compare apples to apples as far as the loan term goes.

2. How soon will you earn back the cost of the new loan through the monthly savings when you compare the payments necessary to pay it off in 25 years rather than 30?

Using the same example above, let's answer these two questions. I call this the **Modified Payback Analysis.**

Refinancing with a 30 year fixed pays your closing costs back in only 19 months – but adds 5 years of loan payments at the back end. *Unless...*

You make larger payments to **pay it off in 25 years**. You still save money on your monthly payment, but pay it off in your original time frame.

Modified Payback Analysis			
	Current Loan	Proposed Loan	Accelerated Payoff
Principal Balance:	$ 200,000	$ 200,000	$ 200,000
Interest Rate:	6.000%	5.500%	5.500%
Term (Years):	25.00	30	25.00
Payment:	$ 1,288.60	$ 1,135.58	$ 1,228.17
Monthly Savings:		$ 153.02	$ 60.43
Cost of New Loan:		$ 3,000	$ 3,000
Payback (Months):		19.6	49.6

All we need to do is calculate what you would have to pay each month if you wanted to pay it off in 25 years. In almost all cases you can make larger payments if you wish, have the surplus applied to the principal, and pay your loan off faster. (See Chapter 3, "Choose Your Lender, Nail the Deal", the section on *Managing Your Mortgage*.) In this case, if I made payments on the new loan of $1,228.17 it would be paid off in 25 years. Now the monthly savings is only $60.43, and it would take me 49.6 months to be paid back for my costs.

Now is it a good deal? Probably, if I make the higher payments and if I intend to stay in the property more than 50 months (the new break-even point.)

The Modified Payback Analysis is fairly simple, but it gets to the heart of the matter for folks who are serial refinancers: each time they obtain a new loan they restart the cycle of paying it off.

This method is much better than a simple payback analysis, but it too has limitations. So let's go deeper for my engineer friends.

The In-Depth Analysis

While the Modified Payback Analysis is much better than any simple rule of thumb you can apply, it has two drawbacks:

1. The analysis treats the entire payment as a cost, and as a result the savings you will actually see are understated.

2. The lower your interest rate the faster you are paying down principal and the simple analysis doesn't account for that.

You want to understand two concepts::

1. Treating the entire payment as a cost understates your savings

There are two things you need to know in order to better understand this.

First, your monthly payment is not all cost (*interest*.) It is both cost (*interest)* and investment (*principal*.) The principal portion of your payment that you pay each month is not really a cost, even though it comes out of your checking account every month. Since it is applied to the principal balance of your loan it is really money that you invest in the equity in your property, like taking money out of your checking account and putting it in savings.

The interest you pay each month is your real monthly cost of carrying this loan, but most advisors don't separate this out because the amount applied to principal and the amount applied to interest changes every month, so the analysis become too complex to do easily.

But if we simplify the analysis it doesn't tell the whole story.

2. The lower your interest rate the faster you are paying down principal

Secondly, the lower your interest rate (all things being equal) the more money goes each month toward your principal, even though your total payment is lower. Your actual savings, therefore, are greater than the simple difference between your old payment and your new one. A simple analysis illustrates this nicely:

Principal & Interest As a Function of Interest Rate		
	Existing Loan	Proposed Loan
Principal Balance:	$ 200,000	$ 200,000
Interest Rate:	6.000%	5.500%
Term (Years):	30	30
Payment:	$ 1,199.10	$ 1,135.58
Interest Portion (Month 1):	$ 1,000.00	$ 916.67
Principal Portion:	$ 199.10	$ 218.91
Balance Five Years Later:	$186,109	$184,921

You can see that from the very first month you are paying more principal on the loan at 5.500% than you are at 6.000%, even though your total payment is lower. The lower your interest rate the faster you are paying down your loan in the early years.

The point is that after 30 years the balance on both is $0.00, but after five years the balances aren't the same at all. As the analysis shows, after five years the homeowner with the lower interest rate owes almost $1,200 less than the other homeowner. So, in addition to saving almost $64 per month on his payment, he is an additional $1,200 ahead after five years by virtue of a lower principal balance – he has paid off more of his loan.

In the Modified Payback Analysis, if you kept the new loan and paid it off over 25 or 30 years the analysis is complete as it is. But if you only held the property for another five years and then sold it, the Modified Payback Analysis doesn't account for the difference in the principal balance at the end of that period.

Put simply, these two principles mean that the monthly savings attributable to reducing your interest rate is **greater than the difference in the payments** and that if you refinance you will owe less at the end of your holding period than if you don't. (Assuming you haven't increased your term – see section immediately above.) We should account for this when deciding whether you should refinance or not.

Finally, the simple analysis does not account for the time value of money. In principle, we would rather pay *later* than *now*. (If you doubt this, call your lender and tell them you'll send in this month's payment next month. They will gently, but clearly explain this principle to you.) So if I had to pay $3,000 more now and could only realize $3,000 in savings over time, I would not choose to do it.

The way to account for this is to *discount* the different payment schedules to a **present value** by using a **safe rate**. I call this a **Net Present Cost Analysis**. This is simpler than it sounds, and you don't need to be a financial genius.

The concept is actually pretty easy. Think of it this way. Let's say you have so much money in savings that you don't even need to get a mortgage. Your financial advisor says you should have one anyway, but you don't want the hassle of making payments. Got it? Yes, my life isn't like that either. But let's pretend.

Let's set up a savings account that pays our mortgage. You'll need to set aside enough money to pay for the up-front loan costs and then make your mortgage payments as planned. You would do it this way:

1. Open a savings account and put a certain amount of money into it at a reasonable interest rate.
2. Pay all of the up-front out-of-pocket costs associated with the loan from this account.
3. Make all of the payments on the loan from this account every month.

You should have put just enough money into the account so that when you make the last payment on the mortgage, the account is drawn down to $0.00. (Or, if you plan to keep the mortgage less than the full term, you should have just enough money left in the account to pay off the remaining principal balance at the end of your holding period.)

The amount of money that you had to put into the account is the **net present cost** of your mortgage.

You don't want to see what the math looks like, but fortunately financial calculators and spreadsheet programs have a present value calculator. I say it's fortunate because, despite doing fairly well in finance in college, I had no idea what the formula was anymore about one week after finals. Albert Einstein once said he didn't memorize his phone number because he didn't want to clutter his brain with information that he could look up. In this one respect, Einstein and I are very much alike.

So how do you get this information? You can find *Refi Benefit Analysis* and *Net Present Cost* Excel-based calculators at www.loanguide.com. Otherwise, give your mortgage professional or financial planner the following information and ask for an analysis in return. They will need:

- Current loan balance (principal balance)

- Current interest rate

- Remaining term (How many months do you have left to pay)

- Current payment (Principal and interest only – if you don't know, your mortgage professional should be able to figure it out from your mortgage statement. If not, get another advisor!)

- Holding period. How long do you think you will stay in the home or keep the loan?

- Do you foresee any life events that may require reworking your finances in the next few years? (i.e. weddings, college tuition, remodeling or additions, purchase of other real estate such as investment property or vacation home.) This answer may impact your holding period, as you may refinance sooner than you sell your home.

- Safe rate. What is the interest rate that you believe you can earn today on a safe investment? This helps your mortgage professional understand your risk profile.

In return, ask your mortgage professional to provide you with the following:

- Interest rate on the proposed new loan

- Terms (Fixed, adjustable, loan term)

- Costs (More on this later)

- Amortization schedule for the proposed loan

- Payment required to pay the loan off by the same time your current loan would be paid off

Do not take vague responses for an answer. Other than the safe rate, which is personal to you, these questions involve math. There is no judgment involved, and no complex estimate or guesses. A good advisor should be able to give you specific numbers. (There will be some slight variation with non-lender loan costs, but your loan officer should be able to get very close.)

With luck your loan officer will be able to conduct a refinance benefit or a net present cost analysis. If not, get the above information and give it to your financial planner, who should be able to do one. For those who love this kind of thing, the following example would be the analysis that I provide to engineers and financial professionals when I work with them.

Let's start with our running example. We have a $200,000 loan currently at 6.000% with 25 years to run. Our monthly principal and interest payment is $1,288.60. We are considering refinancing with a new 30 year fixed mortgage of $200,000 mortgage at 5.500%. The monthly payment will be $1,135.58. We plan to pay the $3,100 in loan costs out of pocket, and we expect to keep the house another 7 years, at which time we intend to move to a better school district.

We can start out with a simple payback analysis. The monthly savings on our minimum payment will be $1,288.60 - $1,135.58 = $153.02. The savings will be paid back in 20.3 months. ($3,100 / $153.02 = $20.3)

Monthly Savings Analysis		
New Loan Type:	30	Year Amortization
You currently pay	$ 1,288.60	per month in **total payments**
You will be paying	$ 1,135.58	per month in **total payments**
For monthly savings of:	$ 153.02	less in payments
You currently pay	$ 1,000.00	per month in **interest costs**
You will be paying	$ 916.67	per month in **interest costs**
For monthly savings of:	$ 83.33	less in interest

Payback Analysis		
You will recoup your costs in	20.3	months
Results: Payback is less than holding period: indicates GO		

But wait – we noticed that the savings were not all interest, so that analysis is misleading. What about the difference in interest costs? We currently pay $1,000 per month in interest. ($200,000 x 6% / 12 = $1,000.

After refinancing we will be paying $916.67 in interest – at first – on the new loan. ($200,000 x 5.5% / 12 = $916.67.) Our actual *savings* in month one is therefore $83.33. ($1,000 - $916.67 = $83.33) This will take a little longer to pay back, then. It will take 37.2 months. ($3,100 / $83.33 = 37.2)

Since we plan to stay for 7 years, or 84 months, it still looks like a good deal. We'll recoup our costs in 37 months and it's all savings from there.

However, this analysis doesn't take into account the difference in the balances between the existing loan and the proposed loan at the end of the holding period (5 years in this example) or the time value of money. Let's look at this.

Cost + Interest Over holding period
Your current loan will cost you $ 57,180 in interest over the holding period
The proposed loan will cost you $ 56,156 in interest and loan costs
Results: $ 1,024 in savings over your holding period
Proposed loan will save you money: indicates GO

Balance at end of holding period

Your current loan will have a balance of $ 179,864
Your proposed loan will have a balance of $ 184,921
(Recognizes your loan balance may be higher as a result of refinancing)
Results: $ 5,057 higher loan balance at end of holding period
Your savings are less than the differences in balances: Indicates no go
But, if you invest your savings of $ 153.02 per month at 2.25%, you will have **$9,708.07** in the bank at the end of 60 months.

Your total net refi benefit therefore equals: **$ 4,651.23**

This analysis shows you that you will pay $1,024 less in costs (Between the proposed loan costs and interest) over the next five years if you refinance.

However, because you are financing the costs you will owe more on your mortgage in five years - $5,057 higher in fact. You'll save $1,024 in interest costs but owe $5,057 more on your loan. That doesn't sound that great suddenly.

However, remember that (if you make only the minimum payment on the new loan) you also have $153.02 more cash each month to invest or spend. You could spend it and have a great time, or if you invest the savings at 2.25% you'll have an additional $9,708.07 in savings. Now it's looking more attractive.

Notice that this analysis doesn't tell us what to do – rather, it forces us to ask the questions, "How long do we think we'll keep the loan?" and "What will I do with my monthly savings?" We can then make sure there is enough benefit within our window period to see if refinancing makes sense.

Finally, let's consider the *Net Present Cost* of the proposed new loan versus our existing loan. Remember, this is nothing more than mathematically determining how much money we would have to put in the bank today to pay for the loan costs, make the monthly payments, pay the loan off entirely in seven years, and have nothing left.

Discounted Net Present Cost of Alternatives		
Net Present Cost of your current loan(s) over holding period:	$	233,804
Net Present Cost of your proposed loan over holding period:	$	232,747
(Recognizes the time value of money by discounting at a safe rate)		
Results: Proposed loan costs $ **1,057** less in today's dollars		

To make payments on our existing loan for the next five years and then pay it off we would have to deposit $233,804 into a savings account bearing 2.25% interest.

To pay up-front out-of-pocket expenses on the proposed loan, make payments for five years and then pay it off we would have to deposit $232,747 in the same account.

The proposed loan, therefore, costs $1,057 less than our existing loan **in today's dollars**. Remember the question we were asking is "Should I refinance to save money?"

The bottom line(s): We've determined that our payments on the new loan would be $153.02 less than our current payments, and we would be saving $83.33 per month in interest. The proposed loan will cost $3,100 in up-front fees, so we would earn the up-front loan costs back in 37 months, less than half the time we plan on keeping the loan. We determined that over the next five years that the loan fees and interest of the proposed loan would cost us $1,024 less than the interest on our existing loan.

However, if we make only the minimum payment on the new loan, after five years we will owe $5,057 more on our loan than we would have if we hadn't refinanced. However, if we invested the money we are saving from the payment into a safe savings account, we would have $9,708 saved up by the end of five years.

This example was intentionally designed to yield some conflicting results, because in real life it often works out that way. But whatever decision you make about whether to move forward or not on this loan, if you go through this type of analysis you will be making an informed decision. If you do that, you can't really go wrong.

Conclusion

If you are refinancing only to save money, go way beyond the normal rules of thumb, and please don't let an uninformed loan officer sell you using a simple payback analysis.

Refinancing to Modify the Terms of Your Loan

If you are refinancing to change your loan terms, the analysis is much less about math and much more about qualitative questions. Here are some examples that may help you.

A very common inquiry today is a family with an adjustable-rate mortgage who wants a fixed rate-mortgage because it is more stable. That seems simple enough; who wouldn't want a fixed-rate mortgage rather than an adjustable?

But naturally, there is a catch.

If you want to refinance **primarily** to change the terms of your loan -- for instance maybe you have a 5/1 ARM (an *adjustable-rate mortgage* with an interest rate that is fixed for the first five years, and then adjusts annually) that will begin to adjust next year and you want a 30 year fixed -- there is usually not a good compelling **financial** argument for doing so. In other words, in the short term you won't likely save money, and in fact you will probably end up spending more.

For instance, I had a client whom I'll call Raoul. Raoul had a $400,000 mortgage that I had written for him five years earlier. The loan was a 7/1 ARM, meaning that the rate was fixed for seven years at 4.500%, and then would begin to adjust annually. On top of that, it was an interest-only loan, so his minimum required payment was quite low. ($1,500)

Strategically, the reason he chose this loan is that he had two children in high school. The younger child would be finishing college in seven years, just about the time the loan adjusted. (We're assuming he would not be on the 12-year college plan like I was.) At the time we wrote the loan, the adjustable terms afforded a much lower interest rate than a fixed rate would have allowed, and the lower interest-only payment meant that Raoul could afford to make payments on his kids' college tuition. Once the loan adjusted and the interest-only period ended, causing the payment to (possibly) increase, the kids could get good jobs and then **they** could pay the mortgage. Ha-ha! OK, maybe not. But I think Raoul made a reasonable choice given his needs at the time.

Now, during a period when interest rates fell, Raoul asked if I thought he should refinance into a fixed-rate mortgage. It was by no means an easy answer. Interest-only loans are rare now, and in my opinion it's not a good idea to constantly re-work your loan into a new interest-only loan; you'll never pay off your house. But even at historically low interest rates at the time, the best Raoul could hope for would be the same interest rate (4.500% at the time we took his application), $4,000 to $5,000 in up-front fees, and a fully amortized payment of $2,027.) In other words, he would have to spend thousands up front, and his payment would go **up** $527 per month.

The tangible benefits would be that his payment would never adjust and he would begin paying principle, so his mortgage balance would begin to go down. The cost would be thousands of dollars up front and hundreds more each month. There isn't a right or a wrong answer here -- it all depends on what's important to Raoul.

If Raoul simply wanted a fixed rate for the security of it, it could be a good move. The important questions here that only Raoul can answer would be: How long do I intend to stay in this property? Why is the security of a fixed payment important to me? How important is it? Can I afford the higher payment?

If Raoul was going to lose sleep over the possibility of his loan adjusting, maybe spending a little more for a fixed rate would be a wise move. But a good mortgage consultant should help him understand **exactly** how much more the fixed rate will cost over time, and let Raoul make the decision.

Raoul did decide to refinance, by the way, and we happened to hit a nice dip in rates and locked strategically (see Chapter 19, "Money-Savings Strategies") and he ended up in much better shape than we had initially thought. His payment still went up, but less than feared.

Raoul is a good example of when the decision is rightly more emotional than strictly financial. But the financial aspect is important too, so let's talk about how to go about that part of the decision.

What You Should Know Before Deciding

First you should investigate what your risk is if you keep your existing loan with an adjustable rate. The two things you want to know are:

- **When** will it adjust? and

- **How** will it adjust?

The question of when is easy to find out. Look at your original *Note* – you should find it in a package that your escrow officer gave you when you signed final documents -- and it will tell you exactly when your first scheduled adjustment is due. The question of how takes a little more work. When mortgages adjust, the adjustment isn't random and the lender can't just choose any rate they please. The new rate is determined by adding together the values for the *index* and the *margin*. These values are described in your original note in a paragraph about how your adjustment will be determined.

For a full discussion regarding the important features of an adjustable-rate mortgage and a definition of *margin, index* and other relevant terms, see Chapter 12, *Adjustable-Rate Mortgages.*

For this discussion let's say that your note calls for the *12-Month LIBOR* index and a margin of 2.25%. What will your note rate be? Simple add them together. The value of the 12-Month LIBOR as of the date this section is being written is 1.02%. We would calculate your new rate by adding your margin as defined in the contract to the current index value.

Index plus	Margin equals	New Interest Rate	Rounded up to nearest 0.125
1.02% +	2.25% =	3.27%	3.375%

So, 1.02% + 2.25% = 3.27%. Your new interest rate is typically rounded up to the nearest .125%, (1/8%) so your new interest rate, if it were adjusting under these assumptions, would be 3.375%.

You can see why I say that most of the time it does not make financial sense to refinance from an intermediate ARM into a fixed-rate mortgage. In a low-interest rate environment if you have a decent adjustable rate loan and simply keep it your interest rate is likely to go **lower** on the next adjustment, not higher. Moreover, the current fixed rate is invariably higher than your impending adjustment. But of course interest rates will not stay this low forever, and there's the rub. A quick look at the chart below will tell you why you may want to get rid of your adjustable rate. LIBOR isn't normally 1.02% -- it's quite a bit higher.

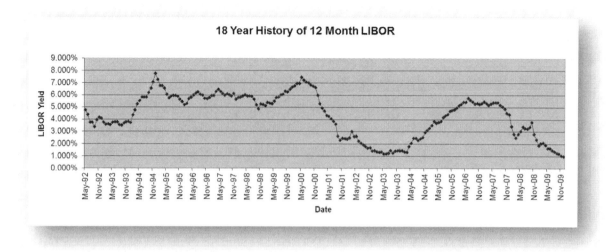

Let's say that over the next 25 years a "typical" LIBOR rate might be 5.000%. If that were the case, then if you keep your adjustable-rate mortgage your interest rate in typical years will be 7.25% (5.000% (index value) plus 2.25% (margin).) This might be considerably higher than the interest rate that you could get on a 30 year fixed today.

So now you know when your loan will adjust, and how it will adjust, or at least about how it will adjust on the next adjustment. But you don't know how it will adjust in the future, and nobody does really. If the security of knowing your payments are fixed forever is important to you, maybe taking on a higher monthly payment in exchange for a fixed rate is a good financial decision. (As it was for Raoul.)

Refinancing to Lower Payments by Extending the Term

Sometimes it's clear that refinancing will not save you money, but you are just desperate for payment relief; you just don't have enough money left over at the end of the month to live comfortably. If you have only a few years left on your mortgage it is possible that you could reduce your payments significantly, even if you can't reduce your interest rate much, by refinancing into a new 30 year fixed. This type of refinancing is far more common than it should be, but on occasion a case comes along where it makes sense.

Another client ("Linda") came to me by referral with a fixed rate loan of 6.125% with a small balance of only about $150,000. (That is a small loan for California.) Her payments were $1,275.94

80

per month. Linda had only 15 years left on her loan but her payments were uncomfortably high for her. When she bought the house she was married and had two incomes to make payments. After her divorce she made payments on her own for a few years, but had no cushion each month.

She wanted to refinance into a new 30 year fixed loan at 5.250% which would lower her payments to $828.31, a huge savings. However, it would extend her loan by 15 years, and if she paid the loan off over 30 years her lifetime cost would actually be much higher with the proposed loan than with her current loan. Should she refinance?

Although she understood the loan would cost her more in the long run, she decided that the monthly savings were the most important factor to her and went ahead.

You can see that when refinancing in order to change the terms of your loan a lot of personal decisions have to be made. As long as Linda made an informed decision, I was willing to work with her.

Conclusion

If you are considering refinancing to change the terms of your mortgage, your first step is to understand your options and the consequences; your mortgage professional should be able to help you make a well-informed decision. Then, before you move forward, run it by your financial planner, or your spouse, or your parents, or your kids, or all of them. But make sure you have looked at all angles before you do something you can't unwind.

Cash Out

If you are considering refinancing in order to pull cash out of your property you obviously have a purpose in mind for the cash. Like refinancing to change your terms, the answer to the question "Should I pull cash out?" depends on the situation.

What Will Your Financial Planner Say?

Most financial planners today would probably advise you to **not** think of your home as a bank account. Yes, it probably will appreciate over time and when it does you will have an inordinate portion of your net worth invested in real estate. However, you will also want to retire one day, and when you do it will serve you well to not have a mortgage payment.

For these reasons, financial planners will tell you not to pull cash out of your home in most cases.

I'm not quite that conservative. For instance, I think it makes sense (in many but not all cases) to pull money out to remodel or expand your home, particularly if your choice is between an addition (or remodel) and selling your home to buy a larger one. When you sell a home and buy up you will spend a great deal on the real estate transactions, between real estate commissions, title costs, inspections, loan fees, etc. It might be cheaper to pull cash out of your existing home to remodel and expand, and you get exactly what you want.

You also might want to pull cash out of your home in order to invest in income property. I have done this myself and have helped a number of clients do so too. This makes sense to me in many cases, as you are using the equity in one property to buy equity in another.

Beyond these two reasons – remodeling or buying investment property -- I believe that pulling cash out of your home to use for other purposes should be used sparingly, if at all. DO NOT pull cash out of your home for any other reason without discussion it at length with your family, your financial advisor, and if necessary, your attorney.

Issues to Consider if You Decide to Move Forward

If you are going to pull cash out of your home for a sensible reason, there are a number of things to consider.

Should you get a new first mortgage, and equity loan, or an equity line?

One of the first decisions you'll need to make is whether to refinance your first or second mortgage, and whether a second mortgage should be an equity loan or an equity line. There are advantages and drawbacks to each approach.

If your existing first mortgage is one that you would like to change anyway because you can reduce your interest rate or improve your terms, then it is probably best to use a new first mortgage to pull cash out.

If you already have an attractive first mortgage you may want to consider using an equity loan or an equity line for the cash out. (See Chapter 17, "Equity Lines.") The advantages include not having to re-write a good mortgage, not re-starting the payment term of your mortgage, and keeping the loans separate may help you separate the debt in your mind. (For instance, if you used an equity loan to purchase a car, perhaps it's a good idea to pay off that equity loan in the same time frame you would a car loan, while leaving your first mortgage untouched.)

If you do opt for a second mortgage, the choice between an equity **loan** (generally a fixed rate for a fixed period) and an equity **line** (an open credit line secured by your home) is an important one. An equity loan is typically a fixed-rate, fixed-term second mortgage. It is much the same as a first mortgage or car loan, with all of the money advanced when the loan closes, and fixed payments over a set period of time.

An equity line is a line of credit using your home as security. You draw the money out only when you need it, and pay interest on the money only when you have drawn it. You can typically continue to pull money out for as long as ten years, after which time you need to pay the entire loan back over a set period of time. The interest rate on equity lines is always adjustable. It is typically based on the Prime Rate plus a margin, and can adjust any time the Prime does – even more than once a month, although that is rare.

So, once you've decided **if** you're going to pull money out of your home you need to decide **how** you'll do it. The quick guide below summarizes the points made above. Because each case is unique, have your mortgage professional prepare a thoughtful analysis for you showing you how much each of these options is likely to cost over the life of your loan.

Pulling Cash Out – Options		
Option	*Advantages*	*Drawbacks*
Refinance (New existing first mortgage)	• If your current terms are not favorable, allows improvement in rate or term • You only have one mortgage and one payment • Rates are typically lower on a first mortgage	• Typically higher fees than for a second mortgage • You "recycle" your first mortgage, add years to paying it off • You must borrow all the money at once, and begin paying it right away.
Equity Loan (Leaves existing mortgage alone)	• If the terms on your existing mortgage are favorable, you get to keep that loan • Payments on an equity loan are fixed, and you have a set amortization period • Acquisition costs are typically lower than a new first mortgage • The interest rate is usually fixed on an equity loan	• The interest rate on an equity loan tends to be higher than a new first mortgage • There are typically higher fees associated with an equity loan compared to an equity line • You must borrow all the money at once, and begin paying it right away.
Equity Line (Leaves existing mortgage alone)	• The interest rate on an equity line tends to be low • There are usually no or very low fees to acquire an equity line • You only draw the money when you need it, and pay no interest on it until you do	• Equity lines tend to be adjustable, and the interest rate can adjust any time. • Human nature is such that we tend to use equity lines like credit cards – once again using long-term debt to pay for short-term items.

There are also certain profiles of folks for whom an equity line makes more sense than a fixed loan. I would suggest if some of the following apply to you, you would do well to consider an equity line:

- You are comfortable with a variable rate if it means your lifetime cost could possibly be lower than a fixed rate.
- You are self-employed and have the need for access to inexpensive working capital from time to time and the ability to pay the line off when cash is flowing well.
- You have "windfall" income (i.e. stock option grants, large annual bonuses, large commissions) from time to time, and are disciplined enough to use the windfalls to pay off your equity line.
- Your income is steady, but more than sufficient to pay off the equity line quickly.
- You have excellent credit and have managed your credit well.
- Your job is very secure.

I like to see equity lines used as **temporary** sources of money. Unless you have a stomach for variable rates, it is not the best vehicle for long-term financing that you pay off slowly.

Borrow Enough for Your Needs

The biggest mistake I've seen someone make is pulling cash out of their home and not pulling enough out. It's an expensive transaction, especially if you rewrite your first mortgage. If you must do it, do it once, not two or three times.

An elderly woman ("Hazel") who was referred to me by her financial planner was having trouble finding the money she needed to enjoy life. She was living on a small fixed income. She had worked hard all her life and could "get by," but not take vacations, go out to eat, or just enjoy her golden years as she should. Her primary home was nearly paid off, and she also owned a vacation home free and clear. She came to me to pull cash out of her primary home to live on.

My difficulty with this request was that she was planning to take on long-term debt to pay for **current** living expenses, and although she could technically afford the payment, at some point the new cash would run out. I also learned that she had two children who both earned a reasonable living, and both used the vacation home on a regular basis.

I suggested that rather than pulling cash out of her home, she either sell her vacation home and invest that cash to provide her with all the income she needed, or that she ask her children to provide some support in exchange for the use of the vacation home.

Apparently her children did not see the wisdom in my suggestion, and told her not only that they could not support her, but that they preferred she not sell the vacation home either, as they enjoyed using it and one of them wanted to live in the property after her passing.

Hazel came back to me and asked that I proceed with the refinance. I thought about declining to do the loan, but that didn't seem to be the right thing to do in this case. Instead, I decided to reduce my fees and give her the best deal possible. (This was also a small loan, so my broker was a little unhappy about how little we were making. I convinced him it was a karma loan.) Hazel decided to take a smaller amount out, though, than her financial planner and I recommended, so as to keep her payment under a certain target level. This turned out to be a HUGE mistake.

We did the loan and Hazel got the best deal on a loan that I've ever done.

One year later, Hazel called and said she had run out of money again. I contacted her financial planner and discussed the situation, and we both agreed that another refinance was a very bad idea. We counseled her and her children, and pointed out several other ways she could raise the money she needed to live comfortably. (All mentioned above.)

I didn't hear from Hazel for a while, but when I did it turned out she had gone to her bank – a large national bank that you know well – and a loan officer there convinced her to pull out a little more money using an *Option ARM*. This allowed her to pull the money out that she wanted and at the same time keep her minimum payments very low. (See Chapter 14, "Option ARMs;" you should be cringing knowing that a senior citizen got one of these loans.) She got the money and a lower payment, but of course she also got one of the subprime toxic loans that contributed to the Great Meltdown. When she came back to me she wanted to get out of her option ARM and into a new fixed-rate loan, but it was too late. She had burned up too much equity in two refinances already, and in the increasing principal of her new sub-prime loan.

I lost touch with Hazel and earnestly hope that her children stepped up to the plate. The lesson I learned was that if you're going to pull cash out, pull enough out for what you need with a good cushion, whether it is a remodel, buying an investment property, or enjoying your golden years. Pull enough out the first time.

Also, raise your children to be kind and generous and then be really nice to them.

Match the Cash Out With the Purpose

The financing that you decide on when you pull money out of your home should match the use for which you're borrowing it. What do I mean by that? Let's use an example.

A very common purpose for cash-out second mortgages is for home improvement. In fact, contractors will actually partner with lenders and offer you a way to finance what they sell.

There is nothing wrong with this necessarily, except that "lenders of convenience" don't always tend to be the best deals. In fact, these loans often have insanely high fees and extremely high APRs. There tends to be one thing about them, however, that is sensible: they are tied in with the specific home improvements you have in mind, so you only borrow as much as you need and you pay it off as the improvement depreciates.

You can do this yourself, of course, and potentially save a lot of money. Simply borrow enough to complete the proposed improvements, and then pay it off **as quickly as** the improvement depreciates. What do I mean by that?

For instance, let's say you need a new furnace, and you have a quote for $10,000. The new furnace has an estimated life span of 15 years. You could finance the furnace with a second mortgage if you needed to. It would be very smart to either get a 15 year loan or, if you ended up with a longer term that you make whatever minimum payment you need to pay it off in 15 years.

$10,000 is not very much money to borrow, however, when you talk about a real estate loan. A more common scenario (at least in Silicon Valley) is to borrow enough to make several major improvements to the property at once. Most homeowners don't replace high-ticket items the first moment they notice they could be replaced. They will patch things up and "limp along" until a number of items of deferred maintenance have accumulated and the need for some critical component becomes urgent, and then pool the repairs together and finance them all.

While your furnace and roof are the largest critical items that eventually wear out and fail, other components also need to be replaced, some more frequently than others. It is fairly common for homeowners – as long as they're borrowing money – to borrow a lot and take care of a number of issues at once.

Let's say that you've decided your roof can't take another winter and it **has** to be replaced. Your furnace is older and you could get another few years out of it, but it is very inefficient. If you're going to replace an older furnace, then updating those single-pane windows might make sense, too, wouldn't it? Your exterior paint is also showing its age, and with winter coming it could make sense to repaint, since the window replacement will probably necessitate touch-up anyway.

Now that you're thinking along those lines, you also notice that a few of your appliances are older and that your kitchen is very outdated as well. If you're going to borrow money, you might as well borrow enough to do it all, right? Right?

Well, yes…maybe. It's absolutely true that if you're going to pull cash out of your home for any reason, pull it all out at once as it is much cheaper in the long run to do one round of financing, rather than several. However, financing feels almost free to a lot of folks, and this is where they ruin their retirement plans with free-wheeling spending.

So the principal of taking out as much as you need the first time must be tempered with reason. Can you actually afford the higher amount? Are you using long-term financing to finance short-term purchases? Does the proposed loan have any impact on your ability down the road to consolidate your loans?

Let's say your home is worth $250,000 and you owe $150,000. (This is a slight variation on our running example.) It is important to remember that when pulling cash out of your home your loan costs will rise noticeably when your loan amount is more than 75% of the value of the property and rise dramatically if the loan amount is more than 80% of the value. (If you can refinance at all at that point.)

If you borrow an additional $50,000 you now owe 80% of your home's value. ($150,000 + $50,000 = $200,000 = $250,000 x 80%.) If you borrow $75,000, which is probably possible, and then a year from now an opportunity arises to refinance your first into a new low rate and consolidate the loans, you may not have enough equity in your property to do the refinance, or it might be very expensive.

This doesn't mean you should never borrow more than 80% of your home's value, just be aware of the consequences; think it through. You could be stuck with the new financing for a while.

As your mortgage advisor if I notice that you are considering putting yourself in a position that might make things difficult for you down the road, I would want to have this conversation with you to be sure you've considered the risks. The decision is yours of course, unless I think that your decision is so bad that it's hurting your family. In that case, I might decline to do the loan.

So how do you handle it if you want to finance improvements with different useful lives?

I recommend four simple steps:

1. Write down everything you have to do, and categorize them into three categories: Must do now, Must do soon, and Optional.

   You'll need to borrow enough to do everything you must do now, so start with that. (Remember, I recommend that you always borrow enough, but never too much.)

2. Then add the items that you must do soon.

   If you borrow that much at the terms and price available at that time, can you afford the payment? Will you be borrowing less than 80% of the home's equity?

3. Then, add the optional items in.

4. Finally, determine if you can pay off the loan at least as fast as the improvements depreciate.

   Be honest with yourself. Can you afford to pay these items off in less time than they depreciate? A new kitchen might be sexy, but foreclosure and homelessness are not.

How do you figure this out? Here's an analysis I use: (This example is set up as if we are using a second mortgage only to pay for the improvements and leaving the first mortgage in place, but you could use this in either case.)

Paying for long-term home improvements

	Loan Amt	Int Rate	Term	Payment			
Proposed Loan:	$ 76,750	8.000%	30	$ 563.16			

Item	Category	Cost	Useful Life (Years)*	Annual Depletion**	Minimum Payment***	Annualized Payment	Lifetime Payments
New Roof	Must Do Now	$ 25,000	30	$ 833.33	$183.44	$2,201	$66,039
Furnace	Must Do Now	$ 10,000	15	$ 666.67	$95.57	$1,147	$17,202
Exterior Paint	Should Do Soon	$ 12,000	10	$ 1,200.00	$145.59	$1,747	$17,471
New Fridge	Should Do Soon	$ 1,000	15	$ 66.67	$9.56	$115	$1,720
New Stove	Should Do Soon	$ 1,000	15	$ 66.67	$9.56	$115	$1,720
New Dishwasher	Should Do Soon	$ 750	10	$ 75.00	$9.10	$109	$1,092
Interior Paint	Optional	$ 1,500	10	$ 150.00	$18.20	$218	$2,184
New Kitch Cabinets	Optional	$ 15,000	25	$ 600.00	$115.77	$1,389	$34,732
New Countertops	Optional	$ 8,000	25	$ 320.00	$61.75	$741	$18,524
Update Electrical Panel	Optional	$ 2,500	30	$ 83.33	$18.34	$220	$6,604
Total Repairs:		$ 76,750			$ 666.87		$167,287

* How long will this item last before you need to replace it again? The maximum depreciation period should be no more than the maximum term of your proposed loan. (Since you have to pay it off at least that fast.)

** The cost of the improvement divided by its useful life. This is the amount of money this item costs you each year that you own it.

*** This is the minimum payment to pay off each improvement's portion of the loan by the end of that particular improvement's useful life.

Note that the minimum payment for the loan per the terms with the bank is $563.16.

That's important, of course. But if we pay only that much we'll be paying off short-term improvements (i.e. exterior paint) with long-term debt. Your home will need to be repainted in ten years, but you'll be paying off your current paint job for 30.

If we want to pay for each improvement over that item's lifetime, we can come up with a minimum payment that will pay off the entire loan before all the improvements are used up. We simply calculate the payment to pay off the portion of the loan committed to each improvement over that item's useful life, add up the individual payments, and make that payment each month.

In this analysis we need to make monthly payments of $666.87 (rather than the $563.16 the bank expects) initially to pay the loan off fast enough so that we have paid off each improvement before it wears out and needs replacing again.

So, the first question to ask yourself is "Can I afford to make a payment of $666.87?"

Next, compare the "Cost" column to the "Lifetime Payments." This shows you the true cost of financing over time. Scary, isn't it? If you could pay for your roof in cash you would pay a total of $25,000. When you finance it and pay it off over time your total payments will be $66,039! Note that the longer you stretch out your payments, the greater the premium you pay for financing over your lifetime.

Since the "Must Do Now" items are really not optional if you can't pay cash you have to finance them. The "Should Do Soon" items are small enough that if you are disciplined you might be able to save enough to pay cash for them.

Note that the optional items – these examples are very typical when someone is at this point – are usually somewhat expensive and long-term items, which means they add a great deal to your lifetime cost. If you don't really need them and especially if you can't afford the higher payment, now is the time to be prudent and back off. You could always buckle down, save, and pay cash down the road.

Finally, you might have realized that if you continued paying the higher amount after you've "paid off" the shorter-term improvements you would pay the entire loan off early. (18 + years by my calculation.) You could back off and pay less as you paid certain items off" but then is it such a bad thing to pay your loan off early?

Bad Reasons to Pull Cash Out

An excellent example of a bad reason to pull cash out, in my opinion, is to buy a car. It is quite attractive to do so because your monthly mortgage payment will often go up only a few dollars, or possibly not at all. But when you look at the larger picture you have borrowed money for 30 years for an asset you will own for five to ten. You will be paying off that car long after you have donated it to a charity benefiting homeless dogs.

> Let's say we have a $200,000 mortgage at 6.000% with 25 years left to run on it. Our payments are $1,288.60. We can refinance and pull out $30,000 for a new car with a new 30-year loan at 5.5%. Our new payment is $1,305.91. The car is nearly free!
>
> Except that we just added five years to the loan and will be paying for the car for 30 years.

Another example is quite common these days, unfortunately so. A couple came to me ("Violet and Ralph") and wanted to roll their credit card debt into their house payment. They had over $150,000 in revolving debt (credit cards), but had equity in their house.

As a rule, I think paying off revolving debt with equity from your home is a bad idea for the same reason paying off a car is. If it is foolish to pay off a car over 30 years, it seems even more foolish to pay off your **shoes** over 30 years. This just seems really wrong. But sometimes one does what one has to; if you can't make the payments what can you do?

In the case of Violet and Ralph, however, there was another kicker. They couldn't afford the proposed loan. They really had no way to make the higher payments. While I am not an attorney and am no expert at legal matters (please do not take my advice on legal matters – I am ignorant on the subject) I understand that in most cases when you file bankruptcy your unsecured debts – like revolving charge cards -- are cleared away, while your secured debts – like your mortgage and car payment -- are not. If you have about as large a mortgage as you can afford and lots of unsecured credit card debt that you can't afford, what are your options?

1. File bankruptcy and keep your home and the mortgage you can afford, or
2. Refinance the house to pay off the credit card debt (converting unsecured debt which could be discharged in bankruptcy to secured debt, which cannot) and try to figure out how to make the payments.

My recommendation if you are in this case is don't come to see me first. See an attorney first to understand your options. Or else come to me and I'll refer you to an excellent attorney.

What really irritates me about these cases is that most loan officers will show you an analysis that demonstrates how refinancing will lower your monthly bills, without of course explaining how it will ruin your life.

Violet and Ralph had such a loan officer who recommended an Option ARM mortgage to consolidate their bills. Because I had handled financing for them in the past, they wanted my opinion.

I explained that they would not be able to afford the proposed loan, despite the assurances of the loan officer and the very low start rate and payment. I recommended that they talk to a bankruptcy attorney to review their options. They let me know they wanted the loan, and I declined to write it for them. They acquired it from the other loan officer and sure enough, two years later they lost the house.

The really sad thing is that there are software tools available to loan officers that are specifically designed to help them sell clients on debt-consolidation refinance.

A typical software-driven sales presentation looks like this:

If a loan officer showed you this analysis, would you consolidate $60,100 worth of credit card bills into a new first mortgage while at the same time reducing your interest rate on your mortgage?

Would you want to reduce your monthly payments by **63%?**

Who wouldn't?

Consolidate Your Bills! Save Thousands!

Current Debt Load

Mortgage	Balance	Interest Rate	Payment:
	$200,000	6.000%	$1,199.10

Your Credit Cards	Balance	Interest Rate	Payment
Bank of Avarice	$ 12,500	9.99%	$ 625.00
Gotcha Financial	$ 19,750	17.99%	$ 987.50
Fatcat Savings	$ 9,250	6.99%	$ 462.50
Dewey Cheatem and Howe Finance	$ 18,600	22.99%	$ 930.00
Totals	$ 60,100		$ 3,005

Total Monthly Payments: $4,204.10

Proposed Financing

New First Mortgage	
Pay off existing First:	$200,000
Pay off credit cards:	$ 60,100
Closing Costs:	$ 6,500
Total New First Mortgage:	$266,600
Interest Rate:	5.750%
Term:	30 years
New Monthly Payment:	$1,555.81

Total Monthly Savings: **$2,648.30**

But what if your loan officer showed you the rest of the analysis? What is the effect of paying off your credit cards over 30 years, even at a significantly reduced interest rate?

How about an additional **$51,000** in costs over your lifetime compared to not refinancing and simply paying off your credit cards? (See the expanded analysis below.)

Consolidate Your Bills! Save Thousands!

Current Debt Load Mortgage	Balance	Interest Rate	Payment:		Will be paid in		Lifetime Interest Cost
	$200,000	6.000%	$1,199.10		30.00	years	$ 231,676
Your Credit Cards	Balance	Interest Rate	Payment				
Bank of Avarice	$ 12,500	9.99%	$ 625.00		1.83	years	$ 1,230
Gotcha Financial	$ 19,750	17.99%	$ 987.50		2.00	years	$ 3,904
Fatcat Savings	$ 9,250	6.99%	$ 462.50		1.78	years	$ 613
Dewey Cheatem and Howe Finance	$ 18,600	22.99%	$ 930.00		2.12	years	$ 5,078
Totals	$ 60,100			$ 3.005		Total	$ 242,501

Total Monthly Payments: $4,204.10

Proposed Financing

New First Mortgage
Pay off existing First: $200,000
Pay off credit cards: $ 60,100
Closing Costs: $ 6,500
Total New First Mortgage: $266,600
Interest Rate: 5.750%
Term: 30 years
New Monthly Payment: $1,555.81

Total Monthly Savings: **$2,648.30**

Lifetime Interest Cost Total: $293,490

Lifetime Additional Cost: **$50,989**

Yes, you pay less interest each year, but you pay it for 30 years rather than about 2 as you would on most of your revolving credit cards.

If you were the client and only saw the first analysis, what would you do? It looks pretty attractive to me. But by converting your short-term debt into 30 year, long-term debt the total lifetime interest cost of your debt load rises by nearly $51,000. This is a very high price to pay just to get lower payments on $60,000 worth of credit cards.

Tragically, some marketing companies are making a very good living right now selling software that helps loan officers produce a very compelling sales presentation to mislead consumers into spending thousands of extra dollars on interest. These presentations are used by brokers, mortgage bankers, and national banks.

Just remember that every loan originator out there is either paid by commission, or is paid salary by someone who has a very strong interest in closing deals.

Even I only get paid when I close a transaction, so when I tell you it's not a good idea, you should listen. Really, it's costing me money to tell you not to move forward, so when I do, please consider what I have to say carefully.

Conclusion

Never finance anything for longer than you expect to own or use it. A home is the only exception to this, as even if you haven't paid it off you will (probably) have built equity that you can recover by selling. But everything else should be paid for in cash, or at least paid for before you wear it out.

Debt consolidation almost never makes sense in the long run. It almost always works out to be a very long-term, expensive solution to a short-term problem. Re-read the section above before you choose to go down that path.

Before you make a decision to use the equity in your house for any reason, consult with your financial planner or an attorney, and find a mortgage professional that is comfortable speaking with them. If your loan officer presents you with a super-slick analysis showing how your total monthly payments will go down if you consolidate short-term debt into a mortgage, fire them. Now. Really.

Chapter Seven

Should You Buy an Investment Property?

As with your own personal residence, you only **need** to get a mortgage to buy an investment property if you can't pay cash. Most of us can't, and even those who are able may wish to finance it anyway. The bigger question is whether you should buy investment real estate in the first place – it's not for everyone.

Do not make a decision to buy an investment property lightly. Consult your financial advisor; preferably one who is well versed in real estate investing. (Most financial advisors are very well trained in mutual fund investments, by the way, but know little or nothing about investing in income-producing real estate since it is not generally an investment they are licensed to sell.) Better yet, talk to friends or relatives who own investment property. Ask them about their experience.

So, should you or shouldn't you?

Reasons to Buy an Investment Property

Long-Term Growth

As we discussed in Chapter 5 real estate has traditionally provided relatively reliable appreciation **over the long run**. While there are periods where values correct downward, over time real estate tends to appreciate, whether we are talking about your home or an investment property.

Leverage

The same principle of leverage that applies to your personal residence applies to investment property as well. While perhaps 20% to 25% of the purchase price of the investment comes out of your pocket, the balance is advanced by the lender. You earn appreciation on the whole property, though. (For a full discussion of leverage, see Chapter 5 – "Should You Buy a Home?")

One important difference between real estate as an investment and stocks is that you can also leverage stocks by buying on margin – but the terms of borrowing against your real estate are significantly better than stocks.

Inflation Hedge

Because the price of real estate tends to rise more in inflationary times, real estate has historically been an excellent hedge against inflation. Most financial advisors will tell you not to think of your home that way because, well, it's your home – you'll need to live there regardless of what inflation does, so the increased value looks good on paper but for all practical purposes isn't something you can (or in most cases, should) access.

But investment property is another matter. Inflation tends to result in higher rents, so your cash flow improves, and higher values, which you can access either by selling or by refinancing and pulling cash out. Either way, you have access to more cash to help pay for increases in the price of things.

Cash Flow

In my opinion, a properly structured investment property should yield a positive cash flow. If you pay all cash even badly managed property should yield a positive cash flow most of the time. If you finance your purchase the property will have to generate enough cash flow to pay for all expenses and service the debt.

Getting this right requires that you have a clear and realistic understanding of what you can generate in rent, and what it will cost you to run the property. If your projections are accurate, a well-managed income property can generate a nice return in the form of after-tax cash flow to you, and you should get appreciation above and beyond the cash flow too.

Tax Benefits

Finally, there can be significant tax benefits to owning investment real estate. The exact nature of the benefits that apply to you will depend on your circumstances, so you must consult a tax advisor beforehand. However, in most cases you may be able to depreciate the property to offset some or all of the before-tax income generated by the property. Furthermore, the money you make through appreciation is not taxed while you hold the property, and even when you sell the property, you may be able to defer the taxes by exchanging it for another like-kind investment property.

The details of these tax strategies are beyond the scope of this book, but suffice it to say that the tax benefits can be substantial. Your situation might be unique, and tax laws change over time. Please do consult your tax advisor.

Reasons Not to Buy an Investment Property)

Risk

There are three major risks that you expose yourself to when you own rental real estate: value fluctuation, rental income variance, and legal liability.

Investment Value

As we mentioned before, real estate does not **always** appreciate. It can decline in value too, and when it does it can wipe out your entire initial cash investment. You should not, therefore, "bet the bank" on investment real estate by using all available liquid reserves as your down payment. Make sure that you can afford to lose whatever you risk, or hold on to the property long enough to make back your investment in case you end up investing just before the market declines. No one means to do this, of course, but you might find out that you have done so unwittingly.

Rental Income

Rental income is never steady. In fact, the net income generated from your investment **will** vary substantially. Even if you have bought prudently and structured your investment for positive cash flow in the long run, there will be months where vacancies reduce your income, and expenses increase because something needed to be repaired or replaced.

Consequently, as many investors have found out during the Great Recession, not only might your initial investment be wiped out but you may be required to invest more money for a while in order to support your investment. This is never a happy circumstance for any investor, and differs substantially from the nature of the risk associated with, for instance, investing in mutual funds.

If you can't tolerate losing the initial investment or if you can't afford an occasional negative-income month or two (or three…) then I would not advise you to buy investment real estate.

Legal Liability

People do fall down and hurt themselves on privately owned property all the time. They cut themselves on sharp edges on the stair handrails. They walk through plate glass windows and hurt themselves. And when it's a rental property, they do it a lot more often.

You buy insurance for this. I recommend that you buy the largest insurance policy available for your property, account for the higher cost in your expense projections (which will most likely be higher than what the listing agent projects) and have a very thick skin when attorneys send you letters.

Remember too that you are liable for anything that your property manager says or does. Yes, you might be able to turn around and recover any damages from him or her, but your tenant will probably sue you first.

If you can't afford the insurance or can't stomach spurious claims, then owning rental real estate is probably not for you, because it is likely to happen eventually.

Management Headaches

Every property has occasional management headaches. Even if you have a professional property manager, from time to time you will need to get involved. This again is different than investing in mutual funds. Your mutual fund manager never calls you up to ask what you think about GE stock. But your property manager is very likely to call to ask if they can replace the carpeting in your apartment. If your property is professionally managed usually you will need to approve only extraordinary expenses. However, you will have to get involved once in a while.

You also will need to manage your manager. The best property managers are very professional, but many do the bare minimum. You may be as involved as you like reading reports, discussing the property with your manager, and approving expenditures. I have had the experience, however, where getting the information I needed to make an informed decision was like pulling teeth.

The point is some property managers are not as concerned as you might be about the property. Having a professional manager does not mean you will have no headaches. You will have to invest some time into managing the manager.

High Transaction Cost

A real estate transaction is a costly affair. When you buy real estate you can expect to pay between 1% to 4% of the purchase price for title insurance, escrow services, and loan fees if you have a mortgage. When you sell you can expect to pay from 6% to 9% (or more) of your sale price for real estate commissions, escrow services, transfer taxes, etc. Other investments – such as stocks and mutual funds -- have associated transaction or operating fees, too, but with real estate they are quite high. You must anticipate a fairly large profit and a long holding period to make up for the higher transaction cost.

Illiquidity / Long Sale Cycle Time

If you own stock or mutual funds, you know that it takes you minutes to place an order to sell them. One phone call or a few clicks on the internet, and they're sold. Not so with real estate. It could take **months** to sell a piece of real estate, and even days just to get it on the market through conventional means.

The bottom line is, don't use your last dollar to buy real estate. Even if you see the deal of a lifetime, if you can't afford to not have easy access to your money don't buy it.

Conclusion

The decision to buy rental property is complicated and must be taken seriously. Consult with your financial advisor, other real estate investors (who have been successful at it over a long period of time) and with your family. If you can handle the risk, the headaches and the illiquidity, and look at it as a long-term investment, you can do quite well buying investment real estate.

Chapter Eight

Should You Get a Reverse Mortgage?

You might have heard of a reverse mortgage, but the chances are what you have heard is mostly negative. Some of what you heard was probably true, although today you are largely protected from the nastier practices employed during the early days of reverse mortgages. The truly onerous terms of the reverse mortgage that destroyed the equity in seniors' homes are no longer used.

Today over 10,000 people are turning 62 every day. According to the U.S. Census Bureau more than 80% of seniors aged 65 and over owned their own homes in 2012. Rising home values are offering these seniors an opportunity to use their equity to pay for expenses without the need to make payments or sell their homes until they are ready.

But a reverse mortgage is not for everybody. Before you acquire a reverse mortgage you need to understand how it solves your specific needs, what the risks and costs of a reverse mortgage are, and what your alternatives are.

What is a Reverse Mortgage?

A reverse mortgage is a way to access the equity in your home for living expenses without selling your home or having to make payments on the debt. This is also known as a Home Equity Conversion Mortgage, or HECM, as you are converting the equity in your home into cash.

There are six basic ways a reverse mortgage can be structured:

- **Fixed Payments for As Long As You Occupy Your Home:** Called the *Tenure* payment plan, the lender sends you a monthly payment, and it is added to the balance of your mortgage, plus interest. You never have to make payments (although you can.)

- **Fixed Payments for a Set Period:** Called the *Term* payment plan, this loan gives you monthly payments for a set number of years.

- **Equity Line:** Called a *Line of Credit* payment plan, rather than set monthly payments, you may withdraw any amount that you need (up to your maximum account balance) as you need it for any reason. You make no payments, and your principal balance grows every time you are advanced money, and as your accrued interest is added to the principal balance every month.

- **Combination Fixed Payment / Equity Line:** Called the *Modified Tenure*, You receive fixed payments for as long as you own your home, and can draw an additional amount as needed.

- **Lump Sum:** Called the *Single Disbursement Lump Sum* payment plan, the entire amount of the loan for which you qualify is advanced to you upon closing of the loan. You make no payments, but your principal balance grows over time as your unpaid interest accrues.

Do You Qualify?

To qualify for a reverse mortgage you must be at least 62 years old and have enough equity in your home. You do not need to have a job, verifiable income, savings or even good credit.

What Are the Important Terms?

Fixed or Adjustable?

Most reverse mortgages are written as adjustable-rate loans. If you select the single disbursement lump sum option you will have a fixed-rate loan, but you must take all of the money at once in a lump sum (whether you need it or not) and the *mortgage limit* does not increase as it does with the other options. The benefit, however, is that you have a fixed rate for as long as you have the mortgage. When interest rates are very low, this could be worth considering.

Mortgage Limit

With a conventional mortgage you can borrow (in some cases) up to 97% of your home's value. With a reverse mortgage your principal balance is increasing, not decreasing. Consequently, your mortgage limit (how much of your equity you can access) is initially set quite low compared to a conventional loan. However, since we assume that the value of your home will increase over time, your mortgage limit will also increase over time at a set schedule.

How much you can initially access and how it grows depends on your age when you acquire your reverse mortgage. The older you are the more of your equity you'll have access to. This is because, frankly, you are not as likely to need the money for as long as someone younger. If you are of good Swedish stock and your grandfather lived to be 115, it doesn't matter; you are treated the same as everyone else.

Other factors in determining your initial mortgage limit are the current interest rate, your home's appraised value, and the loan limits set by the Federal Housing Administration (FHA.)

Since there is more than one lender and different structures available for a reverse mortgage the exact amount that you would qualify for varies. You'll need to get a custom quote from a reverse mortgage advisor to get a firm answer.

However, you will find that your *mortgage limit* is likely to be at most 66% of your home's value – and in most cases less -- when you first take it out. Also, the maximum value used to determine your mortgage limit today is $625,500. If your home is worth $1,000,000 (not unusual in the Bay Area) it doesn't matter – your mortgage limit is based on a value of $625,500.

The Limit Increases Over Time

The mortgage limit does increase over time, however, based on your current age, the projected appreciation of your home, and your projected payments over time. The limit will increase for as long as you live in the home and your HECM is active.

Consequently, you cannot outlive your reverse mortgage. As long as at least one qualifying homeowner uses the home as their primary residence and keeps taxes and insurance current the loan will not become due.

> There is some interesting current movement in this area. Under HUD rules as long as one qualifying **borrower** remains in the home they cannot call the loan. However, if a surviving spouse is not on the loan, the lender can, but doesn't have to, call the loan and foreclose if necessary.
>
> Litigation now in process (in early 2014) seeks to change that so surviving spouses who are not also borrowers on the loan cannot be foreclosed upon.

Term

Most folks will choose the tenure payment plan. You'll receive a small monthly payment from your lender, for as long as you live in the home. You will stop living in the home one day, either when you move into assisted living, sell the home to downsize, or when you die.

When the last remaining qualifying borrower passes away or ceases to use the property as their primary residence for twelve months, the loan comes due and must be paid. You have a few months to figure out what you wish to do, but you can no longer keep the mortgage.

Inheritance

When the loan becomes due for any of the above reasons your family can refinance the home into a conventional mortgage (if someone who takes title can qualify) or they can sell the home.

If they sell the home, any balance above and beyond the principal balance of the mortgage at that time belongs to the estate (and thus those to whom the property has been willed.)

If the net proceeds from the sale are less than what is owed to the lender, the lender takes the loss. Today virtually all reverse mortgages are insured by FHA. (This may be changing.) The lender can file a claim with the FHA to be reimbursed for the balance not paid for by the sale of the home.

FHA Insurance

All FHA reverse mortgage products require up-front FHA mortgage insurance. This insurance is expensive, and is the primary contributor to the very high initial expense of reverse mortgages. (See below.) The benefit to you, as a borrower, is the term that we just discussed. If the real estate market collapses, the lender cannot come after you or your family after your death if the equity in the home no longer covers paying off the mortgage in full.

In 2013 HUD made some changes to the up-front insurance costs. If you access less than 60% of your initial mortgage limit in the first year the up-front mortgage insurance premium is now 0.50% of the mortgage limit. If you access 60% or more of the mortgage limit the premium is 2.5% of the mortgage limit.

Reverse mortgages are more likely to serve senior homeowners well if they have enough equity to be able to access it for as long as they need it. This change encourages homeowners to structure the loan in the way that is most likely to be successful in the long run.

Purchasing a Home

You can use a reverse mortgage to purchase a home. Seniors are often on a fixed income and cannot qualify for a conventional mortgage. However, they often have assets in the form of equity in their home or cash in the bank.

A strategy that could be appropriate for seniors looking to downsize, for instance, would be to sell their existing residence, use their proceeds from the sale for a down payment on their new home, and fund the balance needed with a reverse mortgage. Because they don't have to make payments if they don't wish to, they don't have to qualify for the mortgage. Additionally, depending on how they structure the reverse mortgage they might even be able to access the equity that they invested in their home over time.

Reasons to Get a Reverse Mortgage

Let's start by saying that a reverse mortgage is not a good product for every family, and in fact it was sold inappropriately to many families in the past. There are alternatives, which are discussed below. What are legitimate reasons to get a reverse mortgage?

You Need the Money

You might consider getting a reverse mortgage if you really need the money for urgent and important expenses. I would highly discourage someone who wanted a reverse mortgage to pay for European vacations or a new car, for examples. Medical science has come a long way in the last 50 years, and you just never know – you may outlive Grandma by 20 years or more, and you will need to live somewhere.

You Have Abundant Equity

If have only a minor amount of equity in your home a lender might sell you a reverse mortgage, but it would be a temporary solution at best. In fact, it could be very temporary. If you tap out the mortgage limit when you first take out your new reverse mortgage you will have limited ability to access your home's equity in the future.

If you need money now, chances are good that you'll need money in the future, too. For this reason I would prefer to see you have abundant equity in your property, take out only as much as you need now, and have access to more when you need it.

You Can't Qualify for a Conventional Loan

If you can't qualify (or feel you can't pay for) for a conventional mortgage or equity line, a reverse mortgage is probably the only option you have to stay in your home. You do not need to have any income at all, you don't need to have liquid reserves, and you don't even need good credit. You only need to be at least 62 years old, and have enough equity in the home to qualify.

When It Makes Sense

A couple came to me (Audrey and Dan) who were perfect candidates for a reverse mortgage. Audrey and Dan were in their mid-70s, and owned their home of 40 years nearly free and clear. The home's value was quite high (Silicon Valley after all) so they had a ton of equity. They had little in the way of liquid reserves, however, and were experiencing some unusual expenses in the way of medical bills.

They had an equity line on the property but it had a very low limit, and they could project that eventually the credit line would not cover bills in the event of an emergency and their social security income was not going to be able to cover the payments. Additionally, other than some temporary setbacks, they were both healthy and were likely to be able to live in the home for a long time.

We structured a reverse mortgage for Audrey and Dan as a line of credit. We paid off their current conventional equity line and financed the costs of the new loan, but left the lion's share of the new mortgage limit untouched so they could access it when they needed it in the future.

Dan and Audrey probably would have had to sell their home in order to cover medical expenses if the reverse mortgage product were not available. Since it was the home where they raised their children and they were probably seeing $70,000 to $100,000 per year in equity appreciation, the reverse mortgage not only made a lot of sense, but arguably will leave their family a lot more financial options down the road when Dan and Audrey can no longer live on their own.

Reasons Not to Get a Reverse Mortgage

No doubt, like many of the more exotic loan products, reverse mortgages were oversold during the Mortgage Boom. There are hundreds of horror stories about elderly homeowners who were forced to sell their homes or had them forcibly taken away. And some of these stories are true.

Just like with conventional mortgages, educating yourself is the key to making sure your story doesn't become a horror story. What are the costs and risks?

High Cost

There is a very high initial cost to acquiring a reverse mortgage. Besides the normal appraisal, underwriting, title, escrow and recording fees, you might pay an origination fee to the lender or broker, and you'll have to pay for an up-front mortgage insurance premium

> In fact, paying out claims for HECM-related loan losses was the largest single source of loss for HUD during the Mortgage Crisis.
>
> Naturally, while there is support for the program in general, there is a lot of political pressure to reduce losses which are backed by taxpayers.
>
> We may see changes in the cost structure or nature of the insurance coverage soon.

to the FHA.

The **long-term** cost of a reverse mortgage is actually pretty low, however, depending on how it is structured. The implication is that a reverse mortgage is not a good solution to a short-term financial problem.

Uses Up Equity

By this time it is obvious, but needs to be stated: the principal balance of your reverse mortgage will increase over time, eating into your equity. If your home appreciates at the rate anticipated in the initial analysis you will always have equity in your home, and as we discussed in Chapter 5 the value of real estate has always gone up **given enough time**.

When you get a reverse mortgage you take a risk that when you can no longer stay in the home you might not have much equity left when you sell the home or when your heirs inherit it.

You Might Have to Sell Even if You're Still Living

Most folks think that a reverse mortgage comes due when they pass away; this certainly could trigger the loan becoming due. However, not living in the home for 12 consecutive months is also a trigger.

If you become sick or injured and need to be hospitalized for a long time, or need to enter a rehabilitation facility for a while, it is possible that when you are well and ready to move back into your home you will not have that option.

Considerations and Strategy

If you have read other parts of this book you know that you can save considerable money by properly structuring your conventional mortgage. The structure you choose might even be more crucial with a reverse mortgage, as it can impact not only your lifetime costs, but also how fast you use up equity in the property and how long you might be able to draw cash on the loan.

Current Age and Health

The first thing you must consider is your current age and health. The older you are the more you'll be able to draw up-front, and on an ongoing basis. The younger and healthier you are, on the other hand, the more you are likely to need to mortgage to remain open for a long time.

If you think you might want to stay in the home for a long time, the most important thing is to get the lowest possible *margin* that you can. (See Chapter 12 for a discussion of the important terms for adjustable-rate mortgages. You absolutely **must** understand index and margin before taking any adjustable-rate loan, and most reverse mortgages are adjustable-rate loans.)

You have options as to what your margin on your reverse mortgage will be, but there may be an up-front cost associated with a lower margin. Insist that your lender explain all of your options regarding the margin.

As with conventional adjustable-rate mortgages, the higher the margin the higher the interest rate and therefore the ongoing cost of the mortgage is for you. With a reverse mortgage, this also means that your mortgage will eat up your equity faster.

Amount of Equity

If you have a lot of equity in your home when you take out your reverse mortgage you have a lot more options in terms of how you want to structure the mortgage. In this case I would tend to recommend setting it up as a line of credit, as you can take as little, or as much as you need each month and still have plenty of room in your mortgage limit down the road.

If you don't have much equity in the home, and you want to be sure that down the road you'll at least be getting a little bit each month, you are probably better off with a tenure payment plan. The lender will set the monthly allocation at an amount that they can continue to pay no matter how long you stay in the home, so you'll always be able to count on that income. However, in an emergency you will have to find another source of funds, so it would be very important to build up a savings account if you do this.

Alternative Options

There are alternatives to a reverse mortgage, some involving financing and some not.

Conventional Financing

First, if you can qualify for a conventional mortgage it is a much more conservative way to generate the funds you need in retirement. You can get a fixed interest rate, predictable payments, relatively low cost, and you can borrow a much higher percentage of your home equity. The principal balance of the loan will not go up, so you won't be eating into equity over time.

However, you must qualify for a conventional mortgage and you have to take the money all at once and begin paying interest on it, whether you need it now or not.

You'll have to make payments, of course, but if you bank the proceeds of the loan you could of course pay the loan out of that account. Remember, though, you are probably borrowing money at a higher interest rate than you are earning on your savings, so you are paying the lender rent for money you have sitting idle.

Conventional Equity Line

A conventional home equity line of credit can be a terrific alternative to a reverse mortgage. It is **much** less expensive to put in place, and the interest rates are generally decent. You can typically get an equity line for a higher loan-to-value ratio than a reverse mortgage, so your initial credit line is likely to be higher. Finally, unlike a conventional mortgage you only have to pay interest on what you borrow.

You have to make monthly payments on an equity line, but you could draw on the line anytime you need the funds to make the payments, so in effect you can use the equity line to make payments on the equity line.

You do have to qualify for the equity line, however, so you have to have good credit and verifiable income. The initial credit limit will be set when you take it out. You can ask for the line to be increased, but you will probably need more equity and you'll need to qualify for the higher payment. So, you have to assume when you acquire a conventional equity line that your initial credit limit is all you'll ever have.

An equity line also has s fixed draw period, after which time you'll have to start paying it back and can no longer draw on it, even if you owe less than your credit limit. (See Chapter 17 *Equity Lines*.)

Moreover, many families have found over the last few years that their equity lines were frozen when the value of their homes declined. When an equity line is frozen you can no longer withdraw money, even if you still have room left on your original line of credit. Your equity line lender is allowed to do this under the terms of your contract, and could freeze the line for other reasons as well, such as a credit issue that arises in your life. A reverse mortgage, by contrast, cannot be frozen. The initial mortgage limit is set by contract, and the expansion of the mortgage limit is also set, so if you choose anything but the term payment plan your credit limit will rise every year.

So, an equity line will work well as a short-term solution **if** you can qualify, but is not as useful as a reverse mortgage if you have a very long-term horizon, or can't qualify for the equity line.

Sell Your Home

The whole point of a reverse mortgage is to help you avoid selling your home before you want to. Sometimes, however, it might be time for you to sell your home, bank the profit, and find a new living arrangement. You might consider downsizing to a less expensive home, moving in with family, moving to an adult community, or assisted living.

But selling your home comes with costs. Selling your home will likely cost you between 7% to 10% of the selling price for a real estate commission and other selling costs. If you have capital gains on your property over your exclusion, you might have a big income tax bill to pay as well, amounting to as much as 20% of the gain on your property. I have had clients where their taxes exceeded the net proceeds from escrow because they did not seek counseling before selling.

However, if you have discussed this option thoroughly with your family, financial adviser, and accountant, it might be the right alternative for you to a reverse mortgage.

Conclusion

Out of all the different ways you could finance your home, the decision to get a reverse mortgage requires more thought and greater care than any other. This is because it is expensive to acquire, and as a rule will be permanent – you will probably never get out of it.

Unlike conventional mortgages that math is highly dependent on your individual circumstances, so for now I have no tools available for you to analyze your situation. You will need to talk to a reverses mortgage specialist to determine exactly what you qualify for and how much it will cost.

But do arm yourself with the information in this chapter so that you can hold your advisor's feet to the fire. In particular, your advisor should be able to answer the following questions:

- Which payment term do you recommend, and why?
- (If you are getting one of the adjustable-rate options) What will my margin be?
- Can I get a lower margin?
- What is your up-front (borrower-paid) fee?
- Can I get a lower fee?

Ask these questions and demand solid answers, then discuss them again with your accountant or financial adviser, and your family. Then let your home's equity pay for your good life!

Chapter Nine

Types of Mortgages (A Summary)

When looking at mortgages you may be confronted with a confusing array of terms describing the type of mortgage. The type of mortgage offered to you by your lender may or may not really be the best choice. For instance, prior to the Great Meltdown commissions on FHA loans were substantially higher than commissions on conventional loans. Consequently, many borrowers were sold FHA loans when a conventional loan with mortgage insurance would have been a much better deal.

Today in the broker world the broker's compensation should be the same regardless of the type of transaction. However, banks and mortgage bankers may (and do) still charge whatever they want, and often earn more on FHA and VA loans than on conventional loans. Be aware that the product they are offering may benefit them more than you.

What do all these terms mean, and how do you know which is right for you?

Loan categories and types are described in detail in the following chapters. A quick summary, however, is as follows:

Loan Type	Description	Best Used For
Conforming	Loans made by conventional lenders and then sold to Fannie Mae or Freddie Mac. Subject to a loan limit set each year. The current loan limit may be found at www.fanniemae.com.	Purchases or refinances of residential property up to four units. Borrower must have average or better credit, verifiable ongoing income source and at least 3% down payment or 5% equity in the case of a refinance transaction.
High-Balance Conforming	These loans are also purchased by Fannie Mae or Freddie Mac, but the loan amount is higher than the current conforming loan limit. This is a temporary program, and is likely to end in 2014.	Use where conforming loans would be used, except a higher loan amount than the conforming loan limit is needed. High-Balance loans can go to 125% of the area's median home price, up to a maximum of $625,000.
Non-Conforming (AKA Jumbo)	Loans made by conventional lenders and then packaged and sold to private institutional investors. These loans have theoretically unlimited loan amounts. Underwriting guidelines are set by negotiation between the mortgage bankers and investors.	When the loan amount needed exceeds conforming or high-balance conforming loan limits. Credit guidelines and income verification guidelines can be more flexible since it is private-sector money being lent.
Portfolio	Loans made by a banking institution (bank or credit union or mortgage banker) that are *not* sold to institutional investors or to Fannie Mae or Freddie MAC. Instead, the institution keeps these loans "on the books" and services them. These loans have slightly more flexible underwriting guidelines than conventional loans.	These loans are best used for properties that are not generally acceptable to conventional lenders, such as mixed-use or distressed properties, or where a borrower's profile is strong but not "conventional," such as one whose income is derived solely from investments.

Loan Type	Description	Best Used For
FHA	Loans made by conventional lenders and then *insured* (not bought) by the Federal Housing Administration. FHA loans require rather expensive mortgage insurance that must be paid for the life of the loan regardless of equity in the property.	Purchases or refinances where the creditworthiness of the borrower is in question. FHA loans also allow a low down payment, but at this writing so do conventional loans with mortgage insurance.
VA	Loans made by conventional lenders and *guaranteed* by the Veterans Administration. Borrower must be an honorably discharged veteran and have an eligibility certificate issued by the VA. There is *no* mortgage insurance and no down payment required.	If the borrower is a veteran with little or no down payment, regardless of credit history, this is an excellent program.
Private Money (AKA Hard Money)	Loans made by private lenders, usually arranged by a broker. The underwriting terms of these loans could be almost anything an investor is willing to take a chance on. However, current regulations make these loans difficult to arrange for personal residences.	These loans typically require lots of equity in the property. The borrower's creditworthiness and income are not significant factors in most cases, as the lender is looking to the equity in the property to repay the loan in case the loan fails.
Second Mortgages and Equity Lines	Loans made against the equity of the property and made junior to another loan, which could be a conventional or private money loan. Equity Lines are open lines of credit secured against the property, almost always in "second position" behind a senior loan.	These loans are used when you don't want to disturb the existing first mortgage or when you want to keep the new first mortgage under a certain ceiling in a purchase or refinance.

What You Are Quoted and What You Actually Get

Before we talk about the types of loan products we should discuss how you know what you are getting. Most folks, being honest and ethical, naturally believe that what their loan officer tells them they are getting will be exactly what they end up with when they sign final loan documents. Unfortunately, this has not always been the case. Even if you go to a national lender, when you sign the final loan documents you may end up with very different terms than you were first quoted. (I assume that the borrower has been honest and fully disclosed their circumstances to the lender. If not, of course the terms and price could change.)

So how do lenders get away with promising you one thing and delivering something quite different? There are two things you need to know about if you haven't signed loan documents before. First, the signing package is **huge!** Your signing arm will be sore for a week at least. You think I'm kidding, but I'm not. The sheer size of the loan package ensures that you will not read all the detail in the package.

> Today CFPB regulations pretty require that if any term or cost of your loan changes after you have signed your initial disclosures that you be sent new disclosures with the new terms or costs, and you must be given 3 days before the lender can move forward with the loan.
>
> It's an excellent rule, but it is likely there are some compliance issues, and some lenders are ignoring the requirement, so you still have to be vigilant.

A great loan officer who truly partners with you will be there at escrow when you sign the loan documents, and he or she will carefully point out which documents matter, like the note, the deed, and the estimated closing or settlement statement. They will slowly and clearly guide you through these documents to make sure you understand all the terms. If there is anything you don't understand, don't be shy. Ask again. And again. And again, until you clearly understand what you are signing.

A less honest or professional loan officer, however, will make sure you skim over these documents while signing. What you don't notice at this time you will probably never notice until it is far too late.

The second thing you need to know is that when you sign loan documents it is generally too late to change them for a number of reasons. Even if you do notice a change in terms, you probably have a deadline in your purchase contract that you have to meet, or if you are refinancing your rate lock might be about to expire, and you could lose your interest rate if you don't sign. I know many borrowers have signed loan documents for a loan that was nothing like what they were quoted. They may have signed under pressure, and they may have been angry, but they bit the bullet and signed in order to avoid losing more. And their lender knew they would.

Ask the lender to guarantee, in writing, when you first apply for the loan, that the loan documents you will be asked to sign at the end of the process will contain the terms you expect, or shop elsewhere. (An exception is if your rate isn't locked, they can't guarantee that.)

For a detailed review of the important documents that you must sign at closing, read Chapter 20, *Reading the Disclosures*.

So what type of mortgage should you look for? Let's look at each type individually.

Chapter Ten

Conforming and Non-Conforming Loans

For a long time the majority of mortgages written in the U.S. were "conventional" loans, meaning made through normal channels with no government guarantees, insurance or other assistance. These loans could have been either *conforming* or *non-conforming*. Non-conforming was commonly called "jumbo." Conforming simply meant that the loans were underwritten to Fannie Mae or Freddie Mac guidelines. Fannie and Freddie would buy these loans to provide liquidity to the mortgage market.

The Federal National Mortgage Corporation (FNMA, now simply called "Fannie Mae") and the Federal Home Mortgage Corporation (FHMC, or now simply "Freddie Mac") were created in 1938 and 1970 respectively by the Federal Government as government-sponsored quasi-public entities to purchase pools of mortgage loans from institutional lenders – i.e. banks, credit unions and mortgage bankers. Their purpose was and still is to provide liquidity in the mortgage market by providing new funds so that the lenders may originate more mortgage loans, and thus make home ownership more feasible. These companies raise the funds they use to buy pools of mortgages by selling securities (IOU's basically) secured ultimately by the Real Estate which secures the mortgages, and implicitly or explicitly guaranteed by the U.S. government as well. Consequently, they can raise funds at a very low interest rate, and pass that on to the consumer. These two agencies are known in the industry as *Government-Sponsored Entities,* or simply GSEs.

There is a limit on how large a mortgage that will be purchased by these agencies, however. In 2014, for instance, that limit was set at the beginning of the year at $417,000. This is commonly called the *conforming loan limit.* Most of the loans in the U.S. to creditworthy borrowers are purchased by these two organizations. (Read more about them at www.fanniemae.com and www.freddiemac.com.)

Loans that are not written to the guidelines of the GSEs are called *non-conforming loans.* Those which are non-conforming because the loan amount exceeds the conforming loan limit are commonly called *jumbo loans.* Since non-conforming loans aren't purchased by these government-sponsored entities banks need to find other ways of raising the money to fund the loans. These other sources, as it turns out, tend to be more expensive, so non-conforming or jumbo loans have always been a little more expensive than conforming loans.

In 2008 Congress passed the Economic Recovery and Reform Act, which authorized Fannie Mae and Freddie Mac to raise the limit – so far through 2014 only – to account for high-cost areas (like California) where loans larger than $417,000 are needed to finance average homes. The current limit for any given geographic area is 125% of an area's median price, or $625,500, whichever is less. In areas like the San Francisco Bay Area, this change makes a huge difference and allows far more folks to qualify for the less expensive financing.

Fannie and Freddie responded with a new category of loans from $417,050 up to $625,500 called *high-balance conforming.* High-balance conforming loans are typically more expensive than conforming loans, but less so than non-conforming loans.

In summary:

Conforming Loans:	Are made by brokers or institutional lenders, purchased by GSEs, limited to a maximum loan balance of $417,000 (currently) and require average or better credit and verifiable income. These tend to be the lowest-priced loans available.
High-Balance Conforming Loans:	Are made by brokers or institutional lenders, purchased by GSEs, limited to a loan amount greater than $417,000 but less than 125% of the area's average home value or $625,500 (in 2014) and require average or better credit and verifiable income. These loans tend to be more expensive than conforming loans but less expensive than non-conforming (Jumbo) loans.
Non-conforming (Jumbo) Loans:	Are made by brokers or institutional lenders and purchased by Investment Bankers who raise funds from institutional and private investors. Credit and income verification guidelines can (in theory) be much more flexible than agency loans. Because the performance of these loans is not guaranteed by the U.S. government, interest rates tend to be higher than conforming loans.

In most cases you don't have a choice as to which loan you get, other than the choice you exercise by remaining under the respective loan limits. The first strategy in negotiating the best deal possible for you and your family, therefore, is to keep your loan amount within conforming or high-balance conforming guidelines if at all possible.

Your loan options are significantly narrower than they were a few years ago, but you do still have a choice between fixed-rate and adjustable-rate loans, and can choose from among some "flavors" in each category. Let's review the different ways that your loan might be structured in the next few chapters.

Chapter Eleven

Fixed Rate Mortgages

Classic Fixed-Rate Mortgage

A fixed-rate mortgage is generally the most expensive loan you can get over the life of the loan, but it is very simple and carries very little risk. Your interest rate and payments are fixed for the life of the loan. This is the loan you want if:

- You know you'll be in the home a long time
- You have a stable income and don't expect it to go up significantly
- You have very little cash reserves for emergencies
- You have low tolerance for risk
- Interest rates are at or near historic lows when you lock your loan

Not all of these factors need be present for a fixed-rate loan to be a good choice for you. The essential point is that a fixed-rate loan, all things being equal, is more expensive than an adjustable-rate loan, but eliminates the risk of your payment increasing.

So, if you intend to be in your home a long time (and never refinance) then a fixed-rate loan is attractive because the longer you hold the loan the greater your exposure to the risk of high interest rates would be if you had an adjustable-rate loan.

Similarly, if your income is stable and not likely to increase much over the time period over which you expect to own the home, an adjustable-rate loan may carry too much risk; you don't want your payment to rise beyond what you can afford to pay each month.

If your cash reserves are thin, you won't be able to tolerate changes in your payment as much as if you have some savings to take up the slack.

There is an interesting variant of the fixed-rate loan that works well for young families who have just started out, and whose income will probably rise in years to come; a fixed-rate *buy-down*.

Buy-Down

The buy-down loan is a fixed-rate loan where you "buy-down" the interest rate for the first year or two. You do this by paying some of the finance charge in advance as a discount fee. This is a well-established product that fell a bit out of favor during the Mortgage Boom, and in my opinion is under-utilized today.

By paying a higher up-front fee, you still get a 30-year fixed rate loan, except that the rate is reduced 2% in year one and 1% in year two, before rising to the full note rate in year 3. For example, in our running example of our $200,000 loan at 6.000%, your interest rate in year 1 would be 4.000%. It would be 5.000% in year 2, and then it would settle in at 6.000% for the remainder of the loan.

What is the cost of this?

The cost varies, but generally, the up-front cost of the loan increases by about 2.500% of the loan amount, or 2.500 points. In our example of a $200,000 loan amount the fee for a 2/1 buy-down would then be $5,000. What would that buy you?

In year one your payment at 4.000% would be $954.83 compared to $1,191.10 at 6.000%, and in year two your payment would be $1,073.64. Your total savings in the first two years would therefore be ($236.27 x 12) + ($117.46 x 12) = $4,244.76. However, a larger portion of your payment would go toward your principal in the first two years (as a result of the lower interest rate), so your total savings are actually more than that. (All things being equal, the lower your interest rate the faster you are paying your principal balance down, even at the same amortization.)

On the face of it a buy-down may not seem like a good deal. In our example, you have to pay $5,000 up front to save $4,244.76 (plus a little) in the first two years. However, it allows for a much lower payment in the first two critical years when you are adjusting to the new payment, plus spending lots of money on your new home.

There are three ways to pay for the buy-down.

1) You can bring in more cash and pay for it. I don't generally recommend this, as if you have that cash lying around I would recommend that you just bank it and use it to help with payments the first two years, or use it to buy down the interest rate.

2) In a *buyers' market* you can ask the seller to pay for it. This can work great, as sellers are often sympathetic to the concept of needing cash the first year you own your home – after all, they were once in the same position.

3) You can ask the lender to pay for it by taking a higher interest rate. You always have the option to trade off up-front costs against your interest rate. (See Chapter 21, *Negotiating the Deal, Trade-Off of Rates vs. Fees.*) You might choose to pay for the $5,000 in costs by taking a higher interest rate.

Let's take a look at how that third option works.

In our example, let's assume you choose a permanent interest rate of 6.750% rather than 6.000%. You always have a choice to trade off your up-front loan costs against your interest rate. Take a higher rate, you'll get lower fees. Pay higher fees, you should get a lower interest rate.

If we assume on the day you lock your loan the loan fee for an interest rate of 6.000% is -0-, then if you were willing to accept an interest rate of 6.750% the lender might give you a credit of about 2.5 points, or $5,000, which you can use to pay for other closing costs – your buy-down, for instance.

If you paid for your buy-down cost this way you would pay 4.750%, in year one, 5.750% in year two, and then your loan would cycle for the remainder of the 30 years to 6.750%. If you believed you were not going to be in the house more than 5 years, you could assume that you wouldn't have to pay the higher interest rate very long. However, if you ended up staying longer than you thought, your interest rate is a known quantity, unlike an adjustable rate. See the example below.

How Does a Lender-Funded Buydown Work?

| | 30 Year Fixed | 30 Year Fixed 2/1 Buydown | | |
		Year 1	Year 2	Years 3 - 30
Loan Amount:	$ 200,000	$ 200,000	$ 200,000	$ 200,000
Interest rate:	6.000%	4.750%	5.750%	6.750%
Term:	30	30	30	30
Payment:	$1,199.10	$1,043.29	$1,167.15	$1,297.20
Difference in Monthly Payment:		$ (155.81)	$ (31.96)	$ 98.10
Annual Savings (Cost):		$ 1,869.68	$ 383.46	$ (1,177.14)

In a lender-funded buy-down you accept a higher permanent rate. The higher rate gives you a lower cost, or the lender may give you a credit toward other costs if you choose a high enough interest rate.

In this example we'll take a permanent rate of 6.750% rather than 6.000%, and the loan should cost (on average - it will vary) about 2.500 points less. If we assume that 6.000% would have been zero points on the day we locked, this means that the lender would issue a credit of $5,000 ($200,000 x 2.5%) toward your closing costs in exchange for the 6.750% permanent interest rate – just enough to pay for the interest-rate buy-down in years one and two.

This means that you could choose a conventional 30-year fixed at 6.000% at zero points, or a 2-1 buy down at 6.750% at zero points, since the lender credit of 2.500 points would pay for the buy down fee.

In year one, therefore, your interest rate would be 4.750% (6.750% - 2.000%), in year two your interest rate would be 5.750%, and thereafter your interest rate would be 6.750%.

In this example after about year four your total cumulative payments using a lender-funded buy-down at 6.750% would be about the same as the fixed rate at 6.000%, but with a buy-down your payments are much lower in the early critical years. This could be a conservative alternative to a 5/1 ARM. (See Chapter 12, *Adjustable-Rate Mortgages*.)

The actual relationship between the cost of each increment of interest rate option and the cost to buy that increment varies by the day, the lender, and even the price point. This is meant to be an example, and the difference in the interest rate between a regular fixed loan and a buy-down might be more, or less than, 0.750%.

The buy-down isn't a panacea and there is no magic to it. However, it is a tool that you can use to give a fixed-rate loan some of the same benefits as an adjustable-rate loan, without the same element of risk. It's worth considering.

Shorter Term Mortgages

You could also save substantially by asking for a mortgage with a shorter term. Besides the savings you get just by paying your loan off faster, lenders also offer lower interest rates for shorter term loans, saving you even more. The difference in the interest rates between two different loan terms – 15 years and 30 years, for example – varies widely over time. Sometimes the savings are much greater than others.

The downside, of course, is that the shorter the term of the mortgage the higher the monthly payments. Whether or not a shorter-term mortgage is right for you is not just a question of qualifying, but of affordability. Remember that you can pay any loan off as fast as you want, provided there is no pre-payment penalty. But if you choose a shorter-term loan because it's offered with a lower interest rate, you **must** pay it off fast. Your minimum payment will have to be made, every month, no matter what.

For this reason a shorter-term mortgage is really only a good option, in my opinion, for families with abundant savings and stable employment. If you have a good savings account, in tough times you'll be able to use your savings to tide you through, and with stable employment tough times are less likely to happen.

Today mortgages for 30 years and 15 are most common, but there are also products available for 20 and 10 years. A few lenders offer 25 year loans, but they are rare and not usually competitive.

At least one lender allows you to choose any term you want (in increments of 1 year, between 10 and 30) but the interest rate on this product doesn't change with the term. Since you don't get a benefit from a lower interest rate in this case, and you could select a 30-year loan and pay it off over any term you choose I'm not sure why anyone would choose the flexible-term option. But it makes for a nice marketing pitch.

But back to our discussion: how much can you save if you select a shorter-term loan and a lower interest rate? Let's take a look.

Glancing at one particular rate sheet on the day this is being written, the difference between the terms if we choose an interest rate that would cost zero points are as follows:

30 year term – base interest rate

20 year term – 0.325% better than 30-year fixed

15 year term – 0.750% better than 20-year fixed

10 year term – 0.250% better than 15-year fixed

So let's run a comparison using our running example of a $200,000 mortgage at 6.000%.

Comparison of Different Loan Terms - Payment and Lifetime Cost

	30 year fixed	20 year fixed	15 year fixed	10 year fixed
Loan Amount:	$200,000	$200,000	$200,000	$200,000
Interest Rate:	6.000%	5.625%	4.875%	4.625%
Term:	30	20	15	10
Payment:	$1,199.10	$1,389.93	$1,568.59	$2,084.84
Lifetime Payments:	$431,676	$333,584	$282,347	$250,181
Total Lifetime Cost:	$231,676	$133,584	$82,347	$50,181
Taxes:	$208.33	$208.33	$208.33	$208.33
Insurance:	$60.00	$60.00	$60.00	$60.00

You can see that your payment jumps substantially as your term decreases – but your lifetime costs of carrying the loan go down a surprising amount. The combination of the lower interest rate and the faster pay off of the loan add up to a substantial savings.

A fifteen year fixed will save you almost **$150,000** over the lifetime of the loan compared to a 30 year fixed, but at the cost of another $330 per month in the **minimum** payment.

So should you get a shorter term? It depends. First, it helps to know that to qualify for a loan today your total housing payment cannot equal more than 42% of your gross income (there are exceptions, but this is the standard today) and in the past could not exceed 36% of your gross income.

To be conservative, let's use the 36% figure and use the same property taxes and insurance we used earlier in the book. We'll then compare two different profiles and compare a 30 year fixed to a 20 year fixed loan.

Comparison of Different Loan Terms - Payment and Lifetime Cost

	30 year fixed	20 year fixed	15 year fixed	10 year fixed
Loan Amount:	$200,000	$200,000	$200,000	$200,000
Interest Rate:	6.000%	5.625%	4.875%	4.625%
Term:	30	20	15	10
Payment:	$1,199.10	$1,389.93	$1,568.59	$2,084.84
Lifetime Payments:	$431,676	$333,584	$282,347	$250,181
Total Lifetime Cost:	$231,676	$133,584	$82,347	$50,181
Taxes:	$208.33	$208.33	$208.33	$208.33
Insurance:	$60.00	$60.00	$60.00	$60.00
Total Housing Cost:	$1,467.43	$1,658.27	$1,836.93	$2,353.17
Qualifying Income @ 36%:	$4,076.21	$4,606.29	$5,102.58	$6,536.59

Let's examine two hypothetical cases where it does and doesn't make sense. The first case would be Bob and Mary. Bob and Mary make $3,000 per month each ($6,000 between them), and both work for large organizations in stable jobs. They could qualify for the 30, 20 or 15 year loans, but the 10 year loan would require more income. They would be most comfortable with a 30 year fixed, but the lifetime savings of the 20 year fixed look attractive so they want to consider it. The have the $50,000 for the down payment, plus enough for closing costs, plus another $20,000 in savings.

John and Sue also are considering the 20 year loan. Sue works for a startup high tech company and makes $5,000 per month. John is a stay-at-home dad. They have enough cash for the down payment and closing costs, plus another $6,000 in savings.

When looking at someone's profile to make a recommendation, I always consider how likely it is the client could find themselves in trouble.

I would recommend that Bob and Mary seriously consider the 20 year loan. They certainly bring in enough money to make the payment comfortably, both have stable jobs, and if one of them lost their job they would still at least have half of their income coming in, and they have a reasonable amount of savings to fall back on if they had to. By taking the 20 year loan they would pay their loan off 10 years earlier and have almost $100,000 more (plus interest) in the bank when they retire. (Unless they blow the money on a sailboat.)

John and Sue, on the other hand, are not good candidates in my opinion. Notice that they would qualify for the 20 year loan. However, if Sue lost her job (which is more likely for her than it would be for Bob and Mary) they would have no income coming in, and only a small savings account to fall back on.

Here we see a running theme: you might qualify for a loan, but that doesn't mean it's wise to take it. You have to weigh the risks and be certain you can handle the worst-case scenario.

In the case of John and Sue they could take a 30 year loan and, if things went well for them, make higher payments and pay the loan down on a 20 year schedule, or refinance into a shorter-term loan down the road. But for now, the 20 year loan might be too risky for them.

Chapter Twelve

Adjustable Rate Mortgages (ARMs)

After the Great Mortgage Meltdown of 2007 through 2010 folks are understandably very afraid of adjustable-rate mortgages. Without doubt using an adjustable-rate mortgage entails more risk for the borrower than a fixed-rate mortgage. But they are also cheaper in most cases and, managed properly and used appropriately, can save tens of thousands of dollars over the life of your loan.

The Case for an Adjustable-Rate Mortgage

The only certain benefit of an adjustable-rate mortgage is that the initial interest rate is invariably lower than a fixed-rate mortgage at any given point in time. If you choose an adjustable-rate mortgage you will save money compared to a fixed-rate mortgage every time, at least for the fixed period. (More on that shortly.) The price you pay for these savings is that you take on the risk of interest rates rising. The bank no longer shoulders that risk – you do.

How much can you save and what is the risk?

The difference in interest rates between fixed-rate loans and adjustable-rate loans changes over time. The difference also depends on the type of loan that you choose. Adjustable-rate loans have an initial fixed period during which the interest rate can't adjust. (We're going to explore this more later in this chapter.) That fixed period is commonly 1, 3, 5, 7 or 10 years. The shorter the fixed period is, the greater will be the difference in interest rate compared to a fixed-rate mortgage.

The savings, therefore, are greater when you choose a shorter fixed period. However, your interest rate will begin to float to current market interest rates sooner as well. Let's take a look at how the savings and risk compare.

We're going to work with our $200,000 sample. We already know from earlier chapters that we can get this mortgage for 6.000% as a 30-year fixed. Let's compare this to a 3/1 ARM. A 3/1 ARM means that the initial interest rate would be fixed for 3 years, and thereafter would adjust annually on the anniversary of your mortgage. Contract terms and how to determine how your loan will adjust is described below. For now, let's assume that the difference in the interest rate between a 30-year fixed-rate mortgage and a 3/1 ARM is 1.500%. (This is typical today.) Our initial interest rate for the 3/1 ARM is thus 4.500%. (6.000% – 1.500% = 4.500%)

We will also assume that our loan cannot adjust more than 2.000% after 3 years, 2.000% per year thereafter, and 5.000% over its lifetime. (These terms are described below.) The initial comparison for the first three years looks like this:

Adjustable vs Fixed-Rate Mortgage

Risk vs Benefit

	Fixed-Rate	Adjustable-Rate
Fixed Period:	30	3
Loan Amount:	$ 200,000	$ 200,000
Interest Rate:	6.000%	4.500%
Term:	30	30
Payment:	$ 1,199.10	$ 1,013.37
Initial Monthly Interest Cost:	$ 1,000.00	$ 750.00

This appears pretty simple on the face of it. Our initial payment is about $187 per month less, and we will save $250 in interest the first month. Not bad. For the first three years we are clearly saving money. At the end of year three, however, our payment can change, and change pretty dramatically. It might not change, but it probably will. What if we assume the worst – that our interest rate will rise by 2.000% at the end of year 3? What will happen to our interest rate and payment?

Adjustable vs Fixed-Rate Mortgage
Risk vs Benefit

	Fixed-Rate	Adjustable-Rate
Fixed Period:	30	3
Loan Amount:	$ 200,000	$ 200,000
Interest Rate:	6.000%	4.500%
Term:	30	30
Payment:	$ 1,199.10	$ 1,013.37
Initial Monthly Interest Cost:	$ 1,000.00	$ 750.00
Maximum Interest Rate in year 4:	6.000%	6.500%
Maximum Payment in year 4:	$ 1,199.10	$1,244.70
Mortgage Balance @ End of year 4:	$ 189,229	$ 187,196
Cumulative Payments through year 4:	$ 57,557	$ 51,418
Interest Cost through year 4:	$ 46,786	$ 38,613

Our interest rate is now more than it would be if we had chosen a fixed-rate mortgage. (Remember, we're exploring a worst-case scenario here.) Our payment now rises to $1,244, a full $45 per month more than the fixed-rate option.

But notice something else. The balance of our loan is lower as a result of having a lower interest rate for the first three years. Moreover, by the end of year four we have still paid less than on the adjustable-rate mortgage than the fixed-rate mortgage. We will have paid $6,000 less cumulatively in payments, and more than $8,000 less in interest, even though our interest rate in year four is higher.

Of course, another 2.000% jump in the rate in year five will change the picture a bit.

	Fixed-Rate	Adjustable-Rate
Maximum Interest Rate in year 5:	6.000%	8.500%
Maximum Payment in year 5:	$ 1,199.10	$ 1,490.79
Mortgage Balance @ End of year 5:	$ 186,109	$ 185,139
Cumulative Payments through year 5:	$ 71,946	$ 69,307
Interest Cost through year 5:	$ 58,055	$ 54,446

Now our interest really jumps – all the way to 8.500%. (Again, this is a worst-case scenario. This is as bad as it could possibly get with the assumptions we are using.) Our monthly payment is now almost $300 higher than it would be with the fixed-rate mortgage.

You'll notice, though, that the mortgage balance, cumulative payments and cumulative interest cost by the end of year 5 is still lower than it would be for the fixed rate mortgage.

If we continue the analysis, we'll find that in year 6 the 3/1 ARM will finally have cost us more than a 30-year fixed-rate mortgage – if we assume the worst possible outcome. This is easiest to see graphically:

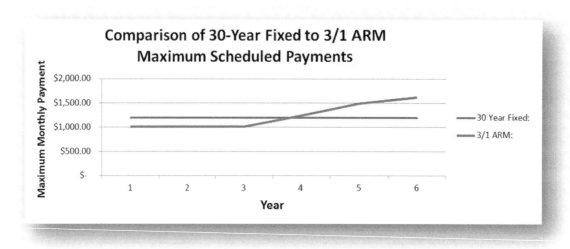

First, you'll see that in year four our payment is slightly higher for the 3/1 ARM, and in year 5 noticeably higher. In year six the interest rate hits the lifetime cap (given the assumptions) and so would never be higher than this.

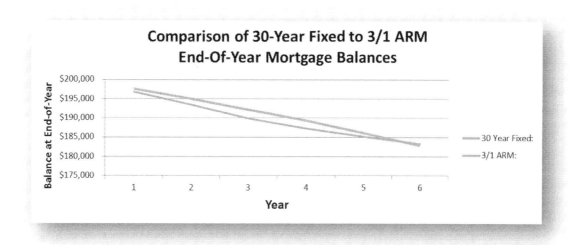

The lower your interest rate the faster you are paying down your mortgage, all things being equal, so the 3/1 ARM with the lower interest rate makes faster progress on paying down the principal balance of our mortgage. As the interest rate rises this changes, of course, and in a worst-case scenario sometime in the middle of year 5 our mortgage balance would be higher with the 3/1 ARM than it would be with the fixed-rate mortgage.

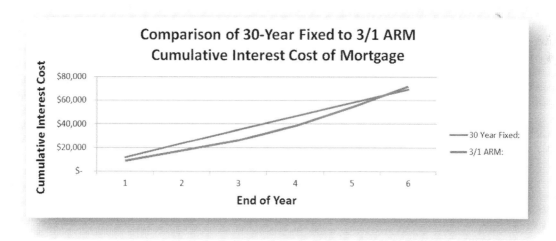

Even under the worst assumptions, we will not have paid more interest on our 3/1 ARM compared to our fixed-rate mortgage until near the end of year five.

The key point in this discussion is that there is a reason to get an adjustable-rate mortgage – it can save you money. In fact, I've never made an adjustable loan where it has actually turned into the worst-case scenario. My clients who hold adjustable-rate mortgages today are finding their loans to be so attractive that it's not an easy decision to refinance out of them.

Especially if you think you have a short time horizon, it is worth considering an adjustable-rate mortgage.

The Case against an Adjustable-Rate Mortgage

To state the obvious, the first reason you would not want an adjustable-rate mortgage is that you are taking on the risk of fluctuations in the interest-rate market. If rates go up the bank is protected, and you pay for it. You have become the insurance company that insures the bank against having unprofitable loans stuck on the books.

If your time horizon is long – say you want to stay in your home long past the time your mortgage will be paid off – then at some point your interest rate on an adjustable-rate mortgage will be higher than it would be for a fixed-rate mortgage. Your lifetime cost might be higher, or lower than a fixed-rate mortgage. Since no one can predict where interest rates will be in the future we don't really know. It is very likely, however, that in some years your payment will be much higher. The longer your time horizon, the greater your exposure will be to higher rates and higher payments.

Finally, between 2009 and early 2013 almost all loans written were fixed-rate loans. If adjustable-rate loans can save you money, why would this be? Interest rates were historically low during this period. Adjustable rates were still lower than fixed-rate loans, but if you can lock a super-low rate in for 30 years, you should probably take it.

When we are in a period where interest rates are so low that they are very likely to rise in the future, the argument for taking a fixed-rate loan becomes very strong.

All of this discussion is simply a long-winded way of saying that an adjustable-rate mortgage will save you money in the early years, and could save you money over the life of your loan, in exchange for you taking on the risk that interest rates will go through the roof.

Important Terms You Must Understand

The key is to understand the important terms of the mortgage. A fixed-rate loan is very simple. When you sign up for an adjustable-rate mortgage, however, you agree to quite a few complex clauses that define how your loan will work over the next 30 years. Sadly, most borrowers have no idea that the clauses even exist, much less where to find them or what they mean. Even worse, some lenders have in the past gone to great lengths to conceal these clauses. So arm yourself if you want an ARM.

There are seven important features to an adjustable-rate mortgage that you should know and understand in advance to be sure that the product is right for you and your family:

- Index
- Margin
- Fixed Period
- Initial Adjustment Cap
- Lifetime Adjustment Cap
- Recurring Adjustment Period
- Pre-Pay Penalty.

This discussion assumes that the loan is neither negatively amortized nor interest-only; those features are discussed separately below.

First, you should know that the only way to be certain about the terms of your proposed loan is to read your *Note*. However, in most cases you don't get to do this until you are signing final loan documents. When you do sign the final package you'll sign dozens of forms, and it is generally too late to change if you don't like the terms.

I recommend that you ask your mortgage advisor at the **beginning** of the process to obtain a copy of the proposed note for you. **Be aware that this is an unusual request**, and he or she may not want to do this. Ask for it anyway, and then read it thoroughly and pay special attention to the terms discussed below so that you fully understand the terms you are being offered.

You may also wish to reference Chapter 20, *Reading the Disclosures*, for a section-by-section analysis of an adjustable-rate note. Here are the specific terms of your mortgage that I want you to understand:

Index

The *index* is a measurement of interest rates, much like the Dow Jones Index is a measurement of stock prices. The index is defined in your *Note*, and it may be something like "The Then-Current Yield on U.S Treasury Certificates with a maturity of One Year" (you might have heard this described as 1-year T-Bills) or "The average of the interbank offered rates for one-year U.S. dollar-denominated deposits in the London market," an index commonly known as 12-Month LIBOR.

What is the significance of this? These indices track the yield that institutional investors are currently earning on relatively short-term investments, and so are good indications of **current** interest rates at any given point in time. The theory is, when your loan adjusts it should reflect whatever interest rates investors (i.e. lenders) are currently demanding. These indices track interest rates pretty well over the long run, and if your interest rate is based on a current index, when it adjusts it should closely reflect the lender's cost of funds. These rates can be tracked by you, by the way; simply do a search for them on the internet for current daily values.

In the last 20 years the value of the most commonly used indices has varied from under 1% to about 8%, so you can see that over the lifetime of a 30 year loan your interest rate could vary substantially.

LIBOR, by the way, has been one of the most commonly used indices in the last ten years because it tends to be highly volatile, and thus rises quickly in rising interest rate environments, protecting the lender better as interest rates rise. It also tends to move lower farther and faster than other indices, so is can work out well for you in low-rate environments. You might remember the chart below from Chapter 6, *Should You Refinance?* which illustrates how LIBOR tracks short-term interest rates.

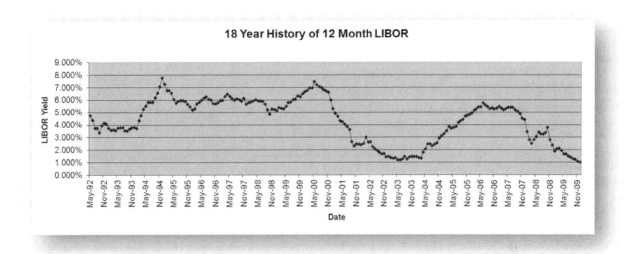

So the first thing you must identify in order to figure out how your interest rate can adjust is the *index* that is defined in your note. But in order to know what your interest rate is going to be when it adjusts, you need to know not only the index, but also the *margin*.

Margin

The *margin* is a percentage that is defined in your note which is added to the *index* to determine your new rate when it adjusts. If you have good credit your margin would typically be between 2.25% and 2.75%.

When the index is hovering around (or even under) 1% as LIBOR did through most of 2009 through 2014, your adjusted rate will be quite low. For example, if the index is at 1.000% on the day your lender calculates your new interest rate and if your margin is 2.25%, your new interest rate for the next period will be 3.25%. This is known as the *fully indexed rate*.

However, if the index goes to 8.000%, your fully indexed rate will be 10.25%, assuming that is not over your *lifetime cap*. (See below) This is why when you first acquire an adjustable-rate loan is much cheaper than a fixed-rate loan; you are taking on the risk of the interest-rate market, instead of the bank. There are ways to manage that risk, however; we'll get to that shortly.

Fixed Period

Whatever adjustable-rate loan program you choose the rate is fixed for a certain period. That period might be as short as one month or as long as ten years. Naturally, the longer your *initial fixed period* is, the more desirable it is for you, but the higher your interest rate will be or the less favorable other terms of your loan will be.

Today it is rare for the initial term to be less than one year, but in the past shorter terms were common, especially with Option ARMs, and we may see shorter fixed terms again in the future.

The way to use this term to your advantage in choosing the loan that's right for you and your family is to match, as closely as possible, the initial fixed period to your needs and plans. For instance, if you look back to our story about Raoul in Chapter 6, he chose an adjustable-rate mortgage with an interest-only feature to keep his payments as low as possible while his children were in college. He chose a seven-year initial fixed period because his youngest child would be graduating from college in seven years. In other words, he matched the terms of the loan with his personal needs, knowing he would be experiencing major cash outflows during this period. By reducing his interest rate compared to a fixed-rate loan, and by taking an interest-only loan rather than fully amortized, and by taking a seven-year initial fixed period, he got the combination of the lowest possible monthly payment with no risk of change for as long as his kids were in college.

A more common scenario is for folks who know that they won't be keeping the loan for more than the fixed period either because they intend to move or because they intend to remodel or expand the home.

A young couple, "Brian and Marge", came to me looking to buy their first home. They had found a terrific deal on a small 3 bedroom, 1 bath home. The home was close to Brian's work and in a decent neighborhood. They intended to have children soon, however, and knew that the home would be too small for them when they did.

At first they assumed that they would keep the home three to five years and then move up. I suggested another alternative: buy this home and expand and remodel it. This would give them greater control over the amenities in the home after remodeling, plus avoid all the transaction costs of selling one home and buying another. Besides, the home they were buying was in an excellent school district, and there were already numerous homes in the neighborhood which had been expanded and remodeled, so they would not be over-improving their home.

Either way, we assumed they had a five-year window period at most for the purpose of the loan they would use to acquire the home. Brian and Marge chose an adjustable-rate mortgage with a five-year fixed period, and at the same time acquired a Home Equity Line of Credit (See Chapter 17, *Equity Lines*) which they didn't need to buy the home, but which afforded them the credit needed for the addition when they got around to it.

Within three years they began their remodeling, paying for it from a combination of savings and the equity line. When they finished their project we consolidated both loans into a new 30-year fixed loan at a time when interest rates were quite low.

In the end, Brian and Marge saved about $16,000 in interest costs in the first four years by having an adjustable-rate mortgage and about $35,000 in transaction costs by not having to sell one home and buy another. $51,000 in savings pays for a lot of improvements. They ended up with plenty of space and exactly what they wanted, and in an excellent school district. The last I heard they had a second baby on the way.

What risks did they take? If their finances had not gone well they might not have been able to do the remodeling, and they might not have been able to move up. In that case, they might have been stuck with a home that was smaller than they wanted and an adjustable loan after the initial fixed period. However, they had a good index and a good margin, so this would have exposed them to some risk but at a manageable level.

I would like you to remember three important points from this discussion:

1) An adjustable-rate mortgage could save you quite a bit of money if you manage the risk properly.

2) You have options regarding the initial fixed-rate period; you can match the period to your specific needs and situation

3) While you can't eliminate risk, you can use the options available to you to manage it while saving money.

Adjustment Caps

So we know you have some control over **when** your loan will first adjust and we know **how** they will calculate your new interest rate, but how do we know the maximum it can adjust?

There will be a clause in your note that will define the maximum your loan may adjust:

- on the initial adjustment *(the Initial Adjustment Cap)*,
- on periodic adjustments after that *(the Periodic Adjustment Cap)*, and
- over the life of the loan *(the Lifetime Cap)*.

Your actual note may not use these terms, so if you don't see them, read through the section on how your loan can adjust carefully, and write down what you **think** these caps are. Then ask your loan officer for confirmation.

While there used to be quite a bit of variance in the amount of the caps depending on the loan, there isn't much anymore. Again, that may change back one day.

Initial Adjustment Cap

The initial adjustment cap limits how much your interest rate can change on the first adjustment date. In the past the initial adjustment cap was the same as the periodic adjustment cap in most notes. From 2008 through 2013 if your fixed-rate period was five years or longer the initial adjustment cap was usually the same as the lifetime cap (which is normally a larger number), but now for various regulatory reasons the initial cap is returning to be equal to the periodic cap. What does this mean?

This means that if you got an adjustable-rate loan between 2008 and 2013, the first time your loan adjusts it **might** adjust (or might have adjusted) to the highest interest rate possible according to your note (which would be your *lifetime cap*.) In most cases, this maximum adjustment is 5% over the start rate. This has implications I'll discuss in a minute. The bottom line is that your loan cannot be adjusted beyond this cap, up or down. So, if your start rate is, say, 4.000%, and your initial adjustment cap is 5.000% over the start rate, on your first adjustment date your rate cannot be set above 9.000%, or below 0.000%. Yes, it could adjust downward, too.

In any event, if the *fully indexed rate* is within the range allowed by the initial adjustment cap, your interest rate will be set at the fully indexed rate when it adjusts the first time. The lender cannot simply choose whatever rate they want to earn. The method to determine your new rate is defined in your contract with them.

Note: After January 2014 most lenders are once again offering the 2% initial adjustment cap, reducing the risk of "payment shock" on your first adjustment.

This is all much simpler than it sounds, and you can actually calculate, with some degree of accuracy, what your new interest rate might be when it adjusts once you get fairly close to your adjustment time. Take a look at the example below. (This calculator is available on www.loanguide.com)

We'll start with our running example of a $200,000 mortgage, but this time we'll assume we have an adjustable-rate mortgage with a starting interest rate of 4.500%, fixed for 5 years. Your initial payment is $1,013.37.

We'll assume that the initial adjustment cap is 2%, the periodic adjustment cap is 2%, and the lifetime cap is 5% over the start rate. We'll also assume that your index is LIBOR and your margin defined in your Note is 2.25%.

The first thing that is important to note is that your interest rate is fixed for five years.

On the 5th anniversary of your loan's start date your interest rate will be adjusted by taking the then-current index value and adding the margin. In the last 20 years LIBOR has ranged between 0.50% and just under 8%. Historically it has spent a lot of time between 5% and 6%, so let's assume that five years from now LIBOR will have returned to 5%. (This is a wild guess, and just an example. Please don't take this to mean LIBOR is going to be 5% five years from the date you are reading this.)

You'll notice that with these assumptions the *fully-indexed rate* jumps all the way from your start of 4.500% rate to 7.250%.

However, remember that the

Initial Adjustment Calculation	
Index Value (Sample):	5.000%
Margin:	2.250%
Fully Indexed Rate:	**7.250%** (Index plus margin)
Maximum Adjustment Cap:	2.000% over the start rate
Maximum New Rate:	**6.500%** (Start rate plus initial cap)
New Adjusted Rate:	**6.500%**
(The *lesser* of the *fully indexed* and *maximum new rate*)	
New Principal Balance:	$182,316 (Reflects paid principal)
New Loan Payment:	**$1,231.01**

maximum *initial adjustment cap* is 2.000% over your start rate, so your new adjusted rate cannot be higher than 6.500%. Your interest rate in year six will therefore be 6.500%, and your new payment will be $1,231.01, an increase of over $200 per month, but less than what it would be without the initial adjustment cap.

From now on your loan will adjust one time per year (in this example.) Your *periodic adjustment cap* is 2%, so your interest rate cannot go up or down more than 2% anytime your interest rate adjusts.

Another year passes, and let's assume that now the economy has weakened again, and that short-term rates have declined.

Now you see the index value has dropped from 5%, where it was on the initial adjustment, to 4.125%. The fully-indexed rate is now 6.375%, which is within 2% of your current interest rate, so your new rate is 6.375% and your new payment is $1,217.20.

Next Annual Adjustment Calculation	
Index Value (Sample):	4.125%
Margin:	2.250%
Fully Indexed Rate:	**6.375%** (Index plus margin)
Maximum Adjustment Cap:	2.000% over current rate
Maximum New Rate:	**8.500%** (Start rate plus initial cap)
New Adjusted Rate:	**6.375%**
(The *lesser* of the *fully indexed* and *maximum new rate*)	
New Principal Balance:	$179,306 (Reflects paid principal)
New Loan Payment:	**$1,217.20**

Next Annual Adjustment Calculation	
Index Value (Sample):	2.125% [9]
Margin:	2.250%
Fully Indexed Rate:	**4.375%** (Index plus margin)
Maximum Adjustment Cap:	2.000% over current rate
Maximum New Rate:	**8.500%** (Start rate plus initial cap)
New Adjusted Rate:	**4.375%**
(The *lesser* of the *fully indexed* and *maximum new rate*)	
New Principal Balance:	$176,094 (Reflects paid principal)
New Loan Payment:	**$988.63**

Finally, let's assume the economy does very poorly again, and LIBOR drops back down to 2.125%, a rate that can happen during tough economic times.

On your next adjustment anniversary your interest rate will go **down** to 4.375%, and your payment will decline to $988.63, a drop of more than $230.

The salient points in this exercise are that your interest rate will not always increase with an adjustable-rate mortgage, and each time it adjusts there are limits as to how far it can adjust when it does.

Periodic Adjustment Cap

After the initial adjustment your adjustable-rate loan will continue to adjust periodically. Today most notes call for an adjustment every 6 or 12 months, and typically limit the periodic interest rate adjustment to no more than 2% per year. If your loan adjusts every six months, then, it usually cannot adjust more than 1% every six months. (Again, up or down.) If your adjustment period is annual, it could adjust as much as 2% up or down each adjustment.

Lifetime Adjustment Cap

Finally, your Note will also define an interest rate above which your loan can **never** adjust, no matter what happens to interest rates. Your risk of higher rates is "capped" at some point. Most conventional adjustable-rate mortgages today cap the interest rate at no more than 5% over the start rate for the life of the loan.

Summary of Adjustment Caps

If you take an adjustable-rate loan in order to save money on your interest costs in the early years you will shoulder some risk of interest rate fluctuations. When you compare your loan offers from various lenders pay close attention to the terms of the how and when your loan adjusts to see just how much of the risk you are being asked to shoulder. While it may not impact your cost today, it could have a significant impact on your family in the years ahead.

Pre-pay penalty

A pre-payment penalty is a fee charged to you if you pay off your loan sooner than expected. Most loans do not have pre-pay penalties, but some of the worst of the loans written during the Mortgage Boom did, and often the terms were quite egregious. Today some loans do still have pre-pay penalties. New laws restrict pre-pay penalties to be no longer than 3 years in most cases, and caps on the amount of the penalties are set as well.

Pre-payment penalties are most common on adjustable-rate mortgages where up-front origination fees are either very low or non-existent. It costs lenders money to make these loans, and they want to make sure that they have at least earned that money back before you pay off the loan.

When Would You Want a Pre-Pay Penalty?

The counter-intuitive implication in this last point is important: accepting a pre-payment penalty with your loan could lower your up-front fees and, if you don't pay it off prior to the expiration of the penalty, could be used to **permanently avoid** some up-front costs. In other words, a pre-payment penalty could actually save you money in the long run, if used intelligently.

New disclosures make it fairly clear whether you do or don't have a pre-pay penalty, but it may not be obvious unless you look for it or it is pointed out. Make a point to have your loan officer point it out.

Common Traps

Misleading Advertising

There are times when ads for mortgage companies drive me crazy.

The worst one is when the ad promotes an interest rate for an adjustable-rate mortgage, but makes it sound like a fixed rate. This is most common with radio ads.

For instance, and ad might promote an interest rate that is a full 1% under the going market rate, and underscore that it is a 30 year loan. (But they don't explicitly state it's a fixed-rate loan.) The ad will then go on to boast that the company offers "no-point, no-fee" loans, and fixed-rate loans. If you don't listen carefully, you'll be led to believe that you can get a 30-year fixed-rate mortgage for a full 1% less than the going rate without paying any fees at all.

A typical script might go like this:

"Because we are a direct lender we can write loans at lower interest rates than anybody. Today we are offering our "Super-Saver" mortgage for only x%! At *Vague Mortgage* we'll help you get a fixed-rate mortgage with no points and no fees!"

Then, in the fast-talk (the radio ad's version of fine print) they will mention that the offer is valid only for a mortgage equal to the conforming maximum loan limit, that the rate is fixed for 3 or 5 years, and of course the infamous "not all borrowers will qualify."

If you call on an ad like this, **start** the conversation with "I'd like to ask you some questions about the loan you advertised, and I'd like you to put the answers in writing to me in an email."

If the loan officer says "no," move on. If they agree, then ask them the following:

Is the mortgage with the interest rate of x that you advertised a 30-year fixed-rate mortgage?

If it isn't, then ask them to give you the following information:

Index:

Margin:

Initial Adjustment Cap:

Periodic Adjustment Cap:

Lifetime Adjustment Cap:

Is there a pre-payment penalty?

Why is this particular index a good choice for my needs?

Be aware, many loan officers will not actually know the answers to these questions. If so, move on. And, as I suggested above, get a copy of the Note in advance.

Annual Percentage Rate (APR)

I explain more in Chapter 20 – "Reading the Disclosures," but for now be aware that the APR on adjustable-rate mortgages isn't very useful. The APR is meant to be a comparative measure of the lifetime cost of two different loans. The problem with the APR for an adjustable-rate mortgage is that you won't know the lifetime cost of your mortgage because your interest rate can – and will – change over time.

We know what your interest rate will be for the introductory fixed period, but after that we can only guess. But we have to guess something in order to give you a number.

So the "proper" way to calculate your APR when giving you your loan disclosures is the assume that when you loan begins to adjust (1, 3, 5, 7 or 10 years from now) the value of the index defined in your Note will be the same as it is on the day we issue your disclosures.

That assumption is absurd. The value of the index changes **by the minute**. What is the likelihood that it will be the same whenever it is time to adjust your interest rate?

So here is the problem. If you are getting a loan when interest rates are very low, the APR will significantly understate the interest costs that you are likely to encounter over the life of your loan. If you acquire your loan when interest rates are very high, the APR is likely to significantly overstate your lifetime costs.

So what do you do? Ignore the APR, and ask about the index, margin and adjustment caps, and use those to compare two competing loan offers.

Changing Loan Terms

With new disclosure laws this should no longer be a problem, but we still hear stories where folks signed documents and later discovered that the documents they signed did not have the same terms as the disclosures they were given.

Read Chapter 20 and use it as a guide to review loan documents **carefully** before you sign them, especially on an adjustable-rate loan.

Chapter Thirteen

Interest-Only Loans

An *Interest Only* loan is one in which the minimum payment required for a certain period (e.g. the first five years) is simply the accrued monthly interest. You may, but do not have to, make payments toward the principal balance of the loan during the interest-only period. For a while interest-only loans were quite common.

Going back to our running example of our $200,000 loan at 6.000%, the fully amortized monthly payment for 30 years was $1,199.10; paying this much each month would pay the loan off in full in 30 years. The initial monthly payment for an interest-only loan, by contrast, would be $1,000 per month. You would **never** pay the loan off or even down with only this payment; you would always owe $200,000 until you began making amortized payments. Since lenders don't make loans forever, at some point they require that you begin paying principal, and that it be paid off in whatever remains of your original 30 years. Consequently, if you make the minimum, interest-only payment during the interest-only period, when you do start making a fully-amortized payment the principal balance is higher on the interest-only loan that it would be if you made a fully-amortized payment. See the example below.

	Fully Amortized Loan Payment	Interest-Only Loan Payment
Starting Principal Balance	$200,000	$200,000
Payment years 1 through 5	$1,199.10	$1,000.00
Balance @ End of Year 5	$186,109	$200,000
Payment years 5 through 30	**$1,199.10**	**$1,288.60**

In this example, by the end of year 5 – the end of the interest-only period – you would have paid off nearly $14,000 in principal had you made fully amortized payments.

If you pay only interest in years 1 through 5 you now have to make larger payments from year 6 on to make up the difference by the end of 30 years. Is an interest-only loan a good idea? I think it's great if used intelligently, as was the case with Raoul in the example in Chapter 6. However, most folks use interest-only loans when buying a home because they cannot afford fully amortized payments. The risk in that as a strategy is that if your circumstances don't improve, eventually you won't be able to afford your own home. In my humble opinion, this is **not** a good idea. A better strategy in this case is to buy a less expensive home that you know you can afford and for which you are qualified using fully amortized payments.

If you only remember one thing from this chapter, remember that the minimum monthly payment on an interest-only loan jumps significantly (almost 30% in the example above) when the interest-only period ends. You would be surprised how many people are surprised when this happens.

Chapter Fourteen

Option ARMs (Neg-Am Loans)

Option ARMs were the worst thing to happen to the mortgage and real estate industries, ever, right?

Not in my opinion.

The original option ARMs were a very useful tool to manage your monthly cash flow, if used intelligently by someone with financial savvy. Moreover, structured properly they carried a much lower interest rate than a conventional fixed loan, or even other adjustable-rate loans. However, they were sold to lots of borrowers who should never have had them.

It doesn't matter much anymore, as this product is not offered today. However, it may make a comeback one day, so if it does, you should know what it is, when to avoid it, and under what circumstances it could save you a lot of money.

Let's start with what an Option ARM is. If you go back far enough, the same product was called a neg-am loan, short for *negative-amortization*. Why was the product description changed? Lenders finally figured out you were much more open to getting an "Option ARM" than a "Negative Amortization loan." If you knew there was no actual difference in terms, would you rather have a neg-am loan or an option ARM? Like any other industry, we get better at marketing our products over time.

In an option ARM you have the right to make a payment that is actually **less** than the interest which accrues each month, at least in the early years of the loan. Unlike an interest-only loan where the principal balance remains the same unless you make additional payments, in an option ARM / negative amortization loan the principal balance of the loan - the amount you owe - can actually **increase** if you make only the minimum payments. (The loan will negatively amortize if you make only the minimum payment.)

These loans were structured in a variety of ways, but there were certain common traits among them. A typical option ARM might have had the following terms: (By now you should be familiar with most of these terms; we'll use our familiar $200,000 loan)

Principal Balance: $200,000	
Start Rate: 2.000%	This appears to be an extremely attractive interest rate – but it's only good for 1 month!
Fixed Period: 1 **month** (Yes, the rate was only fixed for one to three months…)	After one month the interest rate increases to the *fully-indexed rate*, even though your **payment** stays the same.
Payment in Year 1: *$739.24*	Compare this to the $1,199 for the fully amortized loan at 6%, or $1,000 for the interest-only loan. It looks like a bargain. But if your accrued interest in month 2 is $1,000, then *$260.76* is **added** to the loan amount in that month.
1st *payment* change: 12 months	Your **minimum** payment will first change at the end of year one.
Payment Increase Cap: Maximum increase of minimum payment: 7% of the payment, up to $790.99	The most commonly used payment increase was 7% annually, until the end of year 5 or until your minimum payment was equal to a fully amortized payment. Note that you are still not paying for your interest cost if your fully-indexed rate is, say, 6%.
Index: 1 month LIBOR	You may recall that this is one of the most volatile indexes possible, closely tracking the cost of funds for the lender.
Margin: 2.25 to 4.75	This was where borrowers were duped. Most never asked and didn't look at the margin defined by the note, yet this was what guaranteed the bank's profit margin – the higher the margin, the higher the interest rate they earned from the second month onward, but **it didn't affect a borrower's minimum payment**; so few borrowers asked.
Rate can adjust: **monthly**	100% of the risk of interest-rate volatility was borne by the borrower. The loan was not only highly profitable for the lender, but nearly risk-free. (Until borrowers started defaulting.)
Maximum negative amortization: 125% of original loan amount, or $250,000.	However, if interest rates rose dramatically the difference between the payment and the accrued interest was large, the loan balance grew rapidly. To avoid too much risk to themselves lenders capped the negative amortization to (typically) 125%. If the amount owed reached this amount (125% of the original loan balance, or $250,000 in our running example) you had to start making amortized payments even if that meant a substantial increase in your monthly payment.

While these loans could be used wisely to save borrowers thousands of dollars, most were sold to unsuspecting sub-prime borrowers who were enticed by the very low initial payments and the fact that they were led to believe that they could afford a much nicer home than they would have been able to with a 30-year fixed.

In the end these loans ended up not being a very good deal for lenders, either, as when real estate values crashed a lot of their portfolio was made up of loans with increasing principal balances and decreasing security value. As a result, both lenders and borrowers made out poorly and this product is not available today.

So why am I of the opinion that these loans were not that bad? I believe they were a useful product that was used incorrectly. If used by an informed borrower and managed properly on rare occasion they could be a great deal. I turned down dozens of borrowers who wanted this loan when I thought it was a terrible idea, but I did write three of them. All of them worked out, and two of them worked out very well because the borrowers managed them properly. The cases are very different, so I'll tell both stories, as they are excellent examples of when the product works.

1) Ben was a self-employed small businessman who owned a service business. He had cash flow problems from time to time and each time he ended up behind on some bills. He came to me and was currently behind on a few bills at that time, with no real expectation he could catch up.

By now you know that it is a bad idea (usually) to consolidate unsecured debt into secured debt unless there is a real tangible benefit and the outcome is likely to be successful. Ben had a very small balance on his mortgage and large balances on his revolving debt. It would have been a disservice to him to consolidate his debt without a realistic long-term plan.

I gave him a plan to improve his credit situation before I would refinance his house. I asked him to make all his payments consistently for at least six months so that his credit would improve and we could get him a better mortgage. He did all the work; I just supplied the plan. I also wanted to see if he could do it.

He lived frugally, paid his bills, and stayed on plan for six months. He had a lot of equity in his house, so we refinanced and consolidated as much of his remaining debts as possible. We used an Option ARM to give him the flexibility to make lower payments on his house **if** he needed to in order to stay current on bills. I showed him how paying more in discount fees to the lender would bring his *margin* down, and reduce his fully-indexed interest rate, saving him thousands over the first couple of years. His actual interest rate was much lower this way than it would have been with a fixed-rate mortgage or even a fixed-period adjustable.

I then carefully explained the options he would see on his statement every month: the minimum payment, which would result in his principal balance increasing; the interest-only payment, which would at least keep the principal balance steady, and the fully-amortized payment, which would begin paying down the loan amount.

I asked that he pay the fully-amortized payment every month, unless he needed cash for an emergency; our goal was to bring his non-mortgage debt to zero.

Ben was quite smart and did all I asked of him. After three years he had no other debt, he had made the fully-amortized payment almost every month, and his credit score had jumped from the low 600s to over 740. We refinanced him at an opportune time into a 30 year fixed mortgage, and he is doing great.

2) Robert was an architect who wanted to buy a small, older home to rehabilitate and enlarge for resale. He had a healthy practice, but in our area real estate prices and construction costs are quite high. If he used a fixed-rate mortgage he would have had to commit too much of his cash reserves to the down payment, and too much of his monthly income to the monthly payment. He would not have had the cash to do the kind of rehabilitation he wanted.

We structured a low-down-payment option ARM. I did not advise that he bring cash in to buy down the margin because he didn't intend to keep the loan very long, so a super-low interest rate wasn't that important. His fully-indexed interest rate was still much lower than a fixed or a fixed-period ARM. He was able to conserve cash going into the purchase with a lower down payment, and saved considerable money each month on interest cost relative to a 30-year fixed.

I advised Robert to make only the minimum payment each month if he needed cash for construction, as he was upgrading and significantly improving the house, so the rising value would more than offset the rising principal balance of the loan.

Robert took my advice, and even though values didn't rise as much as he thought they would and construction costs amounted to more than he expected, his very low interest cost saved him thousands of dollars and the project was financially successful. His total loan costs were probably $15,000 less over the life of the project than if he had used a fixed rate loan.

You can see that used properly this product can be quite beneficial. However, using an option ARM requires that you, the borrower, be very well informed, have professional guidance on structuring the terms, and properly manage the loan over its lifetime. These factors were rarely in place, and many folks paid dearly for their lack.

If Option ARMs return to the market, do not take one unless you feel you **completely** understand how it works and what the costs and risks really are.

Chapter Fifteen

Private Money (Hard Money)

There has always been a "lender of last resort" for borrowers whose credit is in such dire straits that they simply cannot obtain real estate financing from any conventional sources, or for folks who need to close the loan very fast. The go-to lenders in these circumstances were brokers who handle private money loans, or money lent at high interest rates for short terms, with the money supplied by individual investors. These loans are also knows as "private" or "hard" money loans.

Typical interest rates on private-money loans are 10% to 13% in California, with origination fees running 2 to 4 points. The loans are often written with a three or five year balloon, meaning that the entire amount is due and payable at that time. The security for the loan is strictly equity, since the borrowers are not considered credit-worthy. If you don't make your payments on time the lender takes back the property, sells it, and uses the proceeds to pay back the investor.

Consequently, private-money lenders will typically lend no more than 60% to 70% of the appraised value of a property in order to make sure that they have plenty of security. Private-money loans usually have pre-payment penalties too that could kick up the cost of the financing significantly.

While the terms may seem onerous, there are instances when a private-money loan makes sense. For instance, if you are in foreclosure and need to raise money to bring your loan current to pull it out of foreclosure, a private-money loan could be just the ticket, and may be your only option. Or if you find an outrageous deal on a house but have to close in one week in order to get it, the cost of a private-money loan may be worth it.

However, changes in lending regulations in 2011 - 2013 made private-money loans on personal residences virtually impossible to do. As of 2011, new lending rules prohibit lenders from making loans secured by a personal residence to borrowers without documenting that they are able to repay the loan. This rule has severely diminished private money lending on personal residences at this time, since the entire point of a private-money loan is that the lender's security is the equity in the house, not your ability to repay. This may, and almost certainly will, change again over time, as there are times when private money serves a borrower's needs well.

Private money is still available for investment property, however.

What do you need to consider when dealing with private money? There are four features of private-money loans that can make them less desirable than conventional financing: high interest rates, balloon payments, interest-only payments and pre-payment penalties. The high interest rates we discussed above. As for the rest:

Balloon Payments

Historically a private-money loan was made for a rather short period of time – two to five years was most common. At the end of the term the entire balance of the loan was due and payable. This is known as a balloon payment.

To understand why this was the case it is helpful to remember that the lenders (generally brokers) got their funds for the loans from private individuals. Aunt Jane and Uncle Bob saw earning 10% interest on their money as being quite attractive, but they weren't in the business of lending their money out for 30 years. So, they would invest in a short-term note secured by real estate and when the note paid off in a few years they could reinvest or take their money and run.

From your perspective as a borrower, this meant that if you were to accept a private-money loan you would have to plan to pay it off at the end of the term – either by refinancing into a conventional mortgage, selling the property, or winning the lottery. But remember, there must have been a reason that you went with private money in the first place; perhaps your credit was poor or the property had issues that made it unattractive to a conventional lender. Whatever the reason, there was a deadline, and your property was at serious risk if you didn't have a plan to replace the private money with a conventional loan.

There were many folks who took out a private-money mortgage and then were not able to make the balloon payment and were not qualified to refinance into a conventional mortgage. Those folks often lost their property, or worse many found that the only replacement financing was another private-money loan. These loans have very high transaction fees, and always have a limited term and a balloon payment, so over time folks who moved from one hard-money loan to another ate up their equity in transaction fees, and many eventually lost their homes entirely.

A balloon payment isn't necessarily a toxic loan term, but you should not have a hard-money loan with a balloon payment unless you have a plan in place to replace your loan with a fully-amortized conventional loan at the end of the term.

Interest Only Payments

Private-money loans are most often structured with interest-only payments. The challenge with interest-only payments, as we discussed in Chapter 13, is that the principal balance of the loan never goes down, so you never pay it off.

Private-money loans are meant to be temporary financing anyway, and as mentioned above you really need a plan to get out of it.

Pre-Payment Penalty

Finally, private-money loans have invariably included pre-payment penalties if you pay the loan off early. From the investor's perspective, the pre-payment penalty protects their yield on the investment. They've lent you the money for a certain period of time. If you pay the loan off early their money will be sitting "idle" for a while until another investment comes along. If you pay the loan off at the end of the term as agreed, the investor will have been able to plan ahead and review other investment opportunities.

The pre-payment penalty, therefore, helps them plan their investment strategy.

A pre-payment penalty in California is set by law to be no more than equal to six months interest on the pre-paid balance of the loan. If you paid it off early, you paid the investor the next six month's interest all in one lump sum; the investor thus had plenty of time to review new investments.

From a borrower's perspective, this was a pretty serious cost if you wanted to get out of your loan early. If you sold the property, the penalty would be taken out of your cash proceeds in escrow. If you refinanced into a convention loan, the penalty needed to be paid in escrow (or before,) either in cash or through proceeds of the new loan. In the case of refinancing, you would essentially be paying twice for use of the money for a six-month period: at the higher interest rate for the private money loan through the pre-payment penalty for six months, and at the new rate for the new money you used to replace it.

With new regulations promulgated by the *Consumer Financial Protection Bureau* (CFPB) pre-payment penalties are more restricted now, at least for a while.

Conclusion

I have seen private money used in cases where it was completely unnecessary just because it was easy and fast. I think that's tragic. If someone recommends a hard money loan for you, make sure you've exhausted all other options.

Chapter Sixteen

Second Mortgages

Another product that has faded somewhat from use between 2008 and 2013 but is beginning to make a comeback is second mortgages. They were popular during the Mortgage Boom primarily for two purposes: as a way to purchase a home with less than 20% down and avoid mortgage insurance, and as a way to pull cash out of your home without disturbing your first mortgage.

A second mortgage is exactly what it sounds like – a second mortgage on your home, whose security is considered "junior" to your first mortgage. In other words, in the event of a foreclosure sale, your first mortgage would be paid off first, and then your second mortgage holder would collect whatever proceeds remain.

Options for second mortgages are very similar to first mortgages, in that you can choose fixed or adjustable-rate mortgages, and mortgages amortized over various terms. A common version used during much of the 2000's was an equity line, which is covered in the next section.

Avoiding Mortgage Insurance

Let's look at the first use mentioned above – using a second mortgage to avoid paying mortgage insurance.

Mortgage insurance is discussed in depth in Chapter 18, *"Other Considerations,"* but for the purpose of this discussion it is useful to know that mortgage insurance is an insurance policy which the lender takes out to insure against losses in the event you default on your loan. The cost of this mortgage insurance, besides stricter underwriting guidelines, is an insurance premium which you pay, typically as part of your monthly payment. Mortgage insurance is typically required on any first mortgage in which the loan-to-value ratio is greater than 80%.

If you have one mortgage you only make one payment each month. If you have two mortgages you need to make two payments. If you have one mortgage with mortgage insurance, you essentially also make two payments: your loan payment, plus your mortgage insurance premium. (You will send in only one payment to your lender, however, and your lender will pay the mortgage insurance premium.)

The question then becomes: if you are putting less than 20% down should you get one loan with mortgage insurance or an 80% first loan with the balance made up of a second loan, thereby avoiding mortgage insurance? It depends. Take a look at the analysis below:

The Overly Simple Method

The most common mistake is for people to compare the monthly payment of two loans to the payment of one loan plus mortgage insurance. Why is this a mistake?

As we discussed in Chapter 6 "Should You Refinance?*"* your monthly payment is not all cost. It is part interest, which is a cost, and part principal, which is an investment. This applies to second mortgage as well as first mortgages, so comparing only the monthly payments misstates your true cost.

Let's see what that looks like.

Let's assume for our running example that we only have 10% to put down, instead of the 20% we've been working with. Now we need to borrow $225,000 against our $250,000 purchase price, rather than $250,000.

We have two options. We can either borrow the money in a single loan, and pay for a mortgage insurance policy, or take out two loans, a first and a second, and avoid mortgage insurance.

If we want to use two loans, our first mortgage will be $200,000 (80% of the purchase price to avoid mortgage insurance) and our second loan will be $25,000 (10% to make up the difference.)

The interest rate on the first will be 5.000% and on the second will be 8.000%. We assume the first will be a 30 year fixed-rate loan, and the second a 15 year fixed-rate loan.

The payment on our first mortgage will be $1,073.64.

The payment on our second mortgage is $238.91.

Our total payments will be $1,312.56.

Now let's use mortgage insurance.

We'll have one loan of $225,000 at 5.000%. Our payment will be $1,207.85. But we have to have mortgage insurance; let's assume that will cost $95 per month. Now our total payment will be $1,207.85 + $95 = $1,302.85.

It appears that using one loan with mortgage insurance is less expensive than using two loans to avoid it. However, you remember that the payment is not all cost – it is mostly cost, and a little principal. Paying principal on your mortgage is an investment in your equity, not a cost, so this analysis might misstate the actual difference.

But we do have an app for that.

The Simple Method

We can calculate the exact difference in the **initial monthly cost** between the two options.

We've assumed that the interest rate on our $200,000 first mortgage is 5%. Our initial cost on the loan will be $10,000 per year. (Note that this overstates the cost by a tiny bit, because as you pay down the principal balance your monthly cost of interest declines. However, this is the **simple** method, so bear with me.)

The interest rate on our second mortgage will be 8%. The initial annual cost of the loan is therefore $2,000 ($25,000 x 8%).

If we add the two together, we see that our initial annual cost of the two loans is $12,000, or $1,000 per month.

Let's compare that to using a single loan with mortgage insurance.

Our single loan would have to be $225,000, and we'll assume our interest rate will be 5%. Our mortgage insurance will run $95 per month.

The interest cost on our mortgage is now $11,250 per year ($225,000 x 5%), or $937.50 per month. The mortgage insurance premium is $95, so our initial monthly cost of this financing option is $937.50 + $95 = $1,032.50.

Now it appears that taking two loans is a better deal than taking one with mortgage insurance, despite the fact that we're using the exact same loans in the two analyses.

Like all of the "simple" examples in this book this analysis has some limitations. The primary one is that you are almost certainly paying down your loan balances over time. If so, the calculations and the results change. They don't change by much the first few years, but they do change. Consequently, for the more adventurous it is useful to have a more complex analysis.

Complex Method

Once again, for my Silicon Valley engineer friends…

Since the simple method above at best provides an approximation of the comparative costs for two loans, and then only really for the first year or so, we need a method to compare the lifetime costs of two different ways of doing a loan. There are a few assumptions we need make, and we need to define a few terms:

Loan amount – sounds obvious but I think it had to be stated.

Interest rate – the nominal interest rate as defined by your note.

Loan term – the term over which you intend to pay back your loan.

Holding period – the period over which you intend to keep the loan (may or may not coincide with how long you'll own the property)

Loan costs – **all** of the costs associated with acquiring the proposed loan(s), including title, escrow, recording, appraisal, reconveyance, etc.

There are a few principles that are worth repeating here to help us understand why these things matter:

- First, unless you are making interest-only payments your mortgage payment is not all cost. It is a combination of *interest*, which is a cost, and *principal*, which is really an investment in the equity in the property. (If you pay down your principal balance by $100 this month, you have $100 more equity in the property than you did before.)

- This is important because, all things being equal the lower the interest rate a note carries, the faster the principal balance is being paid down. At a lower interest rate a higher portion of your payment goes to principal, and is an investment in your equity, rather than interest cost.

- Unless you intend to live in the property indefinitely and the loan you are acquiring is likely to be the last one you get, you will probably not pay your loan off. The *holding period* is thus not defined for you. You have to come up with a reasonable estimate for how long you will keep the loan. There could be many factors that influence the holding period of your loan. You might be contemplating life circumstances that will dictate a strategy where you premeditate a refinance, like our friend Raoul in Chapter 6.

The math on this will depend to a great extent what assumptions you are making. To make the complex example as simple as possible, we'll assume that we are looking to refinance and have to decide whether to use mortgage insurance or not. We also assume:

The property value is $250,000

We currently owe $225,000

We could use one loan, but since we owe more than 80% of the value we need mortgage insurance

We can use two loans; we'll assume an 80% first and a 10% fixed-rate second.

The analysis looks like this:

Payment Analysis

	Option One 30 Year Conforming Fixed One loan, mortgage insurance required Zero Points		Option Two 30 Year High-Balance Fixed Two loans Zero Points	
Loan-to-value	90.00%		90.00%	
Total Loans	$ 225,000		$ 225,000	
First Mortgage				
Loan Amount	$ 225,000		$ 200,000	
Loan Type	Fixed		Fixed	
Interest Rate	5.000%		5.000%	
Term (Years)	30		30	
Payment		$ 1,207.85		$ 1,073.64
Mortgage Insurance?	Yes	$ 95.00	No	$ -
Second Mortgage				
Loan Amount	$ -		$ 25,000	
Loan Type	Fixed		Fixed	
Interest Rate	8.000%		8.000%	
Term (Years)	15		15	
Payment		$ -		$ 238.91
Total Monthly Payments:		**$ 1,302.85**		**$ 1,312.56**
First Mortgage Estimated Costs:		$ 3,100	Estimated Costs:	$ 3,000
2nd Mortgage Estimated Costs:		$ -	Estimated Costs:	$ 663
Total Loan Costs		$ 3,100	Total Loan Costs	$ 3,663
Holding Period	5 years			
Bal. @ end of holding period: 1st Mtg.:		$ 206,615		$ 183,657
2nd Mtg.:		$ -		$ 19,692
Total Remaining Principal Balance:		$ 206,615		$ 203,349
Total lifetime payments:		$ 78,171		$ 78,753
Total Principal Paid:		$ 18,385		$ 21,651
Total loan *cost* over holding period:		**$ 62,886**		**$ 60,765**

You'll notice a few things about this analysis that are important:

- The total monthly payments are lower with option one than with option two.
- Consequently the total lifetime payments for option one are lower than they are for option two.

- However, with option two you are paying down the principal balance of the loan faster than you are with option one. Why is that? I assumed that the second mortgage had a 15-year term, which is more common than a 30-year term on second mortgages. Therefore, while the payment is higher you are paying down that portion of the balance faster.

- In fact, while you have paid almost $600 more over 5 years for option two, you have more than $2,000 more equity in your property. Should you sell or refinance at this time, that difference in the principal balance is all profit to you.

- Finally, you'll notice that you still don't have 20% equity in option one, as the loan balance is still over 80% of the original value – **unless** we assume that the property is appreciating, in which case at some point in the five years you would be able to get rid of the mortgage insurance, unless it was an FHA loan. (For more on that, see Chapter 18.)

As a final note with the simple analysis option one – using a single loan with mortgage insurance – appeared to be the less costly option. With the more complex analysis using two loans turns out to be less costly than using one loan with mortgage insurance. When you go shopping for a loan, the overly simple method is the one most likely to be used by your loan officer.

The point isn't that the simple version is irrelevant or wrong. The point is to underscore that your mortgage advisor is, in a very real sense, advising you on what is probably the most significant financial transaction of your life.

Shouldn't he or she be able to walk you through a version of the more complex analysis? I would insist on it.

Pulling Cash Out of Your Home

We're still not through with our discussion of second mortgages. What if you want to pull cash out of your home? Should you use a second mortgage or refinance with a new first?

Obviously, the answer to this depends a lot on your existing first mortgage. If you have a very attractive first mortgage and a new first mortgage would be either higher in interest rate or less attractive in terms, a new first mortgage is probably a very unwise move, and using a second mortgage to pull cash out would make sense.

On the other hand, if you wish to refinance your existing first mortgage anyway now is a very good time to consider whether you want to pull cash out. (For a discussion of the advantages and disadvantages of using one or two loans, see Chapter 6.)

The salient point here is to examine what you are using the money for. As we discussed in Chapter 6, you want to exercise discretion in using the equity in your home. See Chapter 6, and read the section "Match the Cash Out With the Purpose" for a full discussion.

Conclusion

Second mortgages can be a great tool to avoid mortgage insurance or to pull cash out of your home while leaving your first mortgage untouched, but do the analysis thoughtfully.

Using a second mortgage to pull cash out of your home is advisable only if you **really need** to access the equity in your home, can afford the payment, never finance anything longer than you intend to own or use it, and if it does not make sense to refinance your first mortgage.

Chapter Seventeen

Equity Lines

Another way to either buy a home with a lower down payment or to draw money out of your home is to use an equity line. In almost all cases an equity line is written as a second loan on a property, meaning that there is a first mortgage in place, and an equity line is placed behind it. An equity line is a second lien in these instances. An equity line is similar to a mortgage in that your property is mortgaged, or used as collateral for the loan.

However, an equity line differs dramatically from what you think of as a mortgage. An equity line is really a revolving line of credit. You can draw on the line when you need cash, pay it back as you can, and draw more cash out again.

Because I work with a number of financial planners as referral partners, I wrote a lot of equity lines during the Great Mortgage Boom. Used wisely an equity line can be a valuable tool for financial management. After the Great Meltdown fewer lenders offered equity lines through broker channels, and in most cases today I send my clients to credit unions or local banks to get an equity line because they can get a better deal. That is changing back as lenders come back into the market with new products, so moving forward you may have more choices as to where to go to get your equity line.

While equity lines are not for everyone, they can be a great product in certain cases and I highly recommend them for a lot of clients. The terms you need to know about on an equity line are as follows:

Draw Period

An equity line is never open-ended. There is a period during which you may draw money whenever you need, but at the end of the draw period you cannot draw any more cash. The most typical draw period is ten years, although I have seen some with five-year draw periods. This means that you only have the right to draw on the line for ten, or for five years.

During the draw period the minimum payment is typically equal to the accrued interest on the loan. (In other words, payments are interest-only.) If you make only your minimum payment, you will pay no principal down during this period.

Payback Period

Once the draw period is over you enter the payback period. Over this period you must pay back all of the money owed on the loan plus interest. You therefore *must* begin making amortized payments. This period starts when the draw period ends and is typically set at fifteen years, although I have seen ten and twenty year payback periods. During this period your interest rate is still adjustable so your minimum payment may change. You will still receive monthly statements during this period telling you what your fully amortized payment is each month.

Adjustable Rate

All equity lines have adjustable interest rates. By now you know from our discussion about adjustable-rate mortgages that the four most important factors are the *index*, the *margin*, the *adjustment period*, and the *adjustment caps*.

Index

Most equity lines use the Prime Rate as an index. The Prime Rate is the interest rate that major banks charge their most creditworthy large corporate borrowers. This index is a little different than those used for conventional adjustable-rate mortgages, because although it is market-driven in a sense, it tends to track a rate set by the Federal Reserve called the discount rate. This is the rate that the Federal Reserve charges to banks to lend them money for a very short term, and thus closely (in theory) represents the cost of short-term funds to the banks.

Consequently, unlike other market-driven indices the Prime Rate does not adjust daily and does not fluctuate much in the short term. In the long term, however, it can fluctuate dramatically. In the early 1980s the Prime Rate was as high as **21.5%!**

Here is a history of the Prime Rate over the last 18 years:

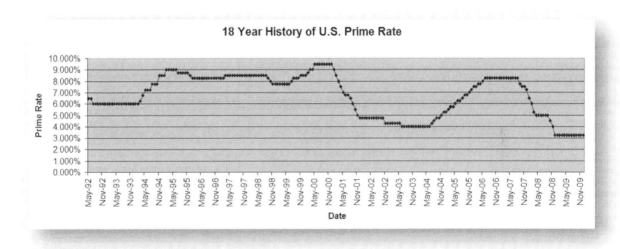

Margin

The margin will be set by your agreement with the bank, just like in an adjustable-rate mortgage. During the Mortgage Boom of the early 2000s it was not uncommon for a highly creditworthy borrower to have a margin as low as -0.25 or on rare occasion even better. This meant that the interest rate on your equity line would be set at 0.25% **lower** than the current index value. At the time, the Prime Rate was typically in the 7% to 9% range, so your rate would have been 6.75% to 8.75% at any given time.

During the Great Recession, however, the Federal Reserve reduced short-term rates that they use as benchmarks to lend to banks (or for banks to lend to each other) to nearly zero in order to lower the cost of borrowing and boost the economy. The Prime Rate, which is set by major banks, tends to run in line with short-term rates. Therefore, the Prime Rate during this period has been running at 3.25%. A borrower with a margin of -0.25%, as an example, was paying only 3.000% on their equity line during this time.

That's a **great** deal for the borrower, and not such a good deal for the lender.

Lenders do learn, and today I don't see any lenders offering an equity line with a margin that low. The lowest permanent margin I could find on the day I searched was + 0.500, for a current fully-indexed rate of 3.75%. (As of the day I searched. By the time you read this I believe short term rates will probably be higher.)

Few borrowers understand how important the margin is to their long-term cost of borrowing, but it is critical to the profitability of the equity line to the lender. Consequently margins vary considerably today. **It is the easiest way for the lender to increase the profitability of the loan without borrowers really understanding how it impacts their cost.** So now more than ever aggressive shopping can save you thousands of dollars over the life of the equity line. Pay attention to the margin you are offered.

Adjustment Period

Most equity lines are written so that the interest rate can adjust daily. Since they are based on the Prime Rate which doesn't adjust daily, however, in practice equity lines adjust infrequently. When the Prime Rate adjusts, your interest rate will adjust the same day. The adjustment period is defined in your Equity Line Agreement, and when your interest rate adjusts your lender will tell you in your monthly statement.

Adjustment Caps

There are typically no periodic adjustment caps with equity lines. However, the Prime Rate is usually adjusted by no more than a quarter point at a time, so in practice your interest rate is not likely to adjust more than 0.250% on any day. (Historically, however, it has adjusted by as much as 0.750% in one day.)

Most equity lines do have a lifetime cap, however, and most are set at 18%. It has been nearly 30 years since the Prime Rate was so high that a typical equity line would yield that high a rate, but it could happen.

Common Traps

Teaser rates

When is the quoted rate not actually your rate? Well, that happened a lot during the Mortgage Boom. This was known as a *teaser rate.* The initial margin (and thus interest rate) you were quoted was only good for a certain period of time, usually for three to six months. After that the interest rate would rise. Lenders would structure a loan offer this way as folks tend to just pay attention to the initial number (the one in a larger, bold font and all caps) and ignore the fine print.

If your loan had a teaser rate your Equity Line Agreement would typically define it as an "Introductory" rate: for example, Prime plus zero. In this case your introductory rate would equal the Prime Rate for the introductory period. After that your *permanent rate* would have a margin greater than your introductory rate; 1.000% higher was pretty common.

In a few cases I used this to my client's advantage. Kim and Dave came to me and wanted to fund an addition on their home. Interest rates were somewhat high and they had a pretty good existing first mortgage, so refinancing their existing first was not an attractive option. As we discussed above an equity line can be an effective way to finance remodeling or an addition, for two very good reasons:

1. You don't need to draw the money out until you need it to pay for something, and
2. You do not pay interest or even make payments until you have drawn the money.

But they had a choice. They could take a permanent rate of Prime + zero, or an introductory rate of Prime – 1.000 for six months, and then the rate would go to Prime + 0.500. We discussed how long it would take to complete the project, and they thought it would take six to nine months.

We waited until they were ready to begin construction and *then* closed on an equity line with an attractive introductory rate. It indeed took about nine months for them to finish the project. In the first six months they paid 1% less in interest than if they had taken the line without the introductory rate. They paid 0.500% more for three months, and then when they finished the project we refinanced them into a new first loan wrapping both the existing first and equity line into a 30-year fixed.

So, watch out for teaser rates, but be aware that you can use them to reduce your borrowing costs in certain cases.

Interest Rate Floor

During the Mortgage Boom lenders never considered that the Prime Rate would drop down to 3.25%. At the time it had bounced between 6.000% and 9.000% for years, with a very short term dip down to 4.000% in 2003. In most years lenders who wrote their equity lines at Prime plus zero were earning 6 to 9% - a respectable yield.

But during the Great Recession the Prime Rate was driven down to 3.25% in an effort to get the economy moving. Lenders had millions of equity lines in place earning between 2.75% and 3.5% - yields that are much too low for those products to be profitable.

Since the Great Meltdown I have noticed most lenders have instituted an *interest rate floor* on their equity lines. This works just like an interest rate cap, except that the interest rate can never go **below** a certain rate. The most common I have seen is a floor of 5%. If your equity-line agreement contains this provision, regardless of how low the Prime Rate goes your interest rate will not go below this level.

Fortunately, plenty of lenders do not have this provision in their agreement, so you have options. You do not need to accept this provision in your equity line. Since some analysts project that interest rates may stay low for a considerable time, avoiding this clause could save you thousands of dollars over the life of your equity line. If at all possible, do NOT accept an equity line with this provision.

Maximum Rate—Lifetime Cap

As we mentioned above most equity lines have a lifetime cap of 18%. There is a problem with this, in my opinion, having to do with whether you can afford the equity line or not

Most lenders will qualify you - determine if you have enough income to pay back the loan - using the assumption that you have drawn the maximum on your equity line and that the interest rate has risen to 12%.

In other words, if you have a $100,000 credit limit on your equity line the lender (for the purpose of underwriting the loan) assumes that you have drawn out the entire amount and that your interest rate has risen all the way to 12%, far above the (say) 3.75% where it sits today. Your **actual** minimum payment at today's rate, assuming you draw the entire amount, would be $100,000 x 3.75% / 12 months = $312.50. For **qualifying** purposes, however, the lender would estimate your payment at $1,000. ($100,000 x 12% per year / 12 months)

This sounds relatively safe, doesn't it? They assume that your payment will be more than three times what it actually will be when you close.

However, most lenders also allow a fairly high debt ratio on their equity-line product. This means that they might allow you to commit 45% (or more) of your gross income to your debt service. (Your minimum monthly housing payment and all other debt obligations total 45% of your gross income. We haven't even accounted for taxes, utilities, food, or buying this book.)

So what happens if interest rates get out of control and the rate on your equity line goes to 18%? Let's take a look.

What Happens to Your Payment When Interest Rates Rise?

	You are qualified... your start rate is 3.750%	But what happens if... your rate rised to 18%?
Equity Line Amount:	$ 100,000	$ 100,000
Interest Rate:	3.750%	18.000%
Payment:	$ 312.50	$ 1,500.00

In our example your initial interest rate is 3.75%, and your payment is only $312.50.

But what if rates spiral out of control? Your rate could go to 18%. If so, you're payment now jumps to $1,500, a huge increase. Your lender thought you could afford a $1,000 payment when they qualified you, but it's much higher than that now.

Can you afford this? Maybe, maybe not.

This is a worst-case scenario. It is not likely to happen. But there were a lot of things that weren't likely to happen that happened anyway in the last few years, and millions of families are paying the price.

Ask your loan officer what the worst-case scenario is, and consider carefully if you think can deal with this. If you feel that the highest payments possible would "put you over the top," lower your sights and buy a less expensive home, or consider using a fixed-rate second mortgage.

The important point to remember is this: pretty much all lenders will have the same lifetime cap, so you probably can't shop and get a better one. The only thing you can do about this is to not borrow more than you can afford to pay in the worst-case scenario; keep the line amount within your affordable range.

Annual Fees

There is considerable difference between the annual fees that lenders charge. Some lenders offer equity lines with no annual fee at all, while others charge as much as $300 per year to keep the line open. However, the annual fee alone does not tell the whole story.

Suppose you are comparing two equity lines, one is at Prime plus zero and has a $50 annual fee. The other is offered at Prime plus 0.25, with no annual fee. Which is a better deal? Say you think you will carry a balance of $20,000 most of the time. The no-fee equity line will cost you an additional $50 per year in interest. ($20,000 x 0.25%.) In this case, the lines are about a wash: a $50 annual fee vs. $50 more in interest per year. Would you reject the line with the annual fee? I know many clients who would.

What if your credit limit on the line was $50,000 and you had to draw out the total amount due to an emergency? (e.g. a really cool sailboat comes on the market and you just have to have it.) Your additional interest cost on the line is now $125. ($50,000 x 0.25%.) If you selected the no-fee equity line at the higher interest rate, you are now spending $125 per year to save $50.

Ask whether your equity line has an annual fee, but don't automatically reject the line because it does. Compare the annual fee of the equity line – a fixed and known cost – with the additional interest cost based on the principal balance that you think you will typically owe.

Up-Front Costs

During the Mortgage Boom you could generally get an equity line either directly from the bank or from a mortgage broker with no up-front costs or fees. After the Mortgage Meltdown most banks stopped offering this product through the broker channel, so mortgage brokers had very few lenders they could work with to acquire an equity line for you.

Consequently, today you pretty much have to go to banks or credit unions to get an equity line, and very few offer true no-fee lines. The up-front fees should be quite limited, though. You might be asked to pay for an appraisal fee in advance, and you might be asked to pay for some title fees or for a processing or administration fee.

A quick search on the internet will reveal that some banks or credit unions are still offering equity lines with no up-front fees, but their annual fees, early closure fees, and margin might mitigate the benefit of that.

As you shop for an equity line, be aware of the up-front fees. Don't automatically reject a bank that charges them; the ongoing fees might make an equity line much more expensive than one from a local bank that charges some reasonable fees up front.

Pre-Payment Penalties / Early Closure Fees

Most equity lines do not have pre-payment penalties. Many, however, have early closure fees. The difference between a pre-payment penalty and an early closure fee is, well, nothing really. They might work a little differently in practice but the net effect is the same; you must pay money if you pay off your equity line before a certain date, regardless of whether it is called a penalty or a fee.

Most of the equity lines I've seen have an early closure fee the first three years, and after that it is waived. The fee can also be quite low compared to many pre-payment penalties, and might be only a couple of hundred dollars.

In practice most folks would rarely close out their line before the early closure fee expires, so while it is good to be aware of it, an early closure fee should rarely be the deal-breaker in choosing between equity lines.

Strategy – What to Consider

Purpose

What are you using the line for? How you intend to use the equity line will often direct you to favor certain terms over others. The purpose of the line will often drive how long you will likely take to pay it off.

Initial draw

How much cash do you need immediately? Some lines require that you draw a large amount initially in order to get the loan with no up-front fees. That's fine if you need it, but not if you don't. Do you need to draw the money out immediately? If not, avoid an equity line where it is required, or you must pay interest to borrow money you don't need, negating one of the best features of the equity line over a fixed loan.

Time Frame

How long will you need the money? I want to stress again that an equity line is not, in my opinion, the best way to borrow money for a long period of time. They all carry adjustable interest rates, and the longer you hold the equity line the longer you expose yourself to the risk of rising rates.

If you need the money you are borrowing for an extended period of time, consider using a fixed-rate equity **loan** rather than an equity line, or refinancing your first mortgage altogether.

Long-Term Plans

Do you intent to close the line when you are done using it? Some folks use an equity line for short-term needs, such as a remodel, and either pay the line off or consolidate their first mortgage and equity line into a new first mortgage when they are done with it.

If you only need to have the cash from the equity line available for a short period of time low up-front fees and a low or no early closure fees are more important than the margin or the annual fees.

Ongoing Use

(Business owners should get a low margin.)

Small business owners often use an equity line as a business line of credit. Your accountant might not want you to commingle personal assets with business, but you will almost certainly save a great deal of money compared to a typical business line of credit.

Some clients now use large lines of credit to buy distressed properties, paying off the line after they have spruced them up and sold them. These clients need large amounts of cash for short periods of time. Using an equity line allows them to move fast on a great deal, avoid fees and costs on a new mortgage, and have the money available again when the project is done.

If you are going to use your line of credit for ongoing cash flow needs the permanent margin and the annual fee could be the most important considerations.

Conclusion

The greatest benefit of an equity line is the flexibility it gives you to access the equity in your home easily and cheaply. The most obvious risk is that your interest rate can rise. The greater risk is that most homeowners use the line to pay for short-term assets or even current living expenses, and don't make a plan to pay it off before the draw period ends, so they are forced to either roll into a new line, or convert the unpaid balance into long-term debt. An equity line is a poor choice for that.

Over time, properly planning and using an equity line can save you thousands of dollars over the life of the line.

Chapter Eighteen

Mortgage Insurance, FHA and VA

There are other issues that you may want to consider that don't fit neatly into the discussions above, but are important for you to know.

Mortgage Insurance

Lenders would prefer that you put 20% down when buying a home because then you have "skin in the game." Because you have made a large commitment, it is not very likely that you will walk away from the home if things suddenly turn bad for you. You will find a way to make the payments to protect your investment.

For instance if you put 20% down on our typical $250,000 home, you have invested $50,000 of your own money into the deal. If you default and the house is taken away from you your loss is quite substantial, and quite painful.

Moreover, the instant equity you bought provides a cushion for the lender. If you default and never bring your loan current, eventually the lender will foreclose. When they do, assuming that the value of your home hasn't changed, they will have plenty of value in the home to pay themselves back. The value of the property is their last line of defense in the event you default on the loan.

To illustrate this, let's assume that you still owe $200,000 when you default. We know from our earlier examples that interest is accruing at about $1,000 per month. Let's assume that it takes nine months to foreclose and the bank runs up $5,000 in legal fees to do so. (Again, keeping it simple.) When the bank takes the house back you know owe $216,000: ($200,000 + (9 x $1,000) + $5,000).

The property is still worth $250,000, but the bank will probably have to discount the price for a quick sale, say 5% or $12,500, for a sale price of $237,500. Commissions and other sale costs will cost the bank 8% of the sale price or so, or $19,000. The bank then nets $218,500, barely more than the $216,000 they are owed, and has just about recovered everything they are owed.

You can see that even at 20% down there is really not an abundance of equity in the property when it comes down to protecting the lender in the event you default and they have to foreclose. So how do folks with less than 20% down buy homes?

This is where the mortgage insurance comes in. Think of it this way: mortgage insurance replaces the insurance that a larger down payment normally provides. The mortgage insurance company, for a fee (an annual insurance premium that you pay for in monthly installments) insures the lender so that if, after a foreclosure is complete the lender has any losses the insurance policy will reimburse the lender for all, or part of that loss.

You noticed just now that there was an insurance premium; who pays for that? You do, of course.

Is mortgage insurance good or bad? Well, it represents an additional cost to buy and finance your home, but it allows you to buy a home with less than 20% down. If you can avoid mortgage insurance by putting more down then by all means avoid mortgage insurance. If you can't, then you either must accept mortgage insurance, use two loans to buy your home (See Chapter 16, *"Second Mortgages- Avoiding Mortgage Insurance."*) or wait until you have saved enough to put 20% down.

You should also know that the perceived risk of default is much greater after the Great Meltdown than it was during the Mortgage Boom. When risk rises, insurance premiums rise too.

This has been the case with mortgage insurance premiums. They have become very expensive, particularly when your down payment is very small.

In Chapter 16 we showed you how to compare a single loan with mortgage insurance to using two loans to avoid mortgage insurance. The analyses we used will help guide you to the solution that produces the lowest calculated cost. But what about the more subjective issues involved in the decision?

There is quite a bit of judgment involved in deciding whether using mortgage insurance is the right solution for you.

In order for this to make sense you have to know how to get rid of mortgage insurance.

Most mortgage insurance policies today are written so that they must remain in place for a **minimum** period of time; two years is most common. They are not automatically removed, though, at that point. You'll have to demonstrate that the principal balance of your mortgage is less than 80% of your home's value so that the lender now has a minimum amount of equity as a buffer against you defaulting on your loan. (Some policies call for a larger equity buffer than 20%.)

An important note here is that if you have private mortgage insurance your lender is not required to let it go – ever. Some lenders require that you keep your mortgage insurance for longer than two years, and some require more than 20% equity in the property before you can remove it. There isn't any good reason for the lender to deny the removal of the insurance policy, but they don't have to. These terms are not typically spelled out in your disclosures, so ask your loan advisor up front what the lender's policy is and, if possible, get it in writing.

Usually when you request that your lender remove your mortgage insurance an appraisal – ordered by the lender but at your cost – is required.

How do you build this equity? Equity is built

> My lender offered me a loan with 5% down and no mortgage insurance. That's a great deal, right?
>
> This product is called *lender-paid mortgage insurance*. The lender charges you a higher interest rate (typically 0.25% to 0.50%) and uses the extra money each month to pay for – you guessed it – a mortgage insurance policy.
>
> Unlike when **you** pay the policy, however, your interest rate premium is forever, unless you refinance or pay off the loan.

when you pay down your mortgage, or when your home appreciates. While we didn't see much of the latter from 2007 through 2012, in most years real estate does appreciate, at least a little.

This is where it gets interesting. With two loans a small portion of your debt is at a higher interest rate. In our example in Chapter 15 the interest rate on the second mortgage is 3.000% higher than the interest rate on the first. (8.000% compared to 5.000%) Simplified, this means that the portion of the down payment provided by the second mortgage costs $750 per year more in interest than if it were all in one loan. ($25,000 x 3% = $750.)

In our example using two loans to avoid mortgage insurance looked favorable. Except…

As one of my most intelligent clients put it, using two loans is a long-term solution to a short-term problem.

If your home is appreciating or if you are paying your mortgage down quickly, then it is highly likely you can get rid of your mortgage insurance in two or three years for nothing more than the cost of an appraisal. When you do, your entire debt load, in the example above, is at the lower interest rate (5% in our example) and you will no longer pay mortgage insurance. From then on you will save money, relative to having two loans.

So now maybe mortgage insurance is looking pretty attractive if we assume that our home will appreciate enough within two to three years to dump the insurance. Except…

A lot of my clients have what I like to call "windfall" income. In our area, this often comes from stock options, large annual bonuses based on company profit or, in some cases, inheritance. If you fit this profile, then two loans could make a lot of sense for you. Why? Because you can acquire two loans to avoid mortgage insurance and as soon as your windfall income arrives you can pay off the higher-cost second mortgage. There is no prepayment penalty in most cases for second mortgages, so you don't have to wait two years as you would to get rid of mortgage insurance.

Of course, you could also take mortgage insurance and use the windfall income to buy down your first mortgage to a point where you can get rid of mortgage insurance, too, but you do have to wait out that minimum term.

One interesting use of this was "Marge and Fred." Marge and Fred were expecting a small inheritance from her grandmother who had passed away. It wasn't due for at least a few months, but it could have been as long as a couple of years. They could count on an amount, but not the timing of it.

Their real estate agent was pushing them to "buy now" before the market went up. Their financial advisor was advising them to wait until the inheritance came in before making any commitments so they could get less expensive financing. They were confused and couldn't make up their minds.

I advised them to not buy a home before the inheritance came in **unless** they found something they loved at a price that was low enough that they could afford whatever payments they had even if the inheritance never came in. I advised them to use two loans so that they could pay the second off if and when the inheritance did come in.

They lowered their range a bit, found something they liked, and used a first and second mortgage to buy the home with 10% down. The inheritance came in within a few months, and they paid off the second and put some money back into savings as a cushion.

The real estate agent had to work a little harder to find a good deal in their new price range on a home that met their needs, and their financial advisor had to live with lower commissions when they withdrew the money from their investment accounts sooner than he recommended. But they got what they wanted and were never "house poor."

There are two important lessons to take from the discussion of whether you should use mortgage insurance or a second mortgage to buy a home with a small down payment:

1. Your loan officer should run a comparison for you of the actual cost of your financing using mortgage insurance versus using two loans, and you should look this over very carefully.

2. The numbers alone don't drive the decision. Look at your situation and at the market in which you are buying. Is your new home likely to appreciate? Do you plan to substantially improve it, thus increasing its value and building equity that way? Do you expect any windfall income? Talk to your real estate agent, talk to your financial advisor, talk to your loan officer, and talk to your family. But remember, *you* drive the bus; we are only supposed to navigate.

FHA Loans

FHA stands for the Federal Housing Administration. It is a department of HUD, the U.S Department of Housing and Urban Development. The stated mission of FHA is to provide access to the housing market, particularly for underserved communities.

FHA is not a lender. FHA does not originate loans, as mortgage brokers and retail lenders do, nor does it buy pools of residential loans as Fannie Mae and Freddie Mac do. Instead, FHA provides insurance against losses for lenders who make loans to underserved borrowers. In the event that a loan defaults and a lender loses money, the insurance policy reimburses the lender for a portion or all of the loss.

In other words, an FHA mortgage guarantee is really just another mortgage insurance product.

The difference is that FHA is not a for-profit organization. Their mission is to enable underserved communities access to home ownership, particularly when for-profit organizations will not.

However, the mission does not include guaranteeing unwise loans (from a lending perspective) or losing money in the long run. The idea is to encourage lenders to serve those who are likely to be able to pay for their mortgage but who do not meet traditional lender guidelines. Specifically, home buyers with very little cash reserve for a down payment or with slightly bruised credit may find that only an FHA-guaranteed loan is available to them.

Consequently the advantage to an FHA-guaranteed loan is that it enables borrowers who would otherwise not qualify for a loan to buy a home. But of course, there is a downside – the cost.

As I mentioned above, FHA is non-profit but they are not in the business of losing money, either. As you can imagine, if they guarantee loans that lenders would otherwise not make, from time to time FHA must pay a claim to a lender when a loan doesn't work out. Where does this money come from?

As with mortgage insurance, it comes from you, the borrower. In addition to annual premiums (paid monthly as part of your mortgage payment) an FHA loan requires an up-front premium to be paid in escrow by you, the borrower. The amount of this premium has varied considerably over the last few years due to the instability of the market, but as of April 1, 2012 the up-front insurance premium is now 1.75% of the loan amount. For example, for a $100,000 mortgage, you would pay a fee in escrow of $1,750. This fee can be financed into the loan amount, even on a purchase, but don't be fooled – you pay for it one way or the other.

Additionally, there is the annual premium to pay (on a monthly basis.) The premium amount varies, but as of this writing is generally between 1.20% and 1.25% of the loan amount on 30 year fixed loans. As an example, if the rate were 1.20% on a $100,000 mortgage, your premium would be $1,200 per year, or $100 per month, included with your monthly payment.

Removing the monthly premium

It used to be that FHA insurance differed from traditional mortgage insurance in that rather than having to keep your mortgage insurance in place for a minimum of two years, you had to pay your FHA premium for a minimum of five years, even if you have plenty of equity in your home.

In 2013 FHA changed their policy. Now the FHA mortgage insurance premium must be paid **for the life of the loan**. No matter how far down you pay your mortgage balance, you cannot remove the insurance premium. The purpose of this change was to encourage borrowers in the future to refinance out of their FHA loans to get the liability of insuring your loan off of the FHA's books.

> One other interesting feature of FHA loans is that when you refinance an FHA loan and pay it off you must pay interest on the old loan through the end of the month in which you pay it off. If you pay off the lender on the 5th of the month, you nevertheless owe the lender for interest through the first of the next month.

Should we ever regain the ability to remove mortgage insurance from an FHA loan, you will probably need 22% equity in your home. (Prior to the rule change the loan needed to amount to no more that 78% of the current appraised value in order to remove the insurance.) So, if you acquire your home with only a 5% down payment, for example, you are not likely to have the equity to remove the MI anyway after only two years, but it's something to consider.

Fannie Mae now offers a very low down-payment option, so the only time an FHA loan is really needed is when your credit score is so low or your debt-to-income ratio so high that you simply can't qualify for conventional financing. If that's the case, perhaps it is better to clean up your credit first or lower your sights and buy a less expensive home anyway.

VA Loans

Like FHA, the *Veterans Administration* does not make loans, but rather guarantees loans made by private lenders such as banks or mortgage bankers.

The idea behind VA loans was to enable veterans to purchase homes when they would otherwise not be able to. Two unique characteristics of loans guaranteed by the VA are that they require no down payment at all, and they require no monthly mortgage-insurance premium. However, there is an up-front funding fee which can be substantial, although it can be financed into the loan.

These loans are a terrific deal for honorably-discharged veterans.

There are fairly complicated rules for eligibility. A veteran must first go to his or her local VA office to apply for a certificate of eligibility. Then they can go to any lender (bank, banker or broker) to obtain the loan.

The interest rates and fees of a VA loan are roughly comparable to a conventional loan. Other than the down-payment requirement, for the most part the requirements for qualifying for a loan are comparable to a conventional loan as well. You will need reasonable credit and a verifiable source of sufficient income to support the monthly payments.

Chapter Nineteen

Money-Saving Strategies

The purpose of this chapter is to provide you a quick guide to matching your mortgage product and price with your specific situation. When you go to acquire financing, what should you consider in deciding what kind of loan to get and what terms will have the greatest impact on your lifetime borrowing cost?

It all depends on your profile and your family's needs. The reason that there are so many products to choose from is that each one can be a very smart way to go in different circumstances.

I recently had the experience of needing an attorney to deal with a real estate matter regarding an elderly friend of the family. The details aren't important, but suffice it to say that an attorney was really needed, and the situation involved a mortgage default, a property with abundant equity, a senior citizen who was not taking care of his business in the manner he had before, and a large nest egg that we were not sure was secure.

What did we need? A foreclosure attorney? A real estate attorney? A trust attorney? An elder law attorney? A financial advisor?

We went to a real estate attorney who wanted to fight the foreclosure action.

We went to a trust attorney who wanted to draw up a trust.

We went to an elder law attorney who wanted to create a living will.

There is an old saying that if the only tool you have is a hammer, every problem looks like a nail. In this case, we found that each attorney wanted to focus in on his specialty, treating all the other issues in the case as secondary.

Like attorneys, most loan officers are taught how to sell a certain product or at best a few products. They are taught how to look for the ways it would benefit you in your situation, how to explain and demonstrate the benefits, and how to close the deal for that particular loan product. Not surprisingly, most of the loans they sell will be the type they have been taught to sell. When the only tool you have is a hammer, every problem looks like a nail.

While there are certainly honest, well-rounded loan officers out there with access to a broad array of fairly priced products, there are also others who are not well versed in all the options you might want to consider. It is not that those loan officers are particularly dishonest (although some might be) but that they simply have been trained to do things a certain way and sell a certain product.

So it is up to you to make sure that you understand what your needs are. Consider the following factors as some of the most important issues when choosing the right loan product and the right price structure.

Holding Period

Probably the most important factor in choosing the right mortgage product is your holding period. Your holding period for this purpose is the anticipated time you will keep the mortgage. Notice that I didn't say how long you will keep the house; it's the mortgage that is important here.

During the Mortgage Boom the holding period for the house and the holding period for the mortgage were almost never the same. There were many reasons for this.

The most common was that many folks kept on refinancing as interest rates rolled down. This became such common practice that many folks started off with the assumption that they would refinance within three years. (Some refinanced every six months!) Today that is rare.

Some folks bought homes knowing they would remodel and expand the home, and then refinance to consolidate debt. They knew in advance that their plans were short term.

Conversely, I have had clients that were buying a home they planned to keep for a while, during a period when fixed-rate loans were low. It seemed reasonable to assume they would keep their loan for a long time.

Loan Product Recommendation

If you think your holding period will be short, consider using an adjustable-rate mortgage. Adjustable mortgages can have a fixed period for one to ten years. During this initial fixed period your interest rate won't change. Your savings over the first few years compared to a fixed-rate loan can be substantial, and if you are not likely to keep the loan very long the risk associated with the adjustable rate doesn't matter. But do match the fixed period of your adjustable-rate loan with your anticipated holding period. (Think back to Raoul in Chapter 6.)

If you think your holding period will be lengthy, consider getting a fixed-rate mortgage especially if it is indicated by one of the other criterion below.

Loan Price Recommendation

As you will see later in this chapter you always have the option to trade off your up-front costs against your interest rate. In other words, all things being equal you can take a higher interest rate at lower costs (possibly even zero) or pay costs in exchange for a lower interest rate.

If you anticipate a short holding period don't pay costs; take the higher interest rate instead. You'll make a higher payment, but you'll be ahead for the first three to five years.

If, on the other hand, you think your holding period will be lengthy, pay as much as you can afford to buy down the interest rate. You'll either pay more cash up front or, if you are financing the costs you'll have a higher mortgage, but you could save thousands over the life of your loan.

Suppose, for example, we have a borrower who wants to refinance a mortgage with a current balance of $200,000 and wants to pay for his loan costs out-of-pocket.

Should he buy down the rate? Let's take a look.

		Option 1		Option 2		Option 3
Holding Period: **24**	months					
Non-recurring loan costs: * $	2,936.00					
Proposed Loan Amount: $		200,000	$	200,000	$	200,000
Interest Rate:		6.000%		5.875%		5.750%
Your Net Points:		(1.625)		(1.000)		(0.375)
In Dollars: $		(3,250)	$	(2,000)	$	(750)
Total Net Loan costs (NRCC): $		-	$	936	$	2,186
Monthly payment: $		1,199.10	$	1,183.08		$1,167.15

Total cost of financing analysis Shows the total *cost* of the financing, including cash outlay up front plus interest over the holding period.

	Option 1	Option 2	Option 3
Total cost of financing over holding period: $	23,715 $	24,150 $	24,900
	Best Option		

Net present cost analysis Accounts for the time value of money; what is total cost in *today's* dollars to pay back the proposed loan?

Assumed safe rate: **2.500%**	Represents your oportunity cost -- set this equal to an investment of similar quality (risk) to you.		

	Option 1	Option 2	Option 3
Mtg Balance @ end of holding period: $	194,936 $	194,821 $	194,702
Net present cost: $	213,481 $	213,932 $	214,697
	Best Option		

In this example of a fixed-rate mortgage the borrower has chosen a holding period of two years – he assumes that he will keep this mortgage for only two years. Why would he do this? Well, he really wants a 15-year mortgage because he's getting closer to retirement, but he still has two kids in school and can't afford the higher payments. However, they'll be out of school in two years and he's highly confident he'll refinance into a 15-year fixed then. If his current interest rate is high enough, even with only a two year holding period it could make sense.

In this example we see an assumed holding period of 24 months. You can see that the total cost of the holding period is best with Option 1. It is better than Option 3, by the way, by almost $1,200. That may not seem like a large difference, but it amounts to $100 per month. That's quite a bit of cash no matter how you look at it.

We can also look at the **net present cost** of the financing. In simple terms, this is what the proposed loan would cost in today's dollars. For a full discussion of a net present cost analysis see Chapter 6, "Should You Refinance?"

In this case we see that Option 1 is cheaper in today's dollars by about $450 than Option 2, but that under Option 1 you would owe $115 more at the end of 24 months.

If we assume a holding period of 24 months, Option 1 is definitely the way to go.

However, if the borrower is highly confident that a 24-month holding period is highly likely, he might want to consider an adjustable loan, too, as that might save him an additional 1% on the interest rate for the first three years, which in this case would amount to $2,000 per year.

But what if our borrower thought he might keep the loan for five years or more? Would the results be different?

	Option 1	Option 2	Option 3
Holding Period: 60 months			
Non-recurring loan costs: * $ 2,936.00			
Proposed Loan Amount:	$ 200,000	$ 200,000	$ 200,000
Interest Rate:	6.000%	5.875%	5.750%
Your Net Points:	(1.625)	(1.000)	(0.375)
In Dollars: $	(3,250)	$ (2,000)	$ (750)
Total Net Loan costs (NRCC): $	-	$ 936	$ 2,186
Monthly payment: $	1,199.10	$ 1,183.08	$1,167.15

Total cost of financing analysis Shows the total *cost* of the financing, including cash outlay up front plus interest over the holding period.

	Option 1	Option 2	Option 3
Total cost of financing over holding period: $	58,055	$ 57,739	$ 57,739
			Best Option

Net present cost analysis Accounts for the time value of money; what is total cost in *today's* dollars to pay back the proposed loan?

Assumed safe rate: 2.500% Represents your opportunity cost -- set this equal to an investment of similar quality (risk) to you.

	Option 1	Option 2	Option 3
Mtg Balance @ end of holding period: $	186,109	$ 185,819	$ 185,524
Net present cost: $	231,827	$ 231,604	$ 231,696
		Best Option	

There is no rule of thumb that will tell you how long you need to keep a loan in order for it to make sense to buy it down. You have to analyze each situation.

In this case if we projected a five-year holding period Option 3 would have the lowest total cost of financing over the holding period. The cost savings isn't huge, but again, why not take the cheapest option?

The Net Present Cost analysis gives us a different answer, however. Why is this? Option 3 has high initial costs, paid out-of-pocket right up front. If you can keep that money in the bank (even earning a whopping 2.500%) it turns out you'll come out ahead taking Option 2's higher interest rate than Option 3's higher cost.

The difference is very small, but it's there. Does this mean our borrower should choose option 2? No, this is **information**. As my engineer friends would say, these are **data points**. They help guide the decision, they don't make the decision.

In reality, most folks don't know with certainty how long they will keep a loan. They would only know a range and what they think is most likely given what they know today. However, by thinking this through you can save your family thousands of dollars that you can use in other ways that are way more fun than paying your mortgage.

Life Stage

Different kinds of financing are generally appropriate at different life stages. Some choices are obvious.

Loan Product Recommendation

For instance, if you have to carry a mortgage into retirement, when your income will be fixed, it is highly advisable at that time to have a fixed-rate mortgage. On the other hand, if you have abundant savings, you can absorb the additional costs of rising interest rates and the long-term savings of an adjustable-rate loan - provided rates stay reasonable - could be an attractive option.

If you are very young and just starting out with your first home, an adjustable-rate mortgage could be a good choice unless contra-indicated by another factor. For instance, if a young couple came to me with good income but where most of it was commission or self-employment, I might recommend an adjustable as it could significantly reduce their costs in the first few critical years and perhaps allow them to buy in a slightly higher price range. If rates did rise down the road, presumably their income would have risen, or they might have the opportunity to work harder to earn more.

(You would be surprised how motivating not knowing whether you can make your next mortgage payment can be.)

On the other hand, if a young couple came to me with fixed incomes that were barely enough to qualify, I would strongly discourage them from using an adjustable-rate mortgage to try to qualify for a higher loan amount. Instead, I would encourage them to lower their sights and buy something they can comfortably afford while saving money for emergencies. Yes, they **can** qualify for a higher priced home with an adjustable mortgage, but **should** they?

While my clients always have the final say, in general I believe that the younger you are the more risk you can tolerate, and the more you can gain by taking risks, such as an adjustable-rate mortgage. However, as you can see it is important to weigh all the factors.

> This is another area where product was sold exactly the way it should not have been. First-time home buyers were often sold adjustable-rate mortgages so they could qualify for a higher loan, and thus a higher purchase price.
>
> If their prospects for greater income in the future were limited, however, they would find themselves in trouble down the road.

Remember our friend Raoul in Chapter 6? If you have kids about to go off to college and the plan is to finance college through the Bank of Mom and Dad, your finance choices may be determined for you. You may have to think short-term, and keep your payments as low as possible, like our friend Raoul.

You should, however, have a plan (like Raoul did) to address your financing needs permanently with more conservative financing once you no longer have large sums of money coming from your pay check to pay for tuition, books and beer.

Loan Price Recommendation

The factors that drive your choices for trading off the up-front cost of your loan against your interest rate are the same as those discussed above when considering the holding period, with a couple of additional notes.

First-time homebuyers usually have just barely enough money to get into their new home. If this is the case with you, be willing to take a loan with lower costs and a higher interest rate, even if you think you'll be holding on to the loan for a while. Remember Chapter 5 where we discussed whether you should buy a home at all – when you buy your first home you will absolutely find yourself short of cash in the first year or two.

And, if you are older, you are likely to be pretty stable in your living situation for a while. This is the perfect time in life to use some extra money to buy down your interest rate in order to drive your payments and lifetime interest cost as low as possible.

Risk Tolerance

We covered risk tolerance in another section of this book, but it might be useful here to reiterate a couple of important points.

Loan Product Recommendation

Some folks have no tolerance for risk. Zero. Even if they have good reserves, a stable and secure income, and have never been without, they **absolutely have to know** what their monthly payment will be. If this is you, get a fixed-rate mortgage. Yes, all things considered this tends to be the most expensive alternative, but anything else will drive you completely crazy. One interesting note, though: in most countries outside the U.S., 30-year fixed mortgages are not available.

If you have some tolerance for risk – provided there is financial benefit to you in exchange – an adjustable-rate mortgage is an excellent product. A three-year ARM could save you as much as 1.5% in interest rate compared to a 30-year fixed. On our $200,000 mortgage, this means a savings of $3,000 per year in interest cost, plus you are paying your mortgage down faster. (See chapter 6, "Should You Refinance?")

Even if your interest rate jumped a full 2% (usually the maximum initial adjustment) your new interest rate would barely be higher than the fixed rate would have been. And even if it again adjusted the maximum amount upward at the end of year 4, it would be close to the end of year 6 before your cumulative loan costs would exceed the cumulative loan costs of a 30-year fixed mortgage.

If you can tolerate risk, therefore, an adjustable-rate mortgage might be an excellent choice for you, especially if your time horizon is somewhat short, since you'll be ahead of the game even after your interest rate begins adjusting for at least two or three years.

For a detailed discussion of exactly what the savings versus risk looks like, see Chapter 12, "Adjustable-Rate Mortgages."

Loan Price Recommendation

My experience in dealing with folks with low risk tolerance is that they are very unlikely to refinance, and they don't move often. If this describes you, then use money to pay costs to buy down your interest rate. In the long run, you will pay far less money to the bank.

Income Pattern and Reserves

Income pattern is directly tied to risk tolerance, or should be. Most folks are paid a salary and have a fairly stable job. (It may not feel like it to you, but it is true for the majority.) If you have a steady income with little or no chance of "windfall" income, such as commissions, large bonuses or stock options, you will tend to have less tolerance for risk than someone who occasionally receives large windfalls. This is especially true if you don't have much in the way of savings to lean on in an emergency.

Loan Product Recommendation

In general, folks with fixed incomes and low savings reserves would be better served with a fixed-rate loan. The irony is that these are the folks that were most often sold adjustable-rate option ARMs during the Mortgage Boom, because they could quality for higher loan amounts with the lower starting interest rate. In other words, the products were sold **exactly** the way they should **not** have been.

Folks with highly variable income might be better able to handle variable mortgage payments, and may find the short-term savings realized by taking an adjustable mortgage very desirable. However, these folks may want to be very cautious about taking a mortgage that is as large as they can possibly quality for, as they may not be able to ramp up their income as much as needed when interest rate rise.

Also, if you are buying a home but don't have a large down payment you may have a choice between taking a loan with mortgage insurance (see Chapter 18) or using two separate loans (see Chapter 16) to finance the purchase. If you have windfall income once in a while, a great way to do this is to use a 75% or 80% first mortgage (the largest available without mortgage insurance) and an equity line to make up the balance. When you realize your windfall you can use that to pay off the equity line – and then use the equity line to draw against when you need cash in the future.

On the other hand, if you have a fixed income that is likely to remain static for a while, take the one loan with mortgage insurance, and pay extra on the principal each month so that you can remove the mortgage insurance once your loan balance drops low enough relative to the value of your home. Talk to your mortgage consultant for more detail on how you would need to do this in your specific case.

Anticipated Life Events

You may have major life events planned in the near future; most folks do. Many don't consider how this might impact their choice of product or price, but in many cases it should. Some examples:

Starting a Business

If you are currently employed but thinking of starting a business your choice of loan product is critical. Particularly now with much more stringent underwriting, once you convert from employed (read: easy to qualify) to self-employed (read: not easy to qualify) you may not be able to get a loan for quite a while. In fact, most lenders will want to see two years of positive, sufficient income reflected on tax returns before they will make you a loan. Think about this: you have to be profitable enough to have to report a profit on your tax returns for two years running before you are qualified again. Since it might be three or four years before you are profitable, get a loan you are willing to be stuck with well before you quit your job to start a new business.

Having a Baby

If you are about to have a baby don't quit your job and start a business. I realize that had nothing to do with real estate financing, but it had to be said.

If you're going to have a baby and lose one income for a while, get an adjustable-rate mortgage with an initial fixed period that is longer than the time you want to spend at home.

If you think you want to stay at home indefinitely, get a fixed-rate mortgage.

If you decide you want to have lots of babies, you may want to consider the possibility that you'll want to add on to your house in a few years. If this is the case, then now might be a good time for an adjustable rate mortgage. When the time comes to build on, you are **very** likely to refinance again to pay for the addition. (We're assuming you'll be able to qualify down the road with one income.) So, you are premeditating refinancing within a short enough time that a fixed-term intermediate ARM might be a good product selection for you.

Remodeling or Addition

Speaking of remodeling or expanding, financing this step in your life is always exciting.

However you decide to finance your improvements, one thing is very important: if you need to tear your house apart in order to complete your plans, your house will not be eligible for financing until the work is largely complete. This is important, because if you run out of money half way through, you may have no way to raise the balance of the funds to finish the project.

> Work that would prevent you from financing while it is still in progress would include opening an exterior wall or the roof, or making any necessary component like the kitchen or a bathroom inoperable for a while.

In the past the most common way to finance home improvements was with construction financing. There are some advantages to it, although there are not many sources for this today. The most significant advantage is that the *loan-to-value ratio* is not based on the property's current value, but rather on the value after completion of the proposed improvements. For many folks without abundant equity in their property, this was the only type of financing available to them.

Construction loans are also managed in a unique way. Rather than simply hand you a check when escrow closes, funds are not disbursed until work is done. The lender makes **progress** payments to the contractor as milestones are reached throughout construction. When your contractor asks for payment, the work must be inspected to be sure it is done, and only then will the lender issue a check, and only for the agreed-upon amount for that specific phase of construction. (i.e. foundation, framing, plumbing) This helps you manage the contractor, but also adds some complexity and costs to the process.

When construction is finished, most construction loans have a clause that they have to be paid off at that time. Most of the time this is done with a new loan commonly called a take-out loan, since it "takes out" the construction financing.

> While the money you've borrowed sits idly in an escrow account waiting to be spent on completed phases of construction, you are paying interest on the entire amount. You may or may not be earning interest on the escrow account, but if you are it isn't much.

Construction loans are not widely available today, although that may change over time.

A simpler way to finance construction is to acquire an equity line. There are numerous advantages of this over construction loans. First, they are usually much less expensive to acquire. While they might carry a higher interest rate, that may not be important as they were not designed to be carried very long. Equity lines cost very little, and sometimes nothing, to originate.

Moreover, you won't pay interest charges on money until (and unless) you draw it from the line. With an equity line the **credit** sits unused, and you only pay interest on the funds you have drawn.

However, equity lines require **equity** in your home as-is, before the improvements. Many homeowners don't have enough equity to qualify for a large enough equity line to complete the project.

Finally, you could just refinance your entire mortgage to finance your improvements. A fixed-rate mortgage would only be called for if **all** of the following are true:

- You are confident that you can finish the project with the funds you raise.
- You are certain that you will stay in the home after the improvements are completed for at least a few years.

- Interest rates are low and are not likely to go lower.

In other words, fixed-rate loans are best for permanent, not temporary financing. If you have enough equity in your home to cover your construction cost needs and you're confident this will be a permanent loan, a fixed-rate cash-out loan is a good way to finance home improvements.

Putting Kids through College

Remember our story of Raoul earlier in this book? Hopefully you've saved enough money for your children's college education. But if you haven't, and if you are looking at financing within a few years of needing to pay for college, consider a fixed-term adjustable rate mortgage like the one Raoul got. If you recall, he took an interest-only 7/1 ARM (fixed for seven years before adjusting) because the first adjustment would coincide with his son's graduation from college; after that he could refinance into a fully amortized fixed loan – which he did.

It varies over time, but a 7/1 ARM might save you 0.75% to 1.000% in interest rate compared to a 30-year fixed. On a $350,000 loan (typical in California) this would save you anywhere from $2,625 to $3,500 per year in interest – enough to make a small dent in college costs.

Savings History

I make a distinction between your **savings** and your **savings history**. I've had some clients who made very little money – and yet always had money in the bank. One client came to me looking to buy her first condo. Martha was a single woman, in her 30s, with a high-school education. She worked in an administrative role for a hospital. Because she was looking to buy a home and because her grammar and spelling in her first email to me were perfect, I assumed she was an executive assistant. In our area, a good executive assistant can make quite a good living.

When we finally met, I found out I was wrong. Actually, she was a lower-level admin who made just barely enough money to put her over the poverty line. I thought I had struck out. But an amazing thing happened. First, I ran her credit and she had the second-highest credit score of anyone I've ever worked with. Second, I looked at her bank statements and she had savings. She wasn't wealthy, but she had plenty of cash to buy the home, plus some reserves. She hadn't inherited it or had any sort of windfall. She had saved – every paycheck, no matter what -- $20 or $30 since she started working at 18.

Despite living at close to the poverty line, Martha had established - through living habits that all of us would do very well to emulate - outstanding credit and nice reserves.

I recommended a fixed-rate loan for Martha, because even though it was more expensive I didn't think she could weather a large increase in her payment should she get an adjustable-rate loan and her payment went up. It all worked out great for Martha, and even though a large portion of her pay check now went to housing expenses, she still managed to put $30 of her paycheck – every time, no matter what – into savings.

Martha exemplified what I call a great **savings history**. Some folks have large bank accounts because they get large windfalls and bank it. Others, like Martha, save a little bit every pay check, and no matter what happens to them they will always have enough to survive.

If Martha had had a much larger savings account I might have recommended an adjustable-rate mortgage to lower her housing costs, knowing she would have enough in reserves to make up the difference if her payment rose. However, if Martha's savings had come from a windfall rather than from steady savings, I might have been less inclined to recommend an adjustable-rate mortgage even if she did have reserves, because I would not have been as confident that she would have the reserves when she needed them should her payment rise in the future.

Real Estate Investors

I own investment real estate. I understand clearly how important it is to stabilize as many expenses as you possibly can in order to get your investment to perform as well and as predictably as possible over time. A case can be made for an adjustable-rate mortgage, however.

To understand this you need to understand the connection between interest rates, inflation and the economy. Mortgage interest rates are set by market forces, and reflect investor's assumptions regarding inflation. An investor would not lend money out today if it was going to be worth less when he got it back than it is today. To see why this is, let's say I could buy a sailboat for $100,000. I can't, but I really like this fantasy.

I could either pay $100,000 for the sailboat today, or invest the money and hope that by the time I get it back it will be enough to still buy the sailboat and have a little extra. If I couldn't do that, I would rather just have the sailboat now.

Now let's say that inflation is running pretty high. So high, in fact, that ten years from now the equivalent new sailboat will cost me $200,000. (This equates to 7.2% inflation, by the way.)

If I lend my money out at 7.2% interest and get it back in ten years with interest, all I will be able to do is buy the sailboat I could have bought now. That doesn't interest me, so I must charge more than the inflation rate or it makes no sense for me to invest.

What this means is that when investors believe that inflation is going to increase the cost of borrowing increases, too.

You also need to understand the link between the economy and inflation. When the economy is strong people have jobs. If they are well-paying jobs, when people have jobs they have money. When they have money they buy stuff. When consumers are in a shopping mood, prices of the things they buy begin to rise.

So, when the economy grows, more people are employed and wages rise. When consumers compete for goods they drive up the prices of things like sailboats. When investors believe prices are going to rise they demand higher yields, and you'll pay more in interest rates. (This is highly simplified but covers the fundamentals.)

The point that is important to real estate investors is this:

If interest rates are rising, it is because the economy is strong and workers have jobs and rising wages. If you use an adjustable-rate mortgage for your investment property, when your mortgage payment goes up chances are good so will the rent that you can command for your property. When you use an adjustable-rate loan for an investment property, there is a built-in self-mitigating factor to the risk you take on with the adjustable rate.

The opposite is true, too – when the economy is weak rents tend not to rise, but your interest rate should be very low. This has been the case from 2008 through 2013.

And there is one more important point. Just as it makes sense to diversify your investment portfolio to manage risk, it can make sense for you to diversify your debt portfolio too. I will often recommend that if a client owns multiple properties that they have at least one adjustable-rate loan.

In low-interest-rate environments you will benefit from having lower payments on at least one property. In high-interest-rate environments you will have at least one loan whose payments are fixed and predictable.

Conclusion

A lot of factors combine to tell me a story that helps me understand which product is best for you. Almost every client tells me they want a fixed-rate mortgage at zero points, and I offer the best deal available on that product. But I also give them options, and it surprises many of my clients when they choose something other than a 30 year fixed.

Chapter Twenty

Reading the Disclosures

When you first apply for a loan, and then when you sign loan papers just before your escrow closes, you are presented with a daunting pile of paperwork requiring dozens of signatures. Realistically there is no way you will read and understand every paper you sign, so there are a few things you should know about the disclosures.

First, most disclosures you sign came to being because someone sued a lender claiming they didn't know about or understand some term in the loan papers. So most of the disclosures you sign today are written to clearly disclose your rights in the transaction to you. When you sign the disclosure, you are certifying that you have read the disclosure.

When you do this you essentially give up the ability to claim that you didn't understand what you were signing, because whether you read it or not you have certified, in writing, that you have been informed of your rights and have read and understood what you were signing.

A large share of the disclosures relate to fraud committed by borrowers in the past where lenders lost money. When you sign these disclosures you are certifying that everything you have told or submitted to the lender is true and correct to the best of your knowledge, and you are authorizing the lender to investigate and confirm the information. You are certifying that you understand that if you have submitted false information or documentation in order to induce the lender into making a loan that it otherwise would not have made, you are committing fraud. Examples of this type of disclosure include the "Borrower's Certification," and "4506 – Tax Transcripts Authorization" which authorizes the lender to contact to IRS to confirm that what you reported to them for income is the same as what you have told the lender.

You will also sign forms that affirm you understand the fees and terms of your loan. These disclosures include the application, the "Good Faith Estimate" and the Truth-in-Lending Form.

Finally, you will be signing a legal agreement with the lender. These forms include the "Note" and the "Deed of Trust" or "Mortgage," and are discussed in detail below.

The important thing to remember is that these forms do create legal obligations for you, or limit your legal options should you have a dispute down the road. However, your loan will not be made without the forms, so they are not optional.

What is optional is whether you read and understand them, and there is a way to do this. In every state you are given an initial set of disclosures when you first apply for a loan. The lender has three days from the date of application to provide this.

If any salient terms of the loan (say, the interest rate or cost) change before you sign final loan papers, the lender has to send out new disclosures and wait at least three days before asking you to sign final loan documents.

Then, before you close escrow you are given the final set, with a couple of extra forms to sign. You have the right to spend at least 24 hours to review these documents before signing if you wish. It may not be practical to do so, however, so let's discuss which forms are important and what to look for.

Initial Disclosures – What's Important

Good Faith Estimate

You must be given the Good Faith Estimate within three business days of submitting your application to a lender. This form has evolved dramatically since 2008, and in 2015 will undergo another dramatic revision. For the current form, here is what is important and what to look for.

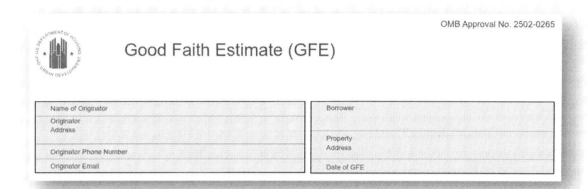

The GFE starts by clearly identifying the originator (the mortgage company or bank,) you, your property address, and the date that the GFE was issued.

Purpose	This GFE gives you an estimate of your settlement charges and loan terms if you are approved for this loan. For more information, see HUD's *Special Information Booklet* on settlement charges, your *Truth-in-Lending Disclosures*, and other consumer information at www.hud.gov/respa. If you decide you would like to proceed with this loan, contact us.
Shopping for your loan	Only you can shop for the best loan for you. Compare this GFE with other loan offers, so you can find the best loan. Use the shopping chart on page 3 to compare all the offers you receive.

This section helps you understand how to use this form to protect yourself and shop for the best possible deal.

Important dates	1. The interest rate for this GFE is available through 02/26/2014 . After this time, the interest rate, some of your loan Origination Charges, and the monthly payment shown below can change until you lock your interest rate.
	2. This estimate for all other settlement charges is available through 03/12/2014
	3. After you lock your interest rate, you must go to settlement within 30 days (your rate lock period) to receive the locked interest rate.
	4. You must lock the interest rate at least 7 days before settlement.

This section discloses important dates to you.

1.   Unless your interest rate is locked, your rate and costs could change at any time without advance notice.

2.   "Other settlement charges" refers to charges from third parties, such as title, escrow, appraisal, recording fees, etc. These fees generally will be the same no matter when you lock, so the quote should be valid for a longer period than the interest rate.

3.   This example assumes you'll be getting a 30 day lock. It could be different, but the purpose is to make sure you know what your mortgage advisor is planning.

4.   You must lock your interest rate at some point, and it cannot be the day before you close, as it takes time to draw final loan documents, have you sign them, review them after signing, etc. Your particular lender will have a minimum amount of time they need. For reasons beyond the scope of this book they can vary dramatically.

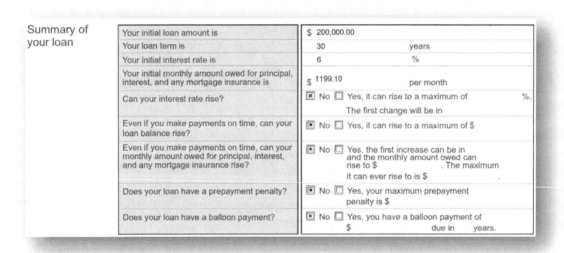

Here is the meat **and** the potatoes of your loan. This will tell you how much you're borrowing, at what interest rate, what your payments will be, and whether:

- The rate is fixed or not
- Whether is it negatively amortizing
- Whether you payments can change
- Whether or not you have a pre-pay penalty, and
- Whether or not you have a balloon payment

Read this section very carefully, as these are the terms of your loan. Your lender may not give you final loan documents that vary **at all** from these terms unless they send you an updated disclosure at least three days before you sign loan documents.

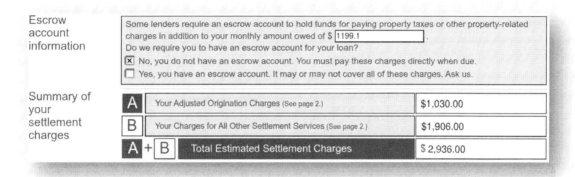

This section tells you whether or not your loan has been set up with an *escrow account* for taxes and insurance. The "Escrow account information" box first reiterates the minimum monthly payment from above (this tells you nothing new) and tells you that either you do not need to have an escrow account, or that you have one. This is a little confusing, as the choice **should** be either that 1 – you either are, or are not **required** to have an escrow account, and 2 – you **have or have not** chosen to have one.

The final section summarizes the charges that are disclosed on the page 2 of the GFE. This section creates more confusion than clarity, in my opinion.

Understanding your estimated settlement charges

Your Adjusted Origination Charges	
1. **Our origination charge** This charge is for getting this loan for you.	$4,030.00
2. **Your credit or charge (points) for the specific interest rate chosen** ☐ The credit or charge for the interest rate of [＿＿＿＿] % is included in "Our origination charge." (See item 1 above.) ☒ You receive a credit of $ [3,000.00] for this interest rate of [6.000] %. This credit **reduces** your settlement charges. ☐ You pay a charge of $ [＿＿＿] for this interest rate of [＿＿＿] %. This charge (points) **increases** your total settlement charges. The tradeoff table on page 3 shows that you can change your total settlement charges by choosing a different interest rate for this loan.	
A Your Adjusted Origination Charges	$ 1,030.00

At the top of page two is a summary of what you will be paying the lender for all services related to originating the loan. Included in this "bucket" of charges are all fees paid to the lender, including underwriting fee, processing fee and administrative fee (if charged).

What is confusing is that if you go to a broker the broker's compensation is also included in "Our origination charges," while if you go to a bank, credit union, or mortgage banker (see Chapter 3 "Choose Your Lender, Nail the Deal") the originator's compensation is **not** included.

So, if you choose to work with a broker a fee is included in the box for "Our origination charge" in box 1 that **you don't pay**. In box 2 you'll notice that you receive a credit of $3,000 (in this example) from the lender that pays for the broker compensation to cover the processing, administrative costs, and loan origination. (You won't be able to see that detail anywhere on this form, though.)

> The lender credit might be greater than the compensation the broker earns, by the way. You would see this happen if you asked for a higher interest rate at a lower net cost. For a detailed discussion of why and under what circumstances this might make sense for you, see Chapter 18, *Money-Savings Strategies.*

The net charges are correct, but the line items can be confusing for most borrowers.

Then the **net** (bottom-line) origination costs that you pay out of pocket are summarized in box A.

The important point in this is that the form isn't very clear and in fact can be very misleading. If you went to the bank and this same loan were being made by them, the origination charge in box 1 would be $1,032, box 2 would be blank, and the total in box A would be the same as it is here.

Clear as mud?

	Your Charges for All Other Settlement Services		
Some of these charges can change at settlement. See the top of page 3 for more information.	3. **Required services that we select** These charges are for services we require to complete your settlement. We will choose the providers of these services.		$525.00
	Service	Charge	
	Appraiser	450	
	Demand Fee From Current Lender	75	

The rest of page two is devoted to all other charges you will see in escrow. Keep in mind that if you are receiving a lender credit that the credit will cover some, or all of these costs, although of course you'll make it up to the lender in your interest payments over time.

Section 3 highlights services from providers that we or the lender must select – you cannot shop for or choose these providers. Generally there is not much variance from one lender to another for these charges. If there is, something might be amiss and you need to ask more questions of one, or all of the lenders who are giving you a quote.

4. **Title services and lender's title insurance** This charge includes the services of a title or settlement agent, for example, and title insurance to protect the lender, if required.	$1,481.00
5. **Owner's title insurance** You may purchase an owner's title insurance policy to protect your interest in the property.	
6. **Required services that you can shop for** These charges are for other services that are required to complete your settlement. We can identify providers of these services or you can shop for them yourself. Our estimates for providing these services are below. Service Charge	

Box 4 is the charge for title and escrow services.

Box 5 shows the charge for the owner's title insurance policy. This policy is generally only needed on a purchase, and it insures you that you are buying what you think you're buying. This insurance policy will pay to correct any deficiencies discovered down the road, such as an encroachment on your property or a claim on your title. This fee **must** be disclosed to you, but **you may or may not be paying it**, depending on your purchase contract and local custom. In many cases the seller will pay this fee, but even so it must be included in this form. Yes, you are right – that's very confusing.

The other thing that is confusing about boxes 4 and 5 is that the Real Estate Settlement and Procedures Act (RESPA) states that you have the right to select your own escrow company. However, it would be extremely impractical in practice so it almost never happens. Plus, if the loan is for a purchase and the seller is paying for the escrow service (as they do in my area) the seller (actually the seller's agent) chooses the escrow company by long-established convention.

The bottom line is that you may have heard you have the right to select your own provider, but it isn't likely the conversation will ever even come up.

Box 6 discloses services that are required but that you can shop for to choose your own provider. You'll notice that this box is blank, which will almost always be the case. It's nice that they put the box there, though.

7.	Government recording charges	
	These charges are for state and local fees to record your loan and title documents.	$120.00
8.	Transfer taxes	
	These charges are for state and local fees on mortgages and home sales.	

Lines 7 and 8 itemize those charges levied by the county or city in which the property is located to record the deeds associated with the transaction. In the case of a refinance this would typically just be a trust deed (in trust deed states, or a mortgage in states that use mortgages.) In the case of a purchase there would also be a grant deed, granting title from the seller to you.

Transfer taxes are generally only charged on purchase transactions. These could be charged by the county, the city, or both. In many cases the seller would pay for some, or all of these charges, but regardless of who pays for them they must be disclosed to you here on this line.

This next section, boxes 9 through 11, itemizes charges that are not related to acquiring your home or your financing, but are actually related to **owning** the home. The distinction is important, as they are ongoing, recurring costs, rather than one-time fees associated with the transaction.

9. Initial deposit for your escrow account	
This charge is held in an escrow account to pay future recurring charges on your property and includes ☐ all property taxes, ☐ all insurance, and ☐ other [＿＿＿＿＿＿] .	$0.00

As disclosed on page 1 of the form you may, or may not be required to have an escrow or impound account. If you are required to have one or choose to have one, you will need to make monthly contributions, but you will also be required to "pre-fund" some portion of it.

When your tax and insurance bills come due there has to be enough money in your escrow account to pay them. Your monthly contributions are not likely to be sufficient the first time your bills come due, so the lender will project what your monthly balances will be, and then ask for an up-front contribution (the initial deposit) so that there will be enough when the time comes. Box 9 shows you how much the initial deposit will be.

10. Daily interest charges	
This charge is for the daily interest on your loan from the day of your settlement until the first day of the next month or the first day of your normal mortgage payment cycle. This amount is $ 30.56 per day for 15 days (if your settlement is 03/16/2014).	$458.33

When you make your payments on your loan you pay interest with each payment that has already accrued. Your March payment pays for interest that accrued in February, for example. Since your payments will be made on the first of each month, if you close escrow in the middle of the month your first payment would have an odd amount of interest due, since a full 30 days would not have passed.

To correct this lender will charge you interest **in advance** in escrow from the day your loan funds until the first of the next month. Then, because you will have already paid for that interest, you will not make a payment the next month. The charge for *pre-paid interest* goes in box 10.

There is one exception. If you close very early in the month (usually before the 6th) a lender may choose to give you a **credit** (to roll you back to the first, rather than forward to the next month) instead of charge you for pre-paid interest. If this happens you will have a payment due on the first of the next month.

11. Homeowner's insurance
This charge is for the insurance you must buy for the property to protect from a loss, such as fire.

Policy	Charge	
Homeowner's Liability Insurance	600	$600.00

You'll need to have homeowner's insurance on your new home, or if you are refinancing you already have homeowner's insurance. When you are purchasing a home you will need to pay one year's premium in advance, in addition to impounding your monthly charge to pay for this in the coming year, if you have an impound / escrow account.

If you are refinancing, you should only need to pay an annual premium in advance if your premium is due within the next 60 or 90 days, depending on the lender.

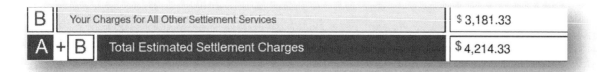

B	Your Charges for All Other Settlement Services	$ 3,181.33
A + B	Total Estimated Settlement Charges	$ 4,214.33

This section simply summarizes the charges itemized above.

Page three of the GFE is meant to help you understand how to review closing documents to ensure you've been given the loan product and pricing that you were promised, and how to compare competing loan offers.

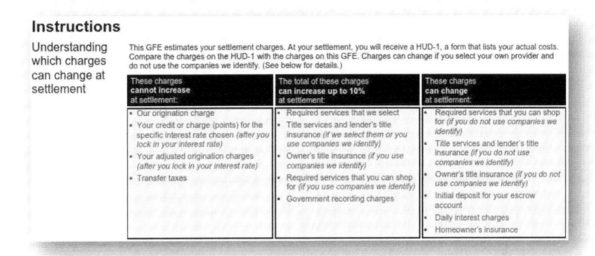

The top of page three simply explains which charges might change by the time you get to settlement and which ones cannot.

Your mortgage company must give you options to pay *points* to get a lower interest rate, or to take a higher interest rate in order to avoid paying for some or all of the loan costs in escrow. This section is where the originator should give you the option you've discussed (as disclosed in the GFE), plus at least one option with higher cost and lower rate, and one with lower cost and higher rate.

Using the shopping chart	Use this chart to compare GFEs from different loan originators. Fill in the information by using a different column for each GFE you receive. By comparing loan offers, you can shop for the best loan.			
	This loan	**Loan 2**	**Loan 3**	**Loan 4**
Loan originator name				
Initial loan amount				
Loan term				
Initial interest rate				
Initial monthly amount owed				
Rate lock period				
Can interest rate rise?				
Can loan balance rise?				
Can monthly amount owed rise?				
Prepayment penalty?				
Balloon payment?				
Total Estimated Settlement Charges				

In the section "Using the shopping cart" your originator should complete only the section for "this loan." The other sections are for you to complete when you shop other providers for competitive loans. The section is meant to give you a concise way to see and evaluate the salient points for your options.

You can find an enhanced Excel-based version of this chart on www.loanguide.com that will help you calculate payments, and help you calculate comparative lifetime costs over the life of your loan options that you are considering.

If you have gotten the impression that I don't particularly like the Good Faith Estimate in its current form, you're very astute. The section titled "Summary of your loan" section on page one is very useful, and the section titled "Using the tradeoff table" on page three is also good. The rest of the form can be quite confusing, however, and even misleading.

Mortgage originators can (and should) provide you with an unofficial form called a *Good Faith Estimate Worksheet* which shows you a complete list of every line item charge associated with origination, title, escrow and recording fees. This worksheet should explain who pays for each fee and how. But note: there is no such thing as a **no cost** or even **a no-point, no fee** loan. You may not pay any charges in escrow, but you will either pay for the costs over time in the form of a higher interest rate, or you will pay for costs by having them built into the loan amount.

The good news is that you should have the option to structure the loan however you want, and a good mortgage advisor can help you figure out which option will cost you the least over time.

Good Faith Estimate Worksheet

Your lender may, but is not required to, provide you with a Good Faith Estimate Worksheet which clarifies exactly what you will be paying for in escrow. While there is no specific format required by law for this worksheet, the estimates in the worksheet must be the same as those used to prepare the good faith estimate. I prefer a worksheet that clearly identifies every line item that you will see when you close escrow and explains what each line item is for. Here's a good example:

Summary of Loan, Escrow and Title Charges and Cash Needed to Close Loan				
Loan Charges				
Origination and Discount		Paid to		*Notes*
Interest Rate:	5.125%			
Discount Fee or (Credit):	$ (1,750.00)			
Fees for Loan Origination				*What does this pay for?*
Appraisal:	$ 500.00	Appraiser	(Estimated)	Provides an estimate of value for the lender
Second Appraisal:	$ -	Appraiser		To confirm the first estimate if needed by underwriter
Appraisal Review:	$ -	Lender		To confirm the first estimate if needed by underwriter
Credit Report:	$ 30.00	Other	(Estimated)	
Tax Service:	$ -	Lender		To monitor whether your taxes are paid on time
Processing:	$ -	Broker		To gather, analyze and submit paperwork to lender
Underwriting / Lender Admin:	$ 1,000.00	Lender	(Estimated)	To review application and docs for compliance
Wire Transfer:	$ -	Lender		To wire money into escrow when ready to fund
Broker Admin:	$ -	Broker		
Flood Cert:	$ -	Lender		To determine if property is in a flood hazard zone
MERS fee:	$ -	Lender		To register loan in nationwide data base
VA Funding Fee	$ -	Lender	(VA loans only)	To pay costs of VA administration
Settlement Services (Title, Escrow, Recording)				
Settlement / Escrow:	$ 625.00	Escrow	(Estimated)	Administrative fee to handle the escrow
Doc Prep:	$ -	Escrow		
Notary:	$ 120.00	Escrow	(Estimated)	To notairze important documents
Owners Title Insurance:	$ -	Title		
Lenders Title Insurance:	$ 495.00	Title	(Estimated)	Insures lender that loan is properly secured
Endorsements:	$ 25.00	Title	(Estimated)	Adds provisions to title insurance (i.e. condo)
Loan Tie-In:	$ 75.00	Escrow	(Estimated)	Confirms recording after the fact
Special Requests:	$ -	Escrow		
Recording Fees:	$ 130.00	Escrow	(Estimated)	Records transaction with County Recorder's Office
Courier	$ 36.00	Escrow	(Estimated)	To deliver urgent files
email Doc Fee	$ -	Escrow		
Other Fees				
Property Inspection	$ 450.00	Other	(Estimated)	Confirms overall condition of property
Pest Inspection:	$ 250.00	Other	(Estimated)	Confirms there is no presence of pests (i.e. termites)
NA:	$ -	Other		
N/A	$ -	Other		
County Transfer Taxes:	$ 137.50	Other	(Estimated)	County charges tax on transfer
City Transfer Taxes:	$ 825.00	Other	(Estimated)	Only some cities charge this
HOA Cert:	$ -	Other		
Total Non-Recurring Loan Costs:	$ 4,698.50			
Lender Charge (Credit) for Interest Rate:	$ (1,750.00)			
Net Loan Costs:	$ 2,948.50			
Pre-Paid Expenses Due in Escrow				
Pre-Paid Interest	$ 427.08			Note: These expenses are for items in connection with *owning the property* and not in
Property Taxes	$ 1,041.67			connection with *acquiring* or *financing* it. They represent either costs that you must fund in
Homeowners Insurance	$ 700.00			advnace (annual insurance premium) and / or ongoing costs for which you are creating a
Mortgage Insurance	$ -			fund to pay later, such as next year's insurance premiums and property taxes as they come
NA	$ -			due.
Flood Insurance:	$ -			
N/A:	$ -			
Total Pre-Paid Expenses:	$ 2,168.75			

There are several things that are important while reviewing this worksheet.

First, fees will vary depending on a lot of factors, including the geographic area in which you live, and your specific circumstances such as credit history, down payment, etc. So, don't rely on this example to determine if your charges are "fair" or not.

However, if you receive competing quotes from two different lenders and there are significant differences between them – especially for non-lender fees such as title, escrow, recording and taxes – ask your lenders why that is. The lender has little or no control over these costs, so they should not vary much no matter what lender you use. A lender may give you a credit toward the costs, but the costs are still paid for in escrow and if you aren't paying for them in cash, you are either paying for them in a higher interest rate or, in the case of a refinance, money added to the loan amount.

If your loan officer omits any costs that you will be paying in escrow, fire them and hire the loan officer who is honest with you about what you will be paying.

Mortgage Loan Disclosure

The Mortgage Loan Disclosure Statement, or MLDS, is a California-specific form, so I won't go into depth in this book. However, it contains most of the information in the GFE, and a version of the GFE worksheet discussed above. For California residents, therefore, it can be useful in reviewing line-item charges estimated in advance, and confirming that the final line-item charges match what was estimated.

Truth-in-Lending

It is arguable that no form in the mortgage disclosure package has caused as much confusion as the Truth-in-Lending form. This form contains uniform disclosures required by the Truth in Lending Act of 1968. The purpose of the disclosures is to allow you to compare competing loan offers so that you can shop for the best loan.

The intention of the Act is very good, but the nature of the disclosures renders it somewhat useless for most borrowers. You have to sign it, however, to document that you have read and understood it, so let's go through it to see what it's about.

TRUTH-IN-LENDING DISCLOSURE STATEMENT
(THIS IS NEITHER A CONTRACT NOR A COMMITMENT TO LEND)

Applicant: **John Customer**	Prepared By: **C2 Financial Corp**
Property Address: **123 Main Street**	**10509 Vista Sorrento Pkwy, Ste 200**
Campbell, CA 95008	**San Diego , CA 92121**
Application No: **Sample**	Date Prepared: **02/25/2014** Ph: **408-348-3442**

ANNUAL PERCENTAGE RATE	FINANCE CHARGE	AMOUNT FINANCED	TOTAL OF PAYMENTS
The cost of your credit as a yearly rate	The dollar amount the credit will cost you	The amount of credit provided to you or on your behalf	The amount you will have paid after making all payments as scheduled
* **6.191** %	$ * **236,207.04**	$ * **195,470.00**	$ * **431,677.04**

This is the top of the TIL. The thing that most confuses borrowers is the Annual Percentage Rate. This particular loan was being written at a *note rate* of 6.000%, so why is the *Annual Percentage Rate* higher than that?

I have heard dozens of different ways to describe this, but the best one is as follows:

Suppose I were to lend you $100 to be paid back over three years in 36 monthly installments at 5.000%. (I am abandoning our running sample for this analysis for simplicity's sake) My math tells me that you would have to pay me $3.00 per month to pay me back my principal of $100 plus 5.000% interest on the outstanding balance every month. By the end of three years you would have paid me $3.00 x 36 = $108. (We'll call this the **Total of Payments**, the last box on the right above.)

Let's say, however, that I decide I need to charge you for the administrative costs of making the loan in the first place. After all, I could just leave the money in the bank and earn the $8 profit in 3 years. So I need to charge you $2.00 to make the loan. I give you $100, but take back $2 at the same time.

Here's the question: How much have I actually lent you? $100, or $98?

The annual percentage rate calculation is based on the idea that I really only lent you $98. But you're still paying me back $3 per month for 36 months. If I only lent you $98 (we'll call this the **Amount Financed** in the box above), rather than $100, what is the effective interest rate of this loan?

Using a spreadsheet because there is no way I can do this math without one, a $98 loan paid back over 36 months at $3.00 per month equals an effective interest rate (we'll call this the **annual percentage rate**) of 5.065%. Notice that it is slightly higher than the 5.000% note rate, as we would expect.

Let's go a little further: we know you will pay back $108 over three years, and I'm advancing you $98 now, so this loan will cost you a total of $108 - $98 = $10. We'll call this the **Finance Charge**, as it is the total cost of financing over the life of the loan, including up-front costs plus interest rate.

And that's it – it's really that simple.

INTEREST RATE AND PAYMENT SUMMARY

	Rate & Monthly Payment
Interest Rate	6.000 %
Principal + Interest Payment	$ 1,199.10
Est. Taxes + Insurance (Escrow)	$ 50.00
Total Est. Monthly Payment	**$ 1,249.10**

Going back to our original example, the next part of the TIL is very simple – it is a reiteration of the note rate, the Principal + Interest Payment, and the escrow payment, if any.

☐ DEMAND FEATURE: This obligation has a demand feature.
☐ VARIABLE RATE FEATURE: This loan contains a variable rate feature. A variable rate disclosure has been provided earlier.

SECURITY: You are giving a security interest in: **123 Main Street, Campbell CA 95008**
☐ The goods or property being purchased ☑ Real property you already own.

The next part of the TIL discloses some important terms.

A **demand feature** means the lender can *call the loan* (demand repayment in full) at any time for any reason. I've never seen a mortgage loan with this clause, but they must have existed at one time.

A **required deposit** refers to a charge for processing or locking the loan (usually non-refundable) at the beginning of the loan process. It is very rare, and should be included in the APR calculation.

A **variable rate feature** is something we already know about. If this box is checked your loan will have a variable (adjustable) rate, and the interest rate and payment can be adjusted in the future (in accordance with the terms of your note – see Chapter 12, "Adjustable-Rate Mortgages.")

The next line reminds you that you are giving a security interest in your property.

FILING FEES: $ **60.00**

LATE CHARGE: If a payment is more than **15** days late, you will be charged **5.000** % of the payment.

PREPAYMENT: If you pay off early, you ☐ may ☑ will not have to pay a penalty.
☐ may ☑ will not be entitled to a refund of part of the finance charge.

The fees are self-explanatory.

The last section discloses whether or not there is a pre-payment penalty, and if you pay off early you will be able to recoup any of the finance charges you would have paid to date. (You won't.)

CREDIT LIFE/CREDIT DISABILITY:
Credit life insurance and credit disability insurance are not required to obtain credit, and will not be provided unless you sign and agree to pay the additional cost.

Type	Premium	Signature	
Credit Life		I want credit life insurance.	Signature:
Credit Disability		I want credit disability insurance.	Signature:
Credit Life and Disability		I want credit life and disability insurance.	Signature:

INSURANCE:
The following insurance is required to obtain credit:
☐ Credit life insurance ☐ Credit disability
☑ Property insurance ☐ Flood insurance

You may obtain the insurance from anyone you want that is acceptable to creditor.
☐ If you purchase ☐ property ☐ flood insurance from creditor
you will pay $ for a one year term.

This section discloses what kinds of insurance you are obligated to carry.

In all cases you will need to carry hazard (homeowner's) insurance, so expect that box to be checked. Flood insurance will be required if you are located in a flood zone.

Credit insurance and credit life insurance are rarely, if ever, required on conventional loans.

ASSUMPTION:

Someone buying your property
☐ may
☐ may, subject to conditions
☑ may not   assume the remainder of your loan on the original terms.

See your contract documents for any additional information about nonpayment, default, any required repayment in full before the scheduled date and prepayment refunds and penalties.

☑ * means an estimate
☐ all dates and numerical disclosures except the late payment disclosures are estimates.

You are not required to complete this agreement merely because you have received these disclosures or signed a loan application.

This section discloses whether someone may assume your loan or not. Fixed-rate loans are not assumable today; adjustable-rate loans might be.

The final disclosure on page one reminds you that you are not obligated to complete the transaction just because you signed this form. You may still have time to shop for a better deal.

One more word about APR: The APR is meant to give you a way to compare apples to apples. It was meant to help you compare two loans of similar terms, where one loan cost more up front, and the other cost less up front but had a higher interest rate. But the APR has one very serious flaw – it only tells you what the comparative cost of two loans would be over the stated term of the loan (say, 30 years.) It can be misleading, however, if you keep the loan for a shorter period.

Let's use our running example of the $250,000 purchase. You have two options:

Option one is a $200,000 30-year fixed loan at 5.000% at and will cost $5,000 to write. The APR on this loan is 5.224%

Option two is a $200,000 30-year fixed loan at 5.375% that will cost $0 in up-front fees.

The APR on this loan is 5.375%, since there are no upfront costs.

Loan one appears to be the better deal. This is true **if** you pay it off as planned over 30 years.

But what if you decide to sell the home after five years? We can calculate the total cost of a loan over an assumed holding period by adding the up-front cost to the interest paid over that period.

On option one your total costs will have been $5,000 + $48,075 = $53,075.

On option two your total costs will have been $0 + $51,808 = $51,808.

If we only keep the property five years, option two is a better deal.

This is a simplified example, but it illustrates that the APR has serious limitations.

Other Disclosures

Other disclosures that you sign mostly ask you to verify that you have been informed of your rights and that you understand them, or ask to you certify that you are giving the lender true information and documentation to the best of your ability and giving them permission to verify it.

The disclosures we examined above verify all of the important terms of your proposed loan. I recommend reading the rest of the disclosures, but they should be self-explanatory.

Closing Disclosures

After your loan has been submitted, examined, underwritten, folded, stapled and mutilated, loan documents are drawn and sent to escrow for you to sign. Many of the forms you sign will look exactly the same as the ones you signed at the beginning, some with minor changes and some with no changes at all.

Let's talk about the forms that will matter to you.

Estimated Settlement Statement

The *Estimated Settlement Statement* is a form produced by and mandated by the Department of Housing and Urban Development. This form is commonly referred to as the HUD-1. The form will list all of the charges that you must pay for the loan and, if applicable, the purchase of the property. It is not a simple form, and many of the line items are combined in one line. Consequently, like some of the other forms you'll sign, this one is of limited value to the consumer.

A simpler and more complete form is the *Estimated Closing Statement* which is described below.

Estimated Closing Statement

Think of the *Estimated Closing Statement* as the final version of the Good Faith Estimate Worksheet that we discussed earlier in the chapter. Like the worksheet, there is not a standardized format. Each escrow company develops its own version of this form. But in general it is a simple, straightforward list of each of the charges you will be paying in escrow, plus credits toward those costs from any source, such as a seller or the lender.

	$ DEBITS	$ CREDITS
FINANCIAL:		
New 1st Trust Deed		327,250.00
TITLE CHARGES:		
Aggregate Recording Charge	95.00	
19-ALTA Short Form Res. Loan (2007) for $327,250.00	625.00	
ALTA Form 8.1-06 - Envir. Prot. Lien $75.00		
Endorsement Fee(s) **ESTIMATE	75.00	
ESCROW CHARGES:		
Escrow Fee	400.00	
Outside Courier/Special Messenger **ESTIMATE	25.00	
Signing Fee **ESTIMATE	125.00	
NEW LOAN CHARGES		
Total Loan Charges: $-1,273.73		
Origination Fee	6,721.88	
Your credit or charge (points) for the specific interest rate chosen		8,616.49
Appraisal Fee * $475.00 by Buyer/Borrower POC		
Credit Report	30.00	
Re-Inspection to Appraiser	100.00	
Verification of Deposit	25.00	
Interest at $46.5877 per day fr 10/22/2013 to 11/1/2013	465.88	
PAYOFFS		
Total Payoff $334,705.29		
Principal Balance	333,181.28	
Interest on Principal Balance at 6.50% fr 10/1/2013 thru 10/24/2013	1,424.01	
Forwarding/Demand Fee	30.00	
Reconveyance Fee	45.00	
Recording Fee	25.00	
MISCELLANEOUS:		
Tax Collector for 1st Installment 2013/2014	1,671.74	
060-081-007		
Hazard Premium	1,013.00	
ESTIMATED BALANCE DUE ESCROW		$10,211.30
ESTIMATED TOTALS	$346,077.79	$346,077.79

You can see that this example contains the same information as the Good Faith Estimate worksheet earlier in the chapter. This is an actual example from my practice. Each fee is individually listed on a single line with a notation as to who is being paid and for what service. Currently this form along with the GFE worksheet is your best way to verify that the charges you were quoted at the beginning of the process are the charges you are paying at the end.

One last note about the GFE, TIL and HUD1: The *Consumer Financial Protection Bureau* (CFPB) understands that these forms are not the most user-friendly. The Bureau has developed a new set of forms that will go into use on August 1, 2015. The first form you will be given in the loan process will be called the **Loan Estimate**. In it you will see will be an estimate of the charges and disclosure of the important terms of the proposed loan. The second form (called a **Closing Disclosure**) will be a confirmation of the charges and terms at closing.

The proposed forms aren't perfect, but they appear to be clear, easy to understand, and most importantly very similar to each other in layout and content, so it will be easy for you to verify that you've been given what you were promised. This will be a dramatic improvement, and will shorten this chapter considerably.

Note

The *Note* and *Deed of Trust* (or *mortgage* in some states) are the two most important documents you will sign.

The Note is also known as a *Promissory Note* because the purpose of the Note is to formalize your promise to pay the lender a specific amount of money over a specific period of time.

The Note is a legal document, and creates a legal obligation on your part when you sign it. Nothing in this book should be construed as legal advice, because I am not an attorney. If you have any concerns or wish to delve deeper into what you are committing to, please consult with a qualified attorney. Having said that...

The terms of the note are spelled out very carefully, so let's review them. The example used in this book is a widely-used Note produced by Fannie Mae. There will be some differences from state-to-state to accommodate state law, and not all lenders will use this exact format. But the essential elements of your note should track these elements fairly closely.

There are slight differences between fixed-rate notes and adjustable-rate notes, so we'll cover fixed-rate notes first, and then point out the differences for adjustable-rate notes.

Fixed-Rate Note

1. BORROWER'S PROMISE TO PAY

In return for a loan that I have received, I promise to pay U.S. $_____ (this amount is called "Principal"), plus interest, to the order of the Lender. The Lender is _____. I will make all payments under this Note in the form of cash, check or money order.

I understand that the Lender may transfer this Note. The Lender or anyone who takes this Note by transfer and who is entitled to receive payments under this Note is called the "Note Holder."

2. INTEREST

Interest will be charged on unpaid principal until the full amount of Principal has been paid. I will pay interest at a yearly rate of _____%.

The interest rate required by this Section 2 is the rate I will pay both before and after any default described in Section 6(B) of this Note.

1. The first section states the principal balance (the actual loan amount), identifies the lender, and clarifies that the lender may assign or transfer the note to another lender.

2. This also identifies the interest rate that will be used to calculate the interest charged for the outstanding (unpaid) balance very month. This is your *Note Rate*.

3. PAYMENTS

(A) Time and Place of Payments

I will pay principal and interest by making a payment every month.

I will make my monthly payment on the _____ day of each month beginning on _____, _____. I will make these payments every month until I have paid all of the principal and interest and any other charges described below that I may owe under this Note. Each monthly payment will be applied as of its scheduled due date and will be applied to interest before Principal. If, on _____, 20____, I still owe amounts under this Note, I will pay those amounts in full on that date, which is called the "Maturity Date."

I will make my monthly payments at _____ or at a different place if required by the Note Holder.

(B) Amount of Monthly Payments

My monthly payment will be in the amount of U.S. $_____.

3. The next section tells you what day of the month your payments will be due (almost always the 1st) and when the **first** payment is due. It tells you where to make the payments, and finally what the amount of the payment will be.

4. BORROWER'S RIGHT TO PREPAY

I have the right to make payments of Principal at any time before they are due. A payment of Principal only is known as a "Prepayment." When I make a Prepayment, I will tell the Note Holder in writing that I am doing so. I may not designate a payment as a Prepayment if I have not made all the monthly payments due under the Note.

I may make a full Prepayment or partial Prepayments without paying a Prepayment charge. The Note Holder will use my Prepayments to reduce the amount of Principal that I owe under this Note. However, the Note Holder may apply my Prepayment to the accrued and unpaid interest on the Prepayment amount, before applying my Prepayment to reduce the Principal amount of the Note. If I make a partial Prepayment, there will be no changes in the due date or in the amount of my monthly payment unless the Note Holder agrees in writing to those changes.

5. LOAN CHARGES

If a law, which applies to this loan and which sets maximum loan charges, is finally interpreted so that the interest or other loan charges collected or to be collected in connection with this loan exceed the permitted limits, then: (a) any such loan charge shall be reduced by the amount necessary to reduce the charge to the permitted limit; and (b) any sums already collected from me which exceeded permitted limits will be refunded to me. The Note Holder may choose to make this refund by reducing the Principal I owe under this Note or by making a direct payment to me. If a refund reduces Principal, the reduction will be treated as a partial Prepayment.

4. This section identifies your right to pre-pay your loan without penalty. You will rarely find a pre-payment penalty today. If you do the terms of the penalty will be spelled out here.

5. This section simply states that if you live in a state which enacts a usury law that – after the fact – makes the loan charges or interest in your loan illegal (in that state) then the lender will refund the difference to you. This would be extraordinarily unlikely.

6. BORROWER'S FAILURE TO PAY AS REQUIRED

(A) Late Charge for Overdue Payments

If the Note Holder has not received the full amount of any monthly payment by the end of _____ calendar days after the date it is due, I will pay a late charge to the Note Holder. The amount of the charge will be _____ % of my overdue payment of principal and interest. I will pay this late charge promptly but only once on each late payment.

(B) Default

If I do not pay the full amount of each monthly payment on the date it is due, I will be in default.

(C) Notice of Default

If I am in default, the Note Holder may send me a written notice telling me that if I do not pay the overdue amount by a certain date, the Note Holder may require me to pay immediately the full amount of Principal which has not been paid and all the interest that I owe on that amount. That date must be at least 30 days after the date on which the notice is mailed to me or delivered by other means.

(D) No Waiver By Note Holder

Even if, at a time when I am in default, the Note Holder does not require me to pay immediately in full as described above, the Note Holder will still have the right to do so if I am in default at a later time.

(E) Payment of Note Holder's Costs and Expenses

If the Note Holder has required me to pay immediately in full as described above, the Note Holder will have the right to be paid back by me for all of its costs and expenses in enforcing this Note to the extent not prohibited by applicable law. Those expenses include, for example, reasonable attorneys' fees.

6. This section clearly spells out what happens if you fail to make payments on time. The consequences are pretty much what you would expect, so make your payments on time.

7. GIVING OF NOTICES

Unless applicable law requires a different method, any notice that must be given to me under this Note will be given by delivering it or by mailing it by first class mail to me at the Property Address above or at a different address if I give the Note Holder a notice of my different address.

Any notice that must be given to the Note Holder under this Note will be given by delivering it or by mailing it by first class mail to the Note Holder at the address stated in Section 3(A) above or at a different address if I am given a notice of that different address.

8. OBLIGATIONS OF PERSONS UNDER THIS NOTE

If more than one person signs this Note, each person is fully and personally obligated to keep all of the promises made in this Note, including the promise to pay the full amount owed. Any person who is a guarantor, surety or endorser of this Note is also obligated to do these things. Any person who takes over these obligations, including the obligations of a guarantor, surety or endorser of this Note, is also obligated to keep all of the promises made in this Note. The Note Holder may enforce its rights under this Note against each person individually or against all of us together. This means that any one of us may be required to pay all of the amounts owed under this Note.

9. WAIVERS

I and any other person who has obligations under this Note waive the rights of Presentment and Notice of Dishonor. "Presentment" means the right to require the Note Holder to demand payment of amounts due. "Notice of Dishonor" means the right to require the Note Holder to give notice to other persons that amounts due have not been paid.

7. This is a housekeeping section. The statements or coupon book will be sent to you at your home. If you wish to give a formal notice to the lender, this section tells you how.

8. This section states that if there is more than one person on the loan, you are both (or all) **each** responsible for the entire debt and all payments. You cannot send in your half of the payment and be "off the hook" for the rest. Each one of you is responsible for the entire debt and the entire payment. In the event that your co-borrower can no longer make payments, it's up to you.

9. Finally, this section reminds you that you have to make payments on the loan whether you receive a statement or not.

10. UNIFORM SECURED NOTE

This Note is a uniform instrument with limited variations in some jurisdictions. In addition to the protections given to the Note Holder under this Note, a Mortgage, Deed of Trust, or Security Deed (the "Security Instrument"), dated the same date as this Note, protects the Note Holder from possible losses which might result if I do not keep the promises which I make in this Note. That Security Instrument describes how and under what conditions I may be required to make immediate payment in full of all amounts I owe under this Note. Some of those conditions are described as follows:

If all or any part of the Property or any Interest in the Property is sold or transferred (or if Borrower is not a natural person and a beneficial interest in Borrower is sold or transferred) without Lender's prior written consent, Lender may require immediate payment in full of all sums secured by this Security Instrument. However, this option shall not be exercised by Lender if such exercise is prohibited by Applicable Law.

10. This section reminds you that the loan will be secured using your real estate as collateral; you are pledging your home (or other real estate) as collateral, and if you default the lender can take it

away from you. The instrument that is used to convey the security interest is called a *Deed of Trust* or a *Mortgage*, depending on what state your property is in. We cover these instruments in the next section.

Finally, the last part of the Note asks for your signature. When you sign this note you could be creating a negotiable instrument. This means that the *Note Holder*, anyone in possession of the Note with your original signature, might be able to claim that you owe them this money, and attempt to collect. Consequently, you will sign only one copy of the Note, and leave all others, including the one you keep, blank.

Adjustable-Rate Note

The first difference between fixed and adjustable-rate notes is that the monthly payment on a fixed-rate note is your permanent payment (in most cases). For the exceptions, see the sections on buy-down mortgages in Chapter 11 and interest-only mortgages in Chapter 13.

In an adjustable-rate note the monthly payment is your **initial** payment, and the note has to define how your interest rate and your payment may change in the future.

3. PAYMENTS

    (A) Time and Place of Payments

    I will pay principal and interest by making a payment every month.

    I will make my monthly payment on the first day of each month beginning on _____, _____. I will make these payments every month until I have paid all of the principal and interest and any other charges described below that I may owe under this Note. Each monthly payment will be applied as of its scheduled due date and will be applied to interest before Principal. If, on _____, 20____, I still owe amounts under this Note, I will pay those amounts in full on that date, which is called the "Maturity Date."

    I will make my monthly payments at _____
_____ or at a different place if required by the Note Holder.

    (B) Amount of My Initial Monthly Payments

    Each of my initial monthly payments will be in the amount of U.S. $_____. This amount may change.

    (C) Monthly Payment Changes

    Changes in my monthly payment will reflect changes in the unpaid principal of my loan and in the interest rate that I must pay. The Note Holder will determine my new interest rate and the changed amount of my monthly payment in accordance with Section 4 of this Note.

3. In this adjustable-rate note the payment is clearly identified as **initial**, and it references the next section where the terms for adjusting the interest rate are clearly identified.

4. INTEREST RATE AND MONTHLY PAYMENT CHANGES

    (A) Change Dates

    The interest rate I will pay may change on the first day of _____, _____, and on that day every 12th month thereafter. Each date on which my interest rate could change is called a "Change Date."

    (B) The Index

    Beginning with the first Change Date, my interest rate will be based on an Index. The "Index" is the weekly average yield on United States Treasury securities adjusted to a constant maturity of one year, as made available by the Federal Reserve Board. The most recent Index figure available as of the date 45 days before each Change Date is called the "Current Index."

    If the Index is no longer available, the Note Holder will choose a new index which is based upon comparable information. The Note Holder will give me notice of this choice.

4. (A) This section identifies the date when your interest rate can be adjusted the first time, and subsequently after that.

(B) It then identifies which *Index* will be used to calculate your new interest rate when your rate adjusts. (See Chapter 12, *Adjustable-Rate Mortgages*) An index such as this measures interest rates in the same way the Dow Jones Average measures stock prices.

    (C) Calculation of Changes

    Before each Change Date, the Note Holder will calculate my new interest rate by adding _____ _____ percentage points (_____ %) to the Current Index. The Note Holder will then round the result of this addition to the nearest one-eighth of one percentage point (0.125%). Subject to the limits stated in Section 4(D) below, this rounded amount will be my new interest rate until the next Change Date.

    The Note Holder will then determine the amount of the monthly payment that would be sufficient to repay the unpaid principal that I am expected to owe at the Change Date in full on the Maturity Date at my new interest rate in substantially equal payments. The result of this calculation will be the new amount of my monthly payment.

    (D) Limits on Interest Rate Changes

    The interest rate I am required to pay at the first Change Date will not be greater than _____ % or less than _____ %. Thereafter, my interest rate will never be increased or decreased on any single Change Date by more than one percentage point (1.0%) from the rate of interest I have been paying for the preceding 12 months. My interest rate will never be greater than _____ %.

    (E) Effective Date of Changes

    My new interest rate will become effective on each Change Date. I will pay the amount of my new monthly payment beginning on the first monthly payment date after the Change Date until the amount of my monthly payment changes again.

    (F) Notice of Changes

    The Note Holder will deliver or mail to me a notice of any changes in my interest rate and the amount of my monthly payment before the effective date of any change. The notice will include information required by law to be given to me and also the title and telephone number of a person who will answer any question I may have regarding the notice.

(C) In this section the exact method for computing your new interest rate is defined. The first blank will contain a number like 2.25% or 2.75%, which will be added to the then-current value of the index defined in the section above it. The new rate is known as your *fully-indexed rate*.

(D) After that, limits on how much your interest rate can adjust on the first adjustment and subsequent adjustments. These are known as your *initial adjustment cap* and your *periodic adjustment cap.*

This section also defines your *lifetime cap*, the maximum interest rate that your loan can ever be.

Deed of Trust / Mortgage

The *Deed of Trust* (or *Trust Deed)* is used in some states, while a *Mortgage* is used in others. (A few states allow either.) The principal difference is that if you secure your property with a mortgage the lender has to sue you in court to foreclose. In a trust deed state you will use a trust deed to provisionally grant title to your property to a trustee. If you go into default, the trustee can sell your home at a trustee's sale without a court trial. The trustee cannot just capriciously do this; he must follow very specific procedures, and allow you certain rights, include the right to redeem your loan and keep your house. Legal advice is beyond the scope of this book. If you need more information regarding your legal rights, consult a qualified attorney.

The salient point is that when you sign a trust deed, you are granting your property to another person who has the right to sell it out from under you if you default. If you sign a mortgage, you are granting a security interest in your property to the lender, who can take the property away from you in a court action.

So, the Trust Deed and the Mortgage are pretty scary, serious documents. And yet, out of hundreds of clients that I've worked with, only **one** has read the Trust Deed from beginning to end.

These documents are very long, are generally written in legalese, and most importantly are required by the lender to make the loan. They aren't negotiable, so it's not like you could ask for modifications or refuse to sign it. You're going to sign it if you want the loan. I personally believe, however, that you ought to know what's in it.

You are pledging your real estate to the lender as security for the loan, to be used in the event you default on the loan. Of course not paying back the money is a default, but there are other ways you could be in default. Let's look at the highlights:

You agree to make all the payments on time and in full.

You agree that you will either pay your property taxes, homeowner's insurance, mortgage insurance (if any) and HOA dues (if any) on time, or that you will establish an impound (escrow) account with the lender, make monthly payments to the lender sufficient to cover taxes and insurance when they are due, and that the lender will make those payments on your behalf from your funds.

You will occupy the property (if you have represented that you will be doing so in order to get the loan.)

You will not intentionally damage or destroy the property, and you will maintain the property in a fashion necessary to protect the property's value and marketability.

You affirm that all the information you gave the lender in order to induce them to lend you the money was true and correct. Note that this means that if the lender finds out **after the loan has been made** that you (or anyone else involved in the transaction) misrepresented information on your application or that you (or anyone else involved in the transaction) falsified any documentation that you will be in a default that you most likely cannot cure. Consider this carefully.

You will not store hazardous substances on the property.

Then, the Trust Deed and Mortgage establish the lender's right to protect itself and to recover the debt owed and the rules and procedures it must follow.

If you have any concerns about the Deed of Trust or Mortgage, ask your lender for a copy of the document you will be asked to sign before the closing date, and review the document with a qualified real estate attorney.

Remember, you can't negotiate terms on this or refuse to sign, so if you want the loan you will sign it. But it's nice to know what you are committing to do and what happens if you fall short in your commitment.

Other Disclosures

There are literally dozens of other disclosures and certifications that you will sign, but most are pretty self-explanatory. The important point is that when you sign them you are either certifying that the information and documentation you gave to the lender was true and correct to the best of your knowledge, or acknowledging that you understand your rights in the transaction.

If you want to read through them by all means, ask for time. You have the right to do so.

Summary

Almost no one reads all the disclosures, because there are so many and because by the time you get the final closing package to sign you probably feel that you are too far in to the process to back out. You only get a mortgage once in a while, and it's a complicated process. A few months after you close escrow you will remember very few details even if you have educated yourself about what you are signing.

However, you have a right to understand what you are signing. You have to sign everything in the package if you want the loan, so you don't have a right to not sign something if you want the loan. But you have the right to preview any document that you want, and you have a right to understand it. Assert those rights.

Chapter Twenty One

Common Marketing Gimmicks

Very smart people sit around thinking up ways to make getting a mortgage seem more attractive, even irresistible. Our industry isn't alone in this; it happens in nearly every industry.

However, since I do what I do, I cringe whenever I hear the puffery many mortgage companies spew in their advertising and promotion. My Grandfather used to call it **horse feathers** in polite company. If you hear any of the following offers, please understand that it is horse feathers.

Automatic Rate Roll-Down after Closing

A very well-known mortgage company came out with this old take on a common practice.

The offer: If you buy a home or refinance with us now, and rates go lower anytime in the next three years, we will happily give you the new, lower rate, at no or minimal cost.

The background: This lender doesn't actually own or even service your loan once you close. They have no ability or authority to simply reduce your interest rate.

What they really mean: They can, however, refinance you again -- provided you qualify -- something that every mortgage company can do. If rates drop far enough, and if your credit and employment picture have not changed, and if your property value has remained stable or increased, and if underwriting guidelines have not become more restrictive…**then** they can, indeed, "reduce your interest rate" by refinancing you.

Is this a good service? Sure. Is it a **unique** service? Not even close. Virtually every broker and banker in the country does this anyway; most just don't frame it as a unique offer to draw you in.

If you lose your job, we'll make your payments.

Actually, I first proposed this service many years ago and it was pooh-poohed by the firm I worked for at the time. Now one of the national banks offers this and advertises it heavily.

The offer: If you get a loan with us and then lose your job anytime within the first (one, two, or three) years, we'll make your payments for you until you become re-employed. (**If** you qualify for this very special program.)

The background: How can any lender, and in particular any small broker, take this kind of risk? It's quite simple. Many insurance companies offer privately-funded unemployment insurance policies for folks who have relatively stable jobs. You could buy this policy yourself. (**If** you qualify.)

What they really mean: They will add in an unemployment insurance policy from a company with whom they've partnered. Because it is part of your loan offer from the beginning and the cost of the premium is built into your fees in escrow, you just might take it.

Is this a good service? Absolutely, if clients understand what it really is and have the option to opt out. Is it unique? While few companies actually do offer this option, almost anyone could, and of course you could go shop for it yourself.

A good analogy would be the extended service warranties offered by car dealers. It's convenient to buy it at the dealership as part of the cost of the car, and it can be financed, and it may bring you peace of mind. However, unless you have an unusual breakdown of some sort it isn't usually a good deal, and you can get a much better price on the same or better insurance policy at your credit union.

Unemployment insurance to cover your mortgage payment is the same way. If it's the right product for you, it's a good offer from the mortgage company. But if insurance to cover your mortgage payment is the right choice for you, ask what the rate and fees would be if you didn't take the "We'll make your payments for you" guarantee, and shop for insurance on your own as well.

Gaming the system

Because I am very up-front with my clients and explain the inner workings of the industry to those who want to hear it, I am sometimes asked by my clients "OK, then how do I game the system?"

There really are no longer any ways to beat the system without taking huge risks for the loan originator, the broker or banker he or she works for, and **you**. *Stated-income* loans are essentially non-existent today, and are not likely to come back in any form that would allow the kind of gaming that was common during the mortgage boom.

However, using intelligent strategy to find the best loan product for you and your family and the best price and rate combination, and then consciously playing the market so that you lock on as favorable a day as possible can save you tens of thousands of dollars over the life of your loan.

Today the system is designed to protect borrowers from incompetent or unethical lenders and to protect the ultimate lenders – investors in mortgage-backed securities – from the type of fraud perpetrated by the investment banks, the banks, the mortgage banking channel and the brokers.

The cost of those protections is that there is much less flexibility in lending left today. If, in the eyes of those who write the rules you cannot afford a mortgage (meaning you are not likely to be able to pay it back as agreed) then you shall not have one.

Even so, if you don't qualify for a mortgage today, a competent, ethical loan officer can help you plan out the adjustments you need to make in order to qualify down the road.

Unlike in the bad old days of lending, today the terms "qualified for…" and "can afford…" mean mostly the same thing. And that's the way it should be.

Chapter Twenty Two

Tools

Most of the excel-based tools used in this book to analyze a problem are available on the book's web site at www.loanguide.com. As much as possible they are designed so that you can use them on your own. If you do use them on your own you are entirely responsible for the results generated by the analysis and any decisions you make as a result of using the analysis.

Rent Vs. Own – Long Term View

If you're in the market to buy a home, you are bound to be shown the simple method (Chapter 5, "Should You Buy a Home?") to show you the difference between renting and owning. As we discussed this has limitations, but is still worth looking at. Since your real estate agent is likely to do this analysis for you, you should be able to do it on your own as well.

The Simple Method

You'll find the following Excel-based tool at www.loanguide.com. It is titled "Homeownership Cost Analysis."

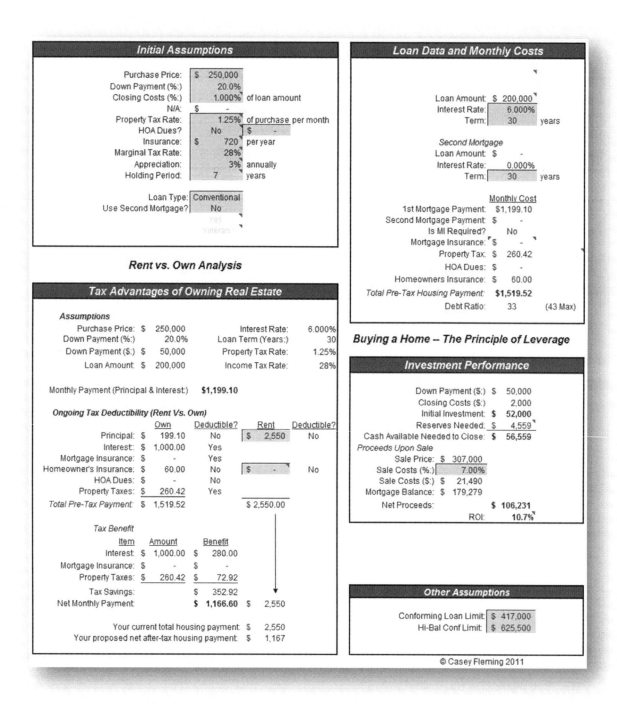

First, please note that you'll only be able to enter data in open, gray-colored fields.

You'll ender your initial assumptions in the top left-hand box. Some of the fields should be self-explanatory. Wherever you see a red triangle you can see hints, instructions and disclosures on that specific field by clicking on that cell or hovering over it. The fields for "Loan Type" and "Use Second Mortgage?" have drop-down lists that you must use for the analysis to work.

Next move to the box on the right, "Loan Data and Monthly Costs." You'll only need to enter in the interest rate and term in years for both loans. Interest-only loans are not generally available today, but if you are contemplating an interest-only loan enter 999 for the term.

At the bottom of this box you'll see what your total monthly housing cost is going to be. This is often where folks get sticker-shock. But it is better that you get that now than later.

Next, in the box that analyzes the tax advantages you will only need to enter the amount of rent you are paying each month (or would have to pay for an equivalent property if you are still living in Hotel Mom and Dad) and the cost of renter's insurance.

Please see Chapter 5 for a full discussion on the limitations of this analysis, and consult your tax advisor for your particular situation.

Finally, we start to take a look at the longer term consequences by showing you how your investment in your down payment and closing costs pays off. *If* the assumptions you've entered in the *Initial Assumptions* box pan out to be true, (and the assumption entered here regarding your sale costs) this calculates your projected annualized return on the investment.

This is a more thorough version of the overly-simple analysis you are likely to be shown when you are considering buying a home. Let's look a little deeper.

The Complex Method

You can look at the long-term effects of home ownership with the tool titled "Rent vs Own Long Term." Enter the same assumptions as you did in the previous analysis. Gray shading means you may enter data in the box, and red triangles will give you hints, instructions and disclosures.

In the results section near the bottom you will see two important data points:

The first is the first year that the cost of owning your home is projected to be less than the cost of renting a similar home. After that – if you have a 30-year fixed-rate mortgage, your costs of owning should always be less than the cost of renting.

The second data point is the year in which you have projected you will have cumulatively spent about the same amount on housing costs.

Rent vs Own, Long Term View	
Assumptions	

Rent		Own	
Monthly Rent:	$ 1,050	Purchase Price:	$ 250,000
Renter's Insurance:	$ 30	Down payment: (%)	20%
		Down Payment: ($)	$ 50,000
Other Assumptions		Loan Amount:	$ 200,000
		Interest Rate:	5.000%
Inflation Rate:	3.00%	Loan Term:	30 years
Property Appreciation:	3.00%	P & I Payment:	$1,073.64
Marginal Tax Rate:	28%	Prop Taxes: (%)	1.25%
		Prop Taxes: ($)	$ 260.42 Increase: 2% annually
Savings Rate:	6.00%	Insurance:	$ 60.00 montlhy
		Total Monthly Housing Pmnt:	$1,394.06

Results

Total housing cost after 30 years

	Annual	Cumulative
Cost of Renting:	$ 30,053	$ 610,250
Cost of Owning:	$ 20,034	$ 495,318

Annual and Cumulative Cost After 5 and 9 years		Renting	Owning
First Year Owning Is Less Than Renting (Annual Cost):	5	$ 14,541	$ 14,478 (Annual)
Years to Break-Even (Cumulative Cost):	9	$ 131,245	$ 130,438 (Cumulative)
Asset Value After 30 years: Renting: $ 254,993			Owning: $606,816

The Annual and Cumulative cost comparison is set by default at 30 years in the field "Total Housing Cost After." If you choose a loan of shorter term, change this field to equal your loan term. Print these results. Then, enter the number of years you expect to own the home, and print those results. Both of these results will give you good information regarding how buying a home will impact your housing costs in the long run.

This information is best presented graphically, however. Look below this box at the bottom of the Excel screen, and you will see two tabs.

Annual and Cumulative Cost After 5 and 9 years	
First Year Owning Is Less Than Renting (Annual Cost):	**5**
Years to Break-Even (Cumulative Cost):	**9**
Asset Value After 30 years: Renting:	**$ 254,993**

Results / Graphs /

Click on the "Graphs" tab to see the results graphically. Here's what you will see:

Long Term Annual Housing CostComparison - Own Vs. Rent

The most surprising thing this shows you is the dramatic savings you'll get once you pay off your home. The second graph shows you how ownership impacts your net worth.

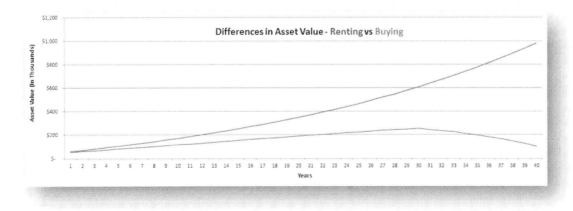

Differences in Asset Value - Renting vs Buying

GFE Loan Comparison

The last page of the current Good Faith Estimate contains a comparison grid that you are instructed to use to compare competing loan options from different lenders. The trouble is that it is not that easy to know what information to put into it, and it doesn't account for total costs of the holding period, especially if you think you'll keep the loan less than the full term of the loan.

Now you have an app for that. This analysis is called "Loan Comparison Shopping Results" and can be found at www.loanguide.com.

Using the Shopping Cart
(From Good Faith Estimate)

	This Loan	Loan 2	Loan 3	Loan 4
Loan originator name	Lender A	Lender B	Lender C	Lender D
Initial loan amount	$200,000	$200,000	$200,000	$200,000
Loan term (years until fully paid off)	30	30	30	30
Initial interest rate	6.000%	5.500%	5.750%	5.375%
Initial monthly amount owed	$1,199.10	$1,135.58	$1,167.15	$1,119.94
Rate lock period (in days)	30	30	30	30
Can interest rates rise?	No	No	No	No
Can loan balances rise?	No	No	No	No
Can monthly amount owed rise?	No	No	No	No
Prepayment penalty?	No	No	No	No
Balloon payment?	No	No	No	No
Total Estimated Settlement Charges	$3,500	$4,200	$3,800	$4,400

How long do you intend to have this loan?	7 years			
Mortgage balance after 7 years:	$179,279	$177,632	$178,467	$177,205
Total payments over 7 years:	$100,724	$95,389	$98,040	$94,075
Total interest paid over 7 years:	$80,003	$73,020	$76,507	$71,280
Total cost of loan over 7 years:	$83,503	$77,220	$80,307	$75,680
Total cost of loan over 30 years:	$435,176	$413,008	$423,972	$407,579

Once again, gray areas are unlocked fields where you can enter data. For this to be a meaningful comparison three things must be true: you must be comparing similar loan offers (i.e. all 30 year fixed loans), the estimated settlement charges must include all fees you will be expected to pay in escrow, not just lender fees (double check this, then triple-check it) and you must get the quotes on the same day within a very short time period, as rates can change by the minute.

The results are clear and hard numbers, but remember from earlier chapters the lowest number isn't always the best option. Sometimes the lowest payment is more important, or the lowest up-front cost. That's a decision only you can make; the purpose of this form is just to give you information.

Refi Benefit Analysis

As you remember from Chapter 6, the payback analysis used by most lenders can be terribly misleading. You absolutely need better tools than that. For those who want something easy to use, but that addresses at least one of the concerns with the (overly) simple payback analysis, you can use the "Modified Payback Analysis" found on www.loanguide.com.

The data entry on this form is very simple. The most important thing is to enter only the principal and interest due on your current loan. If you have an adjustable-rate loan this is probably not a meaningful comparison.

Modified Payback Analysis			
	Current Loan	Proposed Loan	Accelerated Payoff
Principal Balance:	$ 200,000	$ 200,000	$ 200,000
Interest Rate:	6.000%	5.500%	5.500%
Term (Years):	25.00	30	25.00
Payment:	$ 1,288.60	$ 1,135.58	$ 1,228.17
Monthly Savings:		$ 153.02	$ 60.43
Cost of New Loan:		$ 3,000	$ 3,000
Payback (Months):		19.6	49.6

If you have an interest-only loan, enter the amount you would have to pay to fully amortize your loan for a meaningful analysis. Make certain that your loan fees include **all** non-recurring closing costs from all sources, not just lender fees.

If you want to address all of the factors that will impact your lifetime costs, however, you need something a little more than this. Download the "Refi Benefit Analysis" from www.loanguide.com.

If you recall from Chapter 6, the purpose of this analysis is to help you understand how your proposed refinancing is going to impact you financially in the long term, and take into account assumptions such as your holding period.

Start by entering information about your current loan. You should be able to find your current loan balance, interest rate and the monthly principal and interest payment on your monthly statement. (If not, call your lender's servicing department and they can tell you.) The analysis will automatically calculate your remaining term.

Enter the information for your second mortgage only if you want to consolidate the debt on your second into your new loan. Otherwise, leave it blank.

Your Current Loan Data		
Current Property Value:	$	250,000

Your Current First		
Loan Type:	30 Year Fixed	
Current Balance	$	200,000 (est.)
Interest Rate		6.000%
Payments:	$	1,288.60
Term Remaining	25.00	Years

Your Current Second		
Loan Type:		
Current Balance	$	-
Interest Rate		0.000%
Payments:	$	-
Term Remaining	0.00	Years

Total Current Payments $ 1,288.60

Proposed Loan		
No-Cost Loan?		No
Finance Costs?		No
Cost Estimate:	$	3,100
Projected Costs	$	3,100 (Est!)
Projected Points		0.000
In Dollars:	$	-
Total Loan Costs:	$	3,100
Total Loan Amount	$	200,000
Interest Rate		5.500%
Term	30	Years
Requires MI?		No
Mortgage Ins. Premium:	$	-
Payment	$	1,135.58

Next, enter the information about your proposed loan. The "Cost Estimate" field includes **all** non-recurring closing costs from **all** sources – not just lenders fees -- that you will be expected to pay in escrow, except for discount points for the proposed interest rate. Ask your loan officer to give you this data using those exact words. Note that this figure is best extracted from the Good Faith Estimate worksheet, since there may be fees on the actual Good Faith Estimate which you will not actually be paying.

The amount of points should be clearly specified on the Good Faith Estimate.

You will probably need mortgage insurance if your loan-to-value ratio is higher than 80%. Mortgage insurance premiums today are heavily risk-weighted, so your insurance premium must be quoted by your loan officer.

Finally, we need to establish the most important assumption in the analysis – your holding period. How long do you think you'll keep this loan? Is this an intermediate home for you? (Do you plan to move up a few years from now?) Do you think you'll be doing an addition or remodeling? Or is this the last time you'll ever need financing? We want you to really think these questions through.

Other Assumptions		
Holding Period	60	Months
Safe Rate	2.25%	

Finally, enter your "Safe Rate." This is the rate of interest you feel confident you could earn on a relatively risk-free investment for as long as your holding period. This number is used to calculate the net present cost of your proposed loan compared to your existing loan. See Chapter 6 for a full discussion of the theory behind this.

You are done with your part. The results appear in the boxes to the right of the analysis, and guidance on how to read and interpret the analysis appears in Chapter 6. The last box, however, deserves a little discussion.

Amortization Comparison		
Your current loan will be paid off in	25.00	years.
To pay your proposed loan off in the same time you must pay	$1,228.17	per month

This will tell you what kind of payment you would need to pay monthly on your proposed loan in order to pay it off as quickly as you are currently paying your existing loan. There are two ways to use this information. First, note the payment needed to amortize the loan and compare it to your current payment. Second, go back to the input box titled "Proposed Loan" and enter the number of years your current loan will be paid off into the "Term" for the new loan, and review the results again. This will show you how much you can save (if anything) using the proposed loan and aggressive debt-management. (See Chapter 3, "Choose Your Lender, Nail the Deal" for a thorough discussion.)

Paying for Home Improvements

In Chapter 6 "Should You Refinance?" we discuss how it is important to pull out enough money (if you are going to pull money out of your home equity) the first time to do what you need to do. (**Need** to do, not want to do.)

This tool is a nifty way to calculate how much you should pay so that you have paid off all the debt by the time you have used up all the improvements.

Paying for long-term home improvements

	Loan Amt	Int Rate	Term	Payment			
Proposed Loan: $	76,750	8.000%	30	$ 563.16			

Item	Category	Cost	Useful Life (Years)*	Annual Depletion**	Minimum Payment***	Annualized Payment	Lifetime Payments
New Roof	Must Do Now	$ 25,000	30	$ 833.33	$183.44	$2,201	$66,039
Furnace	Must Do Now	$ 10,000	15	$ 666.67	$95.57	$1,147	$17,202
Exterior Paint	Should Do Soon	$ 12,000	10	$ 1,200.00	$145.59	$1,747	$17,471
New Fridge	Should Do Soon	$ 1,000	15	$ 66.67	$9.56	$115	$1,720
New Stove	Should Do Soon	$ 1,000	15	$ 66.67	$9.56	$115	$1,720
New Dishwasher	Should Do Soon	$ 750	10	$ 75.00	$9.10	$109	$1,092
Interior Paint	Optional	$ 1,500	10	$ 150.00	$18.20	$218	$2,184
New Kitch Cabinets	Optional	$ 15,000	25	$ 600.00	$115.77	$1,389	$34,732
New Countertops	Optional	$ 8,000	25	$ 320.00	$61.75	$741	$18,524
Update Electrical Panel	Optional	$ 2,500	30	$ 83.33	$18.34	$220	$6,604
	Total Repairs:	$ 76,750			$ 666.87		$167,287

* How long will this item last before you need to replace it again? The maximum depreciation period should be no more than the maximum term of your proposed loan. (Since you have to pay it off at least that fast.)

** The cost of the improvement divided by its useful life. This is the amount of money this item costs you each year that you own it.

*** This is the minimum payment to pay off each improvement's portion of the loan by the end of that particular improvement's useful life.

Simply enter in all of the home repairs you need or want to make, categorize its importance and urgency, enter the cost you've determined you'll have to pay for it, and finally estimate the useful life for each component.

Then, once you have shopped for your loan, enter in the interest rate and term (number of years) for the loan at the top. The loan amount will automatically be carried up from the sum of the repairs below.

You'll notice that the minimum payment in this example is $563.16. This is the payment needed to pay the loan off in 30 years. But some of your improvements will be used up in less than 30 years, so we calculate in the "Minimum Payment" column what you would need to pay (at a minimum) each month to pay off the portion of the loan used for each individual improvement before the improvement is used up.

In this example, you'll want to make a minimum payment of $666.87 each month so that by the end of year 10, for example, you will have "paid off" your exterior paint, dishwasher, and interior paint – just in time to do it again.

After ten years (in this example) you'll be making payments that will pay the loan off sooner than the original term – but that's really not a bad thing.

Effect of Extra Payments

What if you want to make extra payments? What impact will that have on your lifetime costs? How much more quickly can you pay off your mortgage?

These questions have fairly easy answers. You will find the tool "Effect of Extra Payments" at www.loanguide.com. It looks like this:

Prepared For: Customer			Date:	3/25/2014
Current Principal Balance: $ 200,000			Next Payment Due:	4/1/2014
Current Interest Rate: 6.000%			Extra Payment Now: $ -	
Monthly Pymnt (Princ. & Int. Only): $1,199.11			Extra Payment Monthly: $ -	
Remaining Term: 360 months			Bi Monthly? No	

	Scheduled	Modified	Savings
Total Lifetime Payments:	$ 431,679	$ 431,667	$ -
Total Lifetime Interest Cost:	$ 231,679	$ 231,673	$ -
Total Number of Payments:	360	360	
Years to pay off your loan:	30	30.0	
Date of Last Payment:	4/1/2044	4/1/2044	

Amortization Schedule

Month	Payment	Interest	Principal	Balance
4/1/2014	$ 1,199.11	$ 1,000.00	$ 199.11	$ 199,801
5/1/2014	$ 1,199.11	$ 999.00	$ 200.10	$ 199,601

When you enter in your personal information from your mortgage statement, you set up the spreadsheet to do the calculation for you. Now you can choose bi-monthly payments, a defined extra payment every month, or a one-time payment to determine how much your plan will save you.

Let's assume we want to round up our monthly payment to $1300. We'll be paying an extra $100.89.

Prepared For: Customer			Date:	3/25/2014
Current Principal Balance:	$ 200,000		Next Payment Due:	4/1/2014
Current Interest Rate:	6.000%		Extra Payment Now:	$ -
Monthly Pymnt (Princ. & Int. Only):	$1,199.11		Extra Payment Monthly:	$ 100.89
Remaining Term:	360 months		Bi Monthly?	No

	Scheduled	Modified	Savings
Total Lifetime Payments:	$ 431,679	$ 382,195	$ 49,484
Total Lifetime Interest Cost:	$ 231,679	$ 182,201	$ 49,477
Total Number of Payments:	360	294	
Years to pay off your loan:	30	24.5	
Date of Last Payment:	4/1/2044	10/1/2038	

Amortization Schedule

Month	Payment	Interest	Principal	Balance
4/1/2014	$ 1,300.00	$ 1,000.00	$ 300.00	$ 199,700
5/1/2014	$ 1,300.00	$ 998.50	$ 301.50	$ 199,399

By paying an extra $100.89 per month we pay the loan off in 24.5 years and save $49,477 in interest!

Below this section you will find an amortization schedule so you can examine how the amortization changes over the entire life of the loan.

Other Tools

You can find other tools at www.loanguide.com. Keep in mind that with all of these tools the quality of the results depends entirely on the quality of the information input, and the interpretation of the output.

Your best resource is still an ethical, competent, mortgage advisor. If you have any doubts at all about whether or not your loan officer meets the qualifications highlighted in Chapter 3, do not be afraid to move on to another advisor.

Good luck, and happy homeownership!

Index

Glossary

Adjustable Rate Loan

Also known as a Variable Rate Mortgage, this is a mortgage loan where the interest rate can be adjusted on a periodic basis. The lender cannot adjust the interest rate randomly. The terms of the adjustment calculation are defined in your *Note*.

Annual Percentage Rate)APR)

The effective interest rate that you pay on your loan when accounting for the impact that up-front fees have on your lifetime borrowing costs.

Balloon Payment

A payment due at the end of a loan term when you have not fully amortized the principal balance. (You have not paid the loan down to a zero balance.)

Blended Interest Rate

The effective interest rate that you pay when you have two loans, each at a different interest rate from the other. Your blended interest rate is equivalent to what your interest rate would be if you had one loan with a principal balance equal to the sum of your current loans, and paid the annual interest on your one loan that you do now on two.

Buyer's Market

Describes a market condition where there are more homes for sale than there are buyers. In a buyer's market buyers tend to have more negotiating power than sellers.

Cash-Out Refinance

Refinance where the primary purpose is to access the equity in your home by pulling cash out. Your new loan amount will be higher than the loan you are paying off. Pulling cash out can also be achieved with an equity loan or equity line.

Compounding, Compound Interest

The principle that over time the interest earnings on an investment accelerate if you leave it in the investment. You earn interest on your initial investment, and then in the future you earn interest on your initial investment plus the interest you've earned.

Conforming Loan

A mortgage loan which conforms to the underwriting standards published by Fannie Mae or Freddie Mac. These loans generally are sold to one of these two agencies.

Consumer Financial Protection Bureau

A federal bureau that writes and enforces regulations having to do with consumer finance products of all types. See www.consumerfinance.gov.

Debt Consolidation Loan

A loan used to pay off more than one loan – to *consolidate* two existing loans into one new loan. These are usually sold using a lower monthly payment as an enticement, but can end up costing more in interest over a lifetime.

Deed of Trust

The instrument used in many states in lieu of a mortgage with which you pledge your home as collateral for the loan. In a deed of trust you literally deed your home to a trustee, who can then sell your home without court action in the event of a default.

Equity Line

An open line of credit secured by your real estate. Equity lines are usually secured junior to a conventional mortgage.

Equity Loan

A loan of a fixed term used to pull cash out of your real estate. An equity loan is usually secur3ed junior to a conventional loan.

Escrow Account

An account set up by your lender to deposit monthly payments towards taxes and insurance that are included with your loan payment. When your tax and insurance bills come due the lender pays these bills out of your escrow account. These accounts are typically optional if you have more than 20% equity in your property. See also *Impound Account*.

Estimated Closing Statement

A statement of charges prepared by the escrow company in their own format. The actual itemization of charges should reflect those disclosed in the HUD1, but typically in a more readable format.

Estimated Settlement Statement (Estimated HUD1)

The HUD1 is an accounting of all the charges you will pay in escrow for the cost of the loan, title, escrow, recording fees, and all other fees associated with getting the loan, as well as ongoing fees (such as insurance and taxes) that are due on a recurring basis but some of which are due in escrow. You are given an *estimated* settlement statement before closing for review, and a *final* settlement statement after close of escrow to audit your actual charges.

Fannie Mae

Fannie Mae is a government-owned (as of this writing) organization that purchases pools of mortgages originated, underwritten and funded by mortgage brokers, mortgage bankers, banks or credit unions. By purchasing pools of mortgages Fannie Mae provides liquidity to the mortgage banks to fund more loans, thus making more money available to consumers to purchase homes.

Final Settlement Statement (HUD1)

The HUD1 is an accounting of all the charges you will pay in escrow for the cost of the loan, title, escrow, recording fees, and all other fees associated with getting the loan, as well as ongoing fees (such as insurance and taxes) that are due on a recurring basis but some of which are due in escrow. You are given an *estimated* settlement statement before closing for review, and a *final* settlement statement after close of escrow to audit your actual charges.

Freddie Mac

Freddie Mac is a government-owned (as of this writing) organization that purchases pools of mortgages originated, underwritten and funded by mortgage brokers, mortgage bankers, banks or credit unions. By purchasing pools of mortgages Freddie Mac provides liquidity to the mortgage banks to fund more loans, thus making more money available to consumers to purchase homes.

Fully-indexed rate

When the interest rate on your adjustable-rate loan is ready to be adjusted, the lender takes the value of the then-current *index* and adds the *margin* to determine your fully-indexed rate. This is your new interest rate for the next period. (Usually one year.)

Government-Sponsored Entities (GSEs)

GSE refers to organizations that purchase loans from mortgage banks that assemble large portfolios. These entities are part of, or are backed by the U.S. government. They are known as Fannie Mae, Freddie Mac, and their lesser-known cousin, Ginnie Mae.

The Great Recession

History will inform us more thoroughly about exact dates, but is technically recognized as a period of contraction (or negative economic growth) from December of 2007 through mid-2010. Experientially, however, most people would agree the effects have lasted much longer than that.

Impound Account

An account set up by your lender to deposit monthly payments towards taxes and insurance that are included with your loan payment. When your tax and insurance bills come due the lender pays these bills out of your escrow account. These accounts are typically optional if you have more than 20% equity in your property. See also *Escrow Account*.

Initial Adjustment Cap

The maximum (in terms of percentage) that the interest rate on your adjustable-rate mortgage can increase on the very first periodic adjustment. Most commonly the initial adjustment cap today is 2%, meaning that your interest rate cannot adjust – down or up – more than 2% from the initial start rate on the first adjustment.

Interest-Only Mortgage

A mortgage where your minimum payment is only the interest which accrues each month. If you make only the minimum payment you will be paying no principal on the loan, and thus your principal balance will remain the same. Interest-only mortgages have a specified time period during which you make interest-only payments, and then you must make fully-amortized payments.

Interest Rate Floor

Defined in your Note, the interest rate floor is an interest rate that your adjustable-rate loan cannot go below. This is most often found in equity lines.

Lender-Paid Mortgage Insurance

Mortgage insurance where the premiums are not visible to you, as they are paid by the lender rather than by you. However, the lender charges a premium in the interest rate in order to pay for the insurance, so you pay for it but in a different way than you are used to.

Leverage

The principal that increases your return on the money you've invested in your home. Since you own maybe 20% of your home when you buy it but 100% of the home is appreciating, you are making money on the bank's investment too.

Lifetime Adjustment Cap

The maximum (in terms of percentage) that the interest rate on your adjustable-rate mortgage can increase over the life of your loan. Most commonly today the lifetime cap is 5%, meaning that the interest rate can never exceed your initial interest rate plus 5%.

Loan-to-value ratio

Literally, the ratio of the loan amount to the appraised value of the property. This is one of the key measures of the quality of a loan from the lender's perspective because, in the event that you are unable to make payments and default on the loan, they will foreclose on your home and sell it at auction to recover the money. The more equity you have in your home, the more likely they are to recover all of their money when they foreclose.

Lock, Locking, Interest-Rate Lock

The process whereby you lock in an interest rate at a set price for a given period of time.

Margin

The amount the lender adds to the *index* when determining your *fully-indexed rate* when your adjustable-rate mortgage comes up for adjustment.

Mortgage Banker

1. A company that uses funds on hand to fund loans at closing. These companies might have retail loan officers, or they may work with *mortgage brokers* who originate loans and submit them to the mortgage banker for underwriting and funding. A mortgage banker might have their own internal funds, but more likely carries a line of credit from a major financial institution and draws on that line of credit to fund loans. A mortgage banker then packages these loans together and sells them to a pre-determined investor. The underwriting guidelines used by the mortgage banker are developed by this investor.
2. A person who originates loans and works for the company above.

Mortgage Broker

1. A company that originates mortgage loans but does not underwrite or fund the loans. A mortgage broker takes a loan application, qualifies the borrower, gathers and verifies documentation of income, assets and credit, and then assembles a loan file and submits it to a mortgage banker for underwriting and, once approved, funding.
2. A person who originates loans and works for the company above.

Mortgage Limit

The maximum amount you may access on a reverse mortgage, or Home Equity Conversion Mortgage

Negative amortization loan, or Neg-Am (Same as Option ARM)

An adjustable-rate mortgage where the initial minimum payment is very low; so low, in fact, that it doesn't cover the accruing interest. The loan *negatively amortizes*, meaning that the principal balance of the loan *increases* rather than decreases over time (at least for a while.) This loan was more commonly called an Option ARM during the Mortgage Financing Boom, and is not available today.

Non-Conforming Loan

A mortgage loan which *does not* conform to the underwriting standards published by Fannie Mae or Freddie Mac. These loans generally are *not* sold to one of these two agencies.

Note

The legal agreement between you and your lender, in which the lender promises to lend you the money and you promise to pay it back under very specific terms.

Note Rate

The interest rate defined in your *Note*. This is the actual interest rate that you pay on your loan, without accounting for the impact of fees on your lifetime loan costs.

Option ARM (Same as Negative Amortization Loan)

An adjustable-rate mortgage where the initial minimum payment is very low; so low, in fact, that it doesn't cover the accruing interest. The loan *negatively amortizes*, meaning that the principal balance of the loan *increases* rather than decreases over time (at least for a while.) This loan was originally called a *negative amortization* loan, or neg-am, and is not available today.

Periodic Adjustment Cap

The maximum (in terms of percentage) that the interest rate on your adjustable-rate mortgage can increase on periodic adjustment dates after your initial interest rate adjustment. Most commonly the periodic adjustment cap today is 2% if your loan adjusts annually, or 1% if it adjusts every six months.

Pre-Paid Interest

Interest charges paid in advance when you close escrow on your new loan to "cycle you up" to the first of the upcoming month. If you pay pre-paid interest you will not have to make a payment the first full month that you have your new loan.

Principal, Interest, PITI

Refers to your monthly payment when used this way. The principal is the amount of your monthly payment that goes to reduce principal each month. Interest is the amount that goes to the accrued interest that is now due. PITI stands for Principal, Interest, Taxes and Insurance, and is often used as shorthand for "Your mortgage payment plus impounds."

Point(s)

The price you pay to the lender to "buy" a lower interest rate. These are also known as "discount points" as they compensate the lender for discounting the interest rate to you. One point is equal to 1% of the loan amount.

Pre-payment penalty

A term in a note that protects the lender against the loss of anticipated interest resulting when you pay the loan off early. Today on a primary residence a pre-payment penalty cannot be effective for more than five years, and the maximum allowable penalty by law is a penalty equal to six month's interest.

Principal / Principal Balance

The amount that you owe the bank; the current balance of your loan.

Processing Fee

A fee charged by the loan origination company (bank, mortgage banker or broker) to "process" the paperwork needed to complete the loan application. It is becoming more common for this fee to be built into the origination or discount fee and left off your closing statement as a separate line item.

Rate and Term Refinance

Refinancing your mortgage in order to either reduce your interest rate, or to change the terms of your loan to accomplish a specific goal.

Reverse Mortgage

A mortgage product for seniors with which you may access the equity in your home via a lump-sum payment, scheduled payments, or an equity line without having to make payments on the loan. The principal balance grows until you pay the loan off, typically when you no longer live in the home.

Settlement Charges

All of the charges in escrow charged in escrow or before for all lender and bona fide third party charges such as appraisal, title insurance, escrow fees, notary fees, etc.

Stated-Income Loan

A loan where you do not have to document your income to the lender in order to qualify for the loan. Once common, this is a rare product today and is becoming harder to do while staying compliant with current regulations.

Teaser Rate

Also known as an introductory rate, a teaser rate is an initial interest rate on adjustable-rate loans that is meant to entice you to take the loan. This rate is usually only valid for a short period of time, after which your Note rate, or permanent rate becomes effective.

Underwrite

The process used by a mortgage banker, bank or credit union to determine if your loan application meets the criterion set for a specific loan program. The underwriting process yields one of our possible results:

1. An approval of the loan,
2. A conditional approval – meaning the loan is approved subject to certain conditions being met,
3. A suspense, meaning that the underwriter believes the loan does not qualify for the program but is willing to review more documentation to review it, or
4. A denial.

Underwriting Guidelines

Investors, Fannie Mae, Freddie Mac, or Wall Street investment banks develop underwriting criterion and solicit Mortgage Bankers to find the loans that meet the criterion for the program they have in mind.

Wholesale Lender

A wholesale lender is any lender that works with brokers to offer its products to consumers. Brokers originate the loans and submit a complete loan package to the wholesale lender, who underwrites, approves, and funds the loan, and then pools many mortgages together and sells the pool to raise funds. A wholesale lender might be purely a wholesale lender with no retail loan officers of its own, or it may be a mortgage banker who both works with brokers and who has a retail loan origination staff, or could even be a bank or a credit union, with or without its own retail loan officers.

53024073R00149

Made in the USA
Lexington, KY
18 June 2016